To Benny

Partners forever

Jim Metz

SH # 13697

Tax # 869358

THEY WISHED THEY WERE HONEST

THEY WISHED THEY WERE HONEST

THE KNAPP COMMISSION AND
NEW YORK CITY POLICE CORRUPTION

MICHAEL F. ARMSTRONG

COLUMBIA UNIVERSITY PRESS
NEW YORK

Columbia University Press
Publishers Since 1893
New York   Chichester, West Sussex
cup.columbia.edu

Library of Congress Cataloging-in-Publication Data
Armstrong, Michael F., 1932–
They wished they were honest : the Knapp Commission and
New York City police corruption / Michael F. Armstrong.
p.   cm.
Includes index.
ISBN 978–0–231–15354–6 (cloth : alk. paper) — ISBN 978–0–231–52698–2 (ebook)
1. New York (N.Y.). Knapp Commission. 2. Police corruption—New York (State)—New York
3. Governmental investigations—New York (State)—New York. I. Title.

HV8148.N52A76   2012
364.1'3230883632097471—dc23

2011044777

⊗

Columbia University Press books are printed on permanent
and durable acid-free paper.
This book is printed on paper with recycled content.
Printed in the United States of America

c 10 9 8 7 6 5 4 3 2 1

CONTENTS

Preface   vii

1. The Beginning
   1

2. Staffing and Funding
   12

3. Lurching Into Action
   27

4. Gabe
   35

5. Teddy and Xaviera
   40

6. The Great Meat Robbery
   46

7. George
   51

8. Some Rough Spots
   57

9. Leuci
   61

10. Toody and Muldoon
    72

11. Batman and Robin
    78

12. Waverly Logan
    83

13. Super Thief
88
14. The Freshman
115
15. Phillips at Work
123
16. Problems
133
17. Tank and Slim
139
18. Phillips, in High Gear
148
19. The Dynamic Duo—Again
163
20. The Eve of the Hearings
169
21. The Public Hearings: Phillips's Testimony
178
22. The Public Hearings: Droge, Logan, Tank and Slim, Burkert, etc.
195
23. Serpico
208
24. Aftermath
219
25. Phillips—Epilogue
226
26. Special Prosecutor
235
27. Reflections
243

Index   251

PREFACE

Ten percent of the cops in New York City are absolutely corrupt, ten percent are
absolutely honest, and the other eighty percent—they wish they were honest.
                    —Frank Serpico, New York City police officer, 1959–1972

They were known as "New York's Finest." And they were. Tough, streetwise,
underpaid, brave—often heroic—the police officers in New York City in
1970 rightly viewed themselves as an unappreciated bulwark against crime.

They were also—almost all of them—corrupt.

Without compromising or contradicting the valiant aspect of police work,
another simultaneous reality existed in the New York City Police Department: corruption had become a way of life. Any kid on any corner in Harlem
could report seeing police officers being paid off by gamblers. Bars and nightclubs on the Upper East Side and in Greenwich Village flagrantly violated
a score of easily enforced regulations. Drivers tucked bills in wallets next
to licenses that a cop might ask to see. On the darker side, organized crime
figures seemed to operate without being bothered very much, and a narcotics
trade, then in its adolescence, was maturing with only sporadic interference
from the police.

It was said that corrupt cops were of two kinds: "meat eaters," the in-
corrigible few, who devoted virtually full time to collecting payoffs and who
committed or covered up really serious crimes; and "grass eaters," the vast
majority, who participated in the common, everyday graft indulged in as a
significant sideline by just about everyone "on the job." While some efforts
had been made to catch the "meat eaters," nothing was being done, systemi-
cally, about the "grass eaters." That effort would have to involve cleaning up
the swamp of low-level corruption in which the Department wallowed. This
swamp provided the breeding ground for more significant police crime, and

stifled the natural impulses of the vast majority of cops to do their jobs with integrity and pride. But no one in authority was willing to admit that the swamp existed, much less make any move to clean it up.

Spurred by a newspaper exposé in 1970, the result of public accusations by a young "hippie" cop named Frank Serpico, the city's youthfully charismatic mayor, John V. Lindsay, appointed a commission to investigate corruption in the police department. The commission, which came to be known as the Knapp Commission, after its chairman, Whitman Knapp, conducted a yearlong investigation.

Underfunded and unfamiliar with the ways of the organization it was charged with investigating, the commission's somewhat quixotic goal was to uncover definitive proof of the extent of graft among 32,000 police officers, and bring that proof to public attention. Was police corruption a matter of "a few rotten apples" in an otherwise pure barrel, as police brass and protective politicians routinely proclaimed, or was the disease spread throughout the whole barrel? If, as hearsay accounts indicated, widespread graft existed but was tolerated by higher-ups and public officials who chose to look the other way, public exposure of actual conditions could be the first step on the road to reform. Specific evidence presented in high-visibility public hearings could create pressure on the powers-that-be to focus attention on conditions in the whole barrel, instead of scapegoating a few "rotten apples." But first the commission had to come up with evidence.

Any hope of finding the needed proof rested heavily on being able to persuade or pressure corrupt police officers to describe, firsthand, the graft in which most cops participated and about which all were aware. Prospects of success in this effort seemed remote. Everyone knew that cops don't talk.

These are my recollections, as the Knapp Commission's chief counsel, of its struggles to pierce the legendary "blue wall of silence" and bring to public view serious conditions of corruption in the New York City Police Department.

In the immediate aftermath of the Knapp Commission's efforts, I was besieged by requests to write a book. My consistent answer was "There already is a book—it's called *The Knapp Commission Report*." I felt that behind-the-scenes tales of the Commission's work should not distract attention from its official findings. Now, almost forty years later, the name of the Knapp Commission is no longer on everyone's lips, nor indeed in most people's memories. It has settled, quietly, into its proper place in history, whatever that may be. So I think it can no longer do any harm to recount the human side of the making of that history. Also, a fuller understanding of the events of 1970–72 may be of help in maintaining the vigilance that is required to prevent a resumption of the cycle that has seen New York beset by a police corruption scandal every twenty years since the late nineteenth century.

Most of what I have set forth was committed to writing, in some form, fairly soon after the events occurred. In putting it all together, I have done my best to be accurate, the only minor exceptions being the few occasions when I have, for one reason or another, substituted pseudonyms for real names. My memories have been compared against those of others who participated and, where possible, confirmed by tape transcripts, documents, and the public record. In instances where nothing but memories remain, I have sometimes acquiesced to the recollections of others . . . but, adopted or otherwise, the memories are my own.

THEY WISHED THEY WERE HONEST

1

THE BEGINNING

On April 25, 1970, New Yorkers awoke to a news story on the front page of the *New York Times* that was to keep many people awake for a long time. Written by thirty-seven-year-old investigative reporter David Burnham, the article accused the New York City Police Department of being laced with corruption. It suggested that Mayor John Lindsay, a tall, handsome patrician with an eye on the White House, had deliberately ignored the problem.

Burnham's article was based chiefly on the experiences of a young police officer named Frank Serpico. To most of the cops who knew him, Serpico was a "hippie" if not an outright "weirdo." His beard, longish hair, and Greenwich Village clothes were enough to mark him as strange in a department with a solid tradition of conformity to values and styles that long predated the '60s. Serpico's tendency not to conform became a serious liability when, after five years on the force, he was transferred to the plainclothes division. There, conformity meant considerably more than dressing or talking like your comrades: you also made money the way they did—from graft.

Of the 32,000 men and women in the Department, about 450 were plainclothesmen, charged with enforcing the laws against vice, particularly gambling. These were officers from the patrol force working out of uniform. Detectives were something else. They also worked in "plain" clothes, but they carried gold rather than silver badges, performed investigative as opposed to patrol duties, and served in their own three-thousand-man "Detective Division." A heavy concentration of plainclothesmen were assigned to squads in the city's black and Hispanic ghetto neighborhoods, where gambling was heaviest and where the numbers racket was as well-organized as the New York City Police Department—maybe better. Each day, millions of ghetto dwellers gave anywhere from twenty-five cents to a dollar or two to neighborhood "runners" in the hopes of picking the right three-digit number established daily by a set formula based on published local racetrack betting results. Runners reported to their own local "banks," which in turn reported to established organized crime figures located chiefly in Italian East Harlem. The whole operation was about as secret as the news on the front page of a New York tabloid. Other forms of gambling, like racetrack and sports bookmaking, which the plainclothes division was also supposed to control, operated almost as openly.

The Seventh Division plainclothes squad, to which Serpico had been assigned, was located in the Bronx, in a heavy gambling area overrun with bookies and numbers banks. Serpico soon found that the twenty plainclothesmen in his new squad made no effort to interfere with the activities of the gamblers they were supposed to arrest. Instead, they devoted most of their time to collecting money from them, in return for leaving them alone. The process was known in the trade as putting the gamblers "on the pad." The cops divided responsibility for collecting a specified amount from each gambling spot each month. The money collected was distributed equally among them. Supervisors got an extra half-share. A plainclothesman's day was spent keeping an eye on the gambling establishments, being alert for new spots, attending to collection responsibilities, making enough "show" arrests to keep up some pretense at law enforcement, and punishing gamblers who tried to cheat on their payments. It was a full-time job. No one seemed to think it necessary to do very much to hide what was going on. The corruption was as open as the illegal gambling upon which it fed. Everyone in the squad was expected to do his part, and accept his share of the take.

Serpico did what no other police officer before him had done—he not only refused to accept payoffs, but he decided to blow the whistle.

Aided by a friend with connections, an Amherst-educated cop named David Durk, Serpico tried to report the payoffs to top-level police officers and other City officials. When nothing happened, Durk and Serpico went to *Times* reporter Burnham, claiming that their allegations of payoffs had been ignored by the Department, the City, and even by a top aide to the mayor himself. The *Times* put Burnham's story on the front page. It took hold, and within days police corruption was a hot topic all over the city. Rumblings were heard that Serpico's revelations might be, as Burnham suggested, only the tip of an iceberg that, among other things, could threaten John Lindsay's national political hopes.

Lindsay, aware that the article was coming ↺
days before it was published by appointing a comm.
and make recommendations. The committee consisted ↺
tion Counsel, two district attorneys, the mayor's own comm.
gations, and the police commissioner. After three weeks, having.
complaints of police corruption from the public, the committee pass
potato back to the mayor, saying that they were too closely involved w.
problem and lacked any staff to investigate it. What was needed, they sa.
was an independent commission, made up of prestigious citizens, with its own
investigators and staff.

The mayor called Whitman Knapp. Sixty-one years of age, Knapp knew
a lot about both the City and law enforcement. He had served as a prosecutor under two legendary Manhattan district attorneys, Tom Dewey and
Frank Hogan, rising to be chief of Hogan's Rackets Bureau. Since then, in
a distinguished career as a "name partner" in a prestigious law firm, he had
maintained his ties to people in law enforcement and acquired many political
acquaintances. Educated at Groton, Yale, and Harvard Law School, he lived
and vacationed in all the right places, and was solidly connected in social
circles and the "Establishment."

When he took the call, Knapp thought that the mayor was calling him for
advice. He listened as Lindsay explained that he needed someone to head his
new commission who had intelligence, integrity, experience, a sterling reputation, connections in the city's social community, diplomatic skills, a public
presence, sensitivity, clout, and so on and so on. As Lindsay talked, Knapp
later said, he wondered where in the world they could find anyone with all
these characteristics. Then it dawned on him: "He wants me!" Acknowledg-
ing that he was entirely vulnerable to flattery, Knapp accepted the task.

Knapp looked more like a professor than a big-time lawyer, much less an
investigator of cops. He was of medium height, slender, with wispy gray hair
and an expressive mouth that was molded by his mood, switching quickly
from grin to grimace and—when necessary—back again. During periods of
reflection he would sometimes stare absentmindedly, his light blue eyes mag-
nified by horn-rimmed glasses.

Knapp approached problems with a resoluteness reflecting an extremely
intelligent and creative mind. He had a tendency to jump to conclusions and
form opinions quickly. "Often in error, never in doubt" was his frequently
stated but quite unfair assessment of himself. The fact was that he cherished
doubt, particularly about his own conclusions. In later years, after he became
a federal judge, this quality would serve him well. Now, in 1970, as he set
about establishing the commission that would come to bear his name, he

merely a sharp mind but all the flexibility and openness to new
that he could muster. It helped that Knapp knew the criminal justice
tem from both sides. He colorfully described the trauma of his experience as a prosecutor switching to a role as defense counsel: "It's amazing,"
he said, "how they started to indict innocent people just as soon as I left the
prosecutor's office."

Knapp's task was formidable, and he had no reliable guidelines to tell
him how to go about dealing with it. Not that the problem was a new
one. Corruption was encountered in 1844, as soon as the New York State
legislature created the New York City Police Force as the first municipal
police department in the country. In March 1894 the Lexow Committee[1]
investigated the police department and found systemic extortion and payoffs. The issue would continue to arise just about every twenty years. Seventeen years after Lexow, in 1911, following the Times Square murder of
a gambler who had reported police corruption to the newspapers, a City
legislative committee[2] headed by Henry Curran found systemic monthly
police extortion of various illegal operations. Twenty years later, in 1932,
the Seabury Committee,[3] appointed by the State legislature, made similar
findings, and in 1950, a huge scandal erupted when a notorious gambler
named Harry Gross testified before a grand jury about widespread regular
payoffs to police.[4]

Now, another twenty years had passed, and it was Knapp's turn. The fact
that it had been necessary to explore the problem of police corruption approximately every two decades since before the turn of the century seemed
to indicate that predecessor committees, commissions, and investigators
had not been too successful in finding a long-term solution. Something new
was needed.

Knapp's first concern was to figure out whether he was on a fool's er-
rand. Was the mayor really serious? After all, it was not merely corruption in
the police department that was to be investigated, but whether Mayor Lindsay himself should be faulted for ignoring the problem. Knapp knew that
he could get nowhere if the mayor did not support his efforts at least long

---

1. New York State Senate Committee, chaired by Senator Clarence Lexow.
2. New York City Board of Aldermen.
3. Former Judge Samuel Seabury.
4. Gross recanted his testimony in the middle of a conspiracy trial in which seventy-eight
   police officers had been named as defendants and co-conspirators. The result was that
   the police officers went free and Gross got a twelve-year sentence—but stayed alive.

enough to get the investigation under way. The commission would need approval from the City legislature, authority to take testimony, relaxation of City bureaucratic requirements, cooperation of City personnel, and, most important, adequate funding. All depended on the mayor's support. But why would Lindsay aid an investigation that pointed, at least in part, at City Hall? Whether or not he and his people were ultimately shown to have been involved, the process of looking into the matter could prove embarrassing. On the other hand, it would be a simple matter for him to kill the whole operation at birth, without even being openly obstructive. Inattention or slow action would do the job. Knapp wondered.

When he learned who Lindsay intended to appoint as commissioners, however, Knapp made up his mind that the mayor was for real. Most prominent of Knapp's fellow commissioners was Cyrus Vance. Fifty-four years of age, Vance had been deputy secretary of defense under President Johnson. He had held many other important positions in public life and was now a senior partner at Simpson Thatcher and Bartlett, one of the largest and most prestigious law firms in New York City. A calm man, Vance was as strong as he was thoughtful, and his independence and integrity were beyond doubt. Several years later he would demonstrate these qualities most dramatically by resigning as secretary of state over a difference in principle with President Jimmy Carter. If John Lindsay was looking for "yes men" as commissioners he would never have turned to Cyrus Vance as one of them.

Lindsay's selections for the other commissioners were equally reassuring. Joseph Monserrat, fifty-two, was currently the president of the Board of Education in the City of New York. A feisty little man, Monserrat was a well-known gadfly in city politics. He was acutely aware of the political need for him, as a leader of the Hispanic community, to maintain a public image of independence from the mayor. Franklin Thomas, thirty-seven, African American, was president of the Bedford-Stuyvesant Restoration Corporation, an agency founded by the Kennedy administration to aid in the rehabilitation of ghetto neighborhoods in New York City. An impressive six feet five inches in height and more than 200 well-distributed pounds, Thomas had served as an assistant federal prosecutor in Manhattan and as deputy commissioner for legal affairs in the police department. He would go on in later years to become president of the Ford Foundation. Although Thomas was a quiet man, the force of his personality matched his imposing physical presence. For example, as a young deputy police commissioner he had faced down United Nations ambassador Arthur Goldberg, who had appeared at a precinct house during the noisy booking of a large group of protestors who had been arrested after making a disturbance at the U.N. When Goldberg stridently complained about the slowness of the booking procedure, saying that he had been waiting for forty-five minutes, Thomas coolly asked the former cabinet member and Supreme Court justice, "Do you really think, Mr. Ambassador, that three-quarters of an hour is too long to spend in the protection of the civil rights of thirty American citizens?"

Men of such character and strength, reasoned Knapp, were not the kind of people Lindsay would pick if he were looking for a whitewash. Knapp suggested the final commissioner himself. Arnold Bauman, fifty-six, was another prominent New York attorney. He had held executive positions in both the federal and state prosecutors' offices in Manhattan and was now in law partnership with a former U.S. attorney. Some might think Bauman was outspoken or opinionated, even arrogant, but no one would say he could be pushed around.

The commissioners would receive nominal compensations, and operate part-time, much like the board of directors of a corporation. The day-to-day running of the operation would be handled by a full-time staff, headed by a chief counsel who would be responsible for directing the investigation. Commissioners Frank Thomas and Arnold Bauman, who knew me from my days as an assistant U.S. attorney in Manhattan under Robert Morgenthau—Frank as a colleague and Arnold as an adversary—recommended me.

I was thirty-nine years old, living in a small home in suburban Westchester with my wife and three children. College at Yale and law school at Harvard had been sandwiched around three years as a pilot in the Air Force. After two years as an associate at a large New York City law firm, Cahill Gordon Sonnett Reindel & Ohl, I joined the U.S. Attorney's Office, where I stayed almost six years, and became chief of the Securities Fraud Unit. I returned to Cahill Gordon and had just become partner—a very junior one—when Arnold Bauman called to ask if I would be interested in taking a leave of absence to be chief counsel to the Commission. I was interviewed by Whitman Knapp, and offered the job.

I understand that I was not the Commission's first choice. One or two others turned the position down because, among other reasons, it seemed unlikely that anything could be accomplished. The Commission would have to get very lucky if it was to succeed. Something of an optimist, I felt I could count on breaks going our way. Perhaps the smarter thing would have been to stick to practicing law. But I had enjoyed the time I spent as an assistant U.S. attorney, and here was another chance to do roughly similar work, while striking out in a new direction.

My wife, Joan, was not very enthusiastic. The years I had toiled as an underpaid, overworked prosecutor, spending nights and weekends chasing criminals instead of helping with the children, had meant adventure for me but a great deal of work for her. Although I had now started on the comfortable road of big firm partnership, I was proposing to go back to government pay and hours, leaving her, alone again, to handle the family. Something of an irony underlay the division of our labors. There was no question that Joan would have been at least as good a lawyer as me and my friends—probably a lot better—had the times permitted. For example, after visiting a Saturday class at law school, she had listened for a few minutes to a debate among several of us about a seemingly knotty question posed by the professor. With a sort of puzzled ease, which implied wonder at what all the fuss was about, she quietly asked if it didn't all boil down to . . . the obvious answer, as she explained it. Joan did that kind of thing often. But it was a time when, like all law schools, we had only a handful of women in our class of more than five hundred. Upon my graduation, there simply wasn't any question of who would do what—I would slay dragons and Joan would mind the house and kids.

Now here was one more dragon. Joan graciously gave her support, and I accepted Whit Knapp's offer.

As a first step, Knapp decided that I should meet the mayor. Whit placed a good deal of importance on observing proper formalities, not merely out of a sense of propriety but because he knew how effective courtesy can be in getting what you want. In this case, it was certainly appropriate for Knapp to introduce the mayor to the person who was to run the investigation. In addition, we would never get the necessary approval from the City's legislative bodies without the mayor's support. It was well to build and maintain bridges to him.

There were two problems with this. First, if Frank Serpico was to be believed, the mayor and members of his staff would have to be questioned. Knapp and the other commissioners might be able to stay aloof, keeping on friendly terms with the mayor without involving themselves in the intimate details of any investigation of him. But I would have the job of running the investigation. I could not afford to get too chummy with someone whose integrity and credibility I might have to question. Public officials under scrutiny always say that they welcome tough questions—but they never do. An official who is innocent resents any implication to the contrary while one who is guilty, or even a little guilty, thinks only of the good things he has done and resents bitterly the efforts of an inquisitor to uncover the bad. So I would have to tread a fine line with the mayor—and I was sure he knew it.

Also, I was not a fan of John Lindsay. Although I had never met the man, my opinion of him as a public figure was distinctly unfavorable. The right to cherish irrational biases against public figures is, after all, fundamental in a democracy. One's mind creates mental cardboard figures of celebrities whom one has never met, to worship or detest without needing to be fair, or even accurate. I thoroughly enjoyed disliking the cardboard John Lindsay.

There were, I felt, good reasons for my disapproval of the mayor. Five years earlier he had been elected as a charismatic John Kennedy–like figure who would lead New York City out of the doldrums into which, according to Lindsay, it had fallen under the leadership of his predecessor, Abe Beame, who had been as short and colorless as Lindsay was tall and magnificent. Then, as Lindsay took office, he was greeted with a devastating city-wide transit strike that had been brewing for some time, and began on the day he was sworn in. So the new mayor opened his term walking the streets of New York for six weeks, accompanied by reporters and TV cameras. The citizenry who walked beside him became increasingly impatient with hearing that they were going through some kind of an adventure, which would have a favorable but currently unspecifiable ending.

It quickly became apparent that Lindsay was no match for his adversary, shrill, diminutive, grizzled Transit Authority union boss Michael Quill. An old Irishman with a heavy brogue he reportedly exaggerated on television, Quill put the city through a paralyzing six weeks without public transportation, and then forced Lindsay to agree to terms more favorable to the striking workers than their original demands had been. It was not an impressive performance by the new mayor.

In my opinion, everything had gone downhill from there. Lindsay probably wasn't doing any worse at being mayor than anyone else could have done in a basically impossible job at an impossible time. But he appeared to take himself so seriously, and seemed so swept away by grandiose visions, that people like me tended to judge him against a standard of what he said he could do rather than reality. My bias against Mayor Lindsay stemmed also from an impression I had of him as being too earnest, too self-righteous, and—most of all—lacking a genuine sense of humor.

Unaware of my prejudice against Lindsay, Knapp made an appointment for me to meet him, and Knapp and I arrived at the mayor's office at the designated time. The office was on the first floor of City Hall, a beautiful Federal / French Renaissance building erected in 1812 and located in downtown Manhattan near the Municipal Building and the courthouses, just opposite the Manhattan side of the Brooklyn Bridge. Fronting City Hall Park, the building had an airy, gracious appearance that was reflected in the mayor's own office. It was large and tastefully decorated, with Lindsay's political memorabilia and family photos gracefully distributed about the room.

We were joined, as we waited, by two of the mayor's top aides, Jay Kriegel and Dick Aurellio. Kriegel was the "enfant terrible" of the Lindsay administration. Now thirty-one years old, he had joined Lindsay soon after graduating from Harvard Law School and now served as the mayor's chief of staff. He had a reputation for being as brilliant as he was abrasive. Thin, birdlike, nervous, constantly moving, his eyes darting about behind large glasses, he thought as fast as, and certainly talked faster than, just about anyone I had ever met. Kriegel had been specifically named by Serpico as the one to whom he had fruitlessly brought information about police corruption. Aurellio was a large, shrewd, friendly man with a moustache and a reputation for being a deft politician. I was not aware of his having had anything to do with the police department or with the charges Serpico had made against the Lindsay administration.

As we waited for Lindsay, our conversation was cordial, if guarded. Finally the mayor arrived, fresh from a pitched battle with the City Council, in which he apparently had been double-crossed. Flopping down on the couch in his office, Lindsay heaved a great sigh. I waited for some ponderous platitude about good government. No such thing. "We have *got* to get back to boss rule in this city," Lindsay exclaimed. "Democracy is no way to run a town like this." With that opening, he proceeded to conduct a relaxed conversation with us about the general goals of the Commission and our plans to achieve them. Lindsay, I resentfully realized, was a good guy. He had a sense of humor after all. The cardboard figure became three-dimensional. I was acutely disappointed. It is maddening to have one's prejudice against a public figure undermined by meeting him.

As we talked, the mayor gave every indication of being dedicated to helping us. The most important commitment was, of course, adequate funding. Lindsay said that he could appropriate, from discretionary funds available to him, a few hundred thousand dollars under the 1970 budget. Presumably this would be enough to get us through the remaining seven months of the year. Knapp pointed out, as he had publicly at the time of his appointment, that the job would certainly take one or two years. Lindsay said that he was legally powerless to give us funding beyond the current year without the approval of both the City Council and the Board of Estimate, but he assured us that we would have adequate funds. He would use the full force of his office to make sure that we could complete what we set out to do.

The meeting was a very heady experience for me. My only prior contacts with political celebrities were with occasional targets of investigations during my time as a prosecutor. I had never hobnobbed on informal terms with someone as prominent as the mayor of New York—much less a mayor with pretensions to be president. I tried to keep in mind that, however charming and apparently helpful this important man might be, he himself might have things to answer for, and I would be the one raising the questions.

Outwardly Lindsay continued to say all the right things. He promised full cooperation not only from himself but from everyone in the City bureaucracy over whom he had any control. He assured Knapp that he would have complete independence in his tactical decisions and in his selection of staff. As for the initial funding, he identified $325,000 that would be immediately available, subject only to pro-forma approval by the Board of Estimate. He promised Knapp that more money would be forthcoming in the future and that the Commission would not run out of funds. Later I discovered that Lindsay was not as good at delivering on promises as he was at making them, and that his intentions may not have been as straightforward as they appeared. For the time being, however, Knapp had no reason to doubt the mayor's full commitment.

Police Commissioner Howard Leary himself was hard to figure. Serving as police chief in Philadelphia, he had been recruited by Lindsay a year earlier to replace Vincent Broderick, who had resigned in opposition to the mayor's establishing a civilian board to review complaints of police brutality. Leary backed Lindsay on the issue—at the time he was virtually alone among the nation's professional policemen in doing so—and got the job. A difficult, enigmatic man, he could be counted on to do what was politically advantageous to him. In this case, that clearly did not mean cooperating with our commission.

Some of the administrative details were taken care of quickly. On May 21, 1970, the mayor issued a brief executive order formally establishing the commission and charging it with the responsibilities of investigating allegations of police corruption and reporting the results. The names of proposed commissioners were set forth in the order. The City Council, one of two City legislative bodies, quickly passed a bill giving the new commission power to issue subpoenas and swear witnesses. It was left to the Board of Estimate to go through the formality of approving Lindsay's proposed allocation of funds.

Right from the start, the new commission ran into a host of difficulties. We could of course expect nothing but obstruction from Commissioner Leary and the Department's hierarchy. They had been implicated in Serpico's charges of a cover-up. Another natural foe, the policemen's union, known as the Patrolman's Benevolent Association, slapped a lawsuit on us as soon as we were created, claiming we were illegally constituted. Strong opposition also arose among powerful political elements friendly to the police. Our efforts to recruit field agents encountered inertia if not outright hostility from organizations accustomed to cooperating with the police. And the City bureaucracy, with which we were obliged to deal for administrative needs, was, well, very bureaucratic.

On the day the City Board of Estimate met to consider our funding appropriation, the PBA lawsuit was dismissed in court. We thought we were on our way.

While the commissioners were meeting for lunch to discuss future plans, the phone rang. It was someone from City Hall with the news that the Board of Estimate had just rejected our budget. Apparently, the borough president of Staten Island, a supposed ally, had been persuaded to change his mind, leaving us with less than the needed two-thirds vote. Whit called Mayor Lindsay. "Hello, John," he said, "I am down here with Mike Armstrong and the commissioners, having lunch. I just wanted to know, who's going to pay for it?"

The mayor consulted with advisers, wise in the ways of political infighting, and then moved swiftly. He rushed back to the Board of Estimate chamber and changed his vote to "No," apparently opposing the Commission's establishment. This action, under a technicality in the rules, gave him the right to request a reconsideration of the Commission's budget bill, which he did. He then called a special meeting the next day to take up the reconsidered bill. For some arcane reason, the rules provided that when a bill such as this one was considered for a second time, a different standard applied, and a simple majority vote would suffice. So the defection of the Staten Island borough president no longer mattered.

The only potential flaw in this maneuver was the fact that the mayor really didn't have the authority to call a special meeting of the Board of Estimate under these circumstances. Fortunately for us, our political opponents didn't figure this out. They came to the meeting, blustering about being tricked, but the bill was passed.

Knapp and his commission began, somewhat unsteadily, to do its job. It was mid-summer of 1970.

2

STAFFING AND FUNDING

With our appropriation in hand, Knapp decided it was time to inform the public that we were officially in business. At a well-attended press conference at the New York headquarters of the National Press Club, Whit announced that we had been funded, introduced me as chief counsel, and stated that our purpose would be to identify whether there were systemic patterns of corruption in the New York City Police Department. He said that we would announce our findings in a final written report and perhaps in public hearings. We would not be saying anything in public until we found something worth saying. He pointedly warned that we would not be making any announcements to the press until our investigation was over.

We had informed the public that we were ready to go. But we had no investigators, no equipment or office, no support staff, and no real idea of how, with a handful of people, we were going to investigate a 32,000-person police department.

The commissioners and I met to figure out how we were to go forward. We quickly agreed on a few basic guidelines. We would not focus on making criminal cases against individuals, but rather with discovering what patterns of corruption, if any, existed. However, the only way convincingly to show the existence of patterns of behavior was by exposing the activities of individuals. We did not have to assemble proof beyond a reasonable doubt against individual cops, but we would have to find out what they were doing. The ultimate evidence, without which some sophisticated professionals said we could not do our job, would be to get—presumably through some sort of coercion—the cooperation of police officers who were actually corrupt themselves and who would tell us what they and their comrades were doing. Here we faced the legendary "blue wall of silence." Cops, we were told, would never "rat" on other cops, regardless of the pressure to which they might be subjected.

With no precedents to guide us, and only a vague idea of what we thought we could specifically accomplish, we set out to build an organization. The first thing to do was to figure out an organizational plan. At the commission level, Knapp would host weekly meetings of the commissioners at his office. I would report on how things were going and seek the commissioners' advice and help, as needed. Each commissioner was to receive one hundred dollars for each meeting he attended.

A necessary guideline was imposed by how much money we had to spend. Lindsay had devoted $325,000 to the venture. Any more would have to be approved legislatively. No one suggested that this would be enough, but it gave us an idea of roughly the size of the organization we could put together for a few months, with the expectation that Lindsay would be able to fulfill his promise of more funds later on.

After some discussion, we agreed on the general outline of what our investigative team would look like. We would need four or five experienced attorneys who would act as direct supervisors of ten or twelve field investigators. Ideally the attorneys would have prosecutorial experience. Diversity was an important issue, not only for moral and political reasons, but because it was apparent that any corruption that did exist was probably more widespread in the minority communities than elsewhere. In these areas there were higher crime rates, more cops on duty, and a higher prevalence of open gambling such as the numbers game. We would need credibility in the African American and Hispanic neighborhoods in order to operate effectively.

Because of the risks involved in hiring cops or ex-cops, it was decided that the investigators would be drawn from the ranks of former or, perhaps, current federal law enforcement officers. Any group, particularly a quasi-military one, engenders a loyalty among its members that makes it difficult for one to turn on another, and this attitude was famously intense in the New York City Police Department. Cops who worked in the Department's anticorruption units were scornfully referred to as "shooflies." There weren't going to be too many of us, and we needed everyone to be fully dedicated, subconsciously as well as consciously.

In addition to the regular investigators, we initially held spots open for two or three "neighborhood investigators." The thought was that we might find people, probably youngsters, in the minority communities who would act as observers and liaison in neighborhoods with which we were unfamiliar.

An office staff, consisting of an office manager, perhaps with an assistant, a secretary, and a receptionist/paralegal, rounded out our minimal personnel needs, as we saw them.

Whit got approval of our outline from the mayor's budgetary people. We now had a plan and set about finding people to make it a reality. Our formidable task was to find people willing to sign on to a highly speculative and, in some quarters, unpopular venture, without even being able to give them assurance that there would be money to pay them.

The first attorneys I persuaded to join were two close friends, Paul Rooney and Otto Obermaier, who had served with me, in the late '60s, as assistant U.S. attorneys for the Southern District of New York in the Manhattan office, then headed by Robert Morgenthau. Both men had just left public service and were embarking on careers in private practice. It would be a few months before they could get things going, and they agreed to spend that time working for the Commission.

Rooney was of medium height and build, had light blue eyes and red hair, combining a certain dapper reserve with a sardonic Irish sense of humor. Several years earlier he had created quite a sensation among his colleagues in Morgenthau's office when he augmented his customary Chesterfield coat and Homburg hat by growing a beard—and a red one at that. It might not seem that a trim, dignified moustache and beard should cause that much of a fuss, but in the U.S. Attorney's Office of the mid-'60s it represented something of a revolution. We were all clean-shaven representatives of the government. We could show individuality in many ways, but it took great courage to defy the edict of Silvio J. Mollo, longtime autocratic chief of the Criminal Division, that we should dress "appropriately." Juries, said Sil, did not expect young prosecutors to look like hippies. We put draft-card burners in jail, we didn't try to look like them!

It seemed an act of particularly defiant insanity that Rooney chose to adorn himself with his beard just prior to trying one of the office's most important cases in years—the prosecution, on influence-peddling charges, of Carmine DeSapio. DeSapio was the New York County Democratic leader, a "Tammany boss" with a reputation for being one of the most powerful politicians in the nation. His image as a sinister political manipulator was greatly enhanced by an unfortunate eye condition that required him always to wear dark glasses, indoors or out. This was an advantage to Rooney, because it made DeSapio look the part of someone who should be indicted. Now Rooney was about to even the scales by appearing before the jury with a beard. I joined most of his friends in urging him to shave. Why risk offending a juror? Why give up the advantage of looking like a clean-cut young prosecutor who wouldn't dream of bringing a case against an innocent man? Paul persisted. He kept his beard—and won the case.

Obermaier was a tall, burly bear of a man, exuding quiet confidence, with an entertaining, self-deprecating sense of humor. He was a true legal scholar, with an encyclopedic memory of every court case he had ever read. In his career as a prosecutor, he had been known not only as a "law man" but as a tough, no-nonsense, and savvy trial attorney. He himself would go on in later years to serve as the U.S. attorney for the Southern District of New York. Otto, like Paul, was a tremendous addition, even if, like Paul, he figured to be with us for only a few months, until he could get his practice started. As much as I wished both of them well, I secretly hoped that they might run into difficulties that would delay the opening of their law offices. In fact, each of them found time to return to help every so often. Paul in particular was able to give the Commission significant chunks of his time during the year that followed.

I could find only one experienced former prosecutor who was able to commit himself to stay with the project until it was completed. Nicholas Scoppetta had served for six years in the Manhattan District Attorney's Office under Frank Hogan. He had tried his hand in private practice and was restlessly gravitating back to where his heart obviously led him, public service. Later he would serve as the City's Department of Investigations commissioner, deputy mayor for criminal justice, law professor at New York University, Child Welfare commissioner, and fire commissioner. He gave us a steady, creative, and experienced capability.

Milton Williams, an African American lawyer working at a City legal services agency, had previously served eight years as a New York City cop, putting himself through college and law school while he was on the job. Sharp and knowledgeable, Williams brought experienced insight not only with respect to the police department, but also regarding the minority communities where police corruption was most prevalent. He was to continue in public service and would wind up as presiding justice of the prestigious Appellate Division, First Department Court in New York.

The final assistant attorney, Nicholas Figueroa, also went on to distinguish himself as a judge on the trial bench, designated in New York as the Supreme Court. Prior to graduating from law school, Figueroa had held a nonlegal position at the U.S. Attorney's Office, under Morgenthau.

As soon as attorneys started coming aboard, we turned to the task of putting together a squad of investigators. Nothing was going to happen for us unless we assembled a group of agents to go out on the streets and collect evidence of what was going on. We hoped to gather a squad of about a dozen investigators, culled chiefly from the ranks of former federal agents whom we had gotten to know during our service as prosecutors.

We also came up with an idea that at first seemed to reflect the most extreme wishful thinking. Maybe we could persuade a few federal law enforcement agencies to *lend* us some agents. We would reimburse the agent's salary while he took a leave of absence in order to work for us. Given the institutional jealousies and turf battles that pervaded law enforcement efforts in those days, the notion appeared to be pie-in-the-sky. But the problem of police corruption certainly affected the federal government's attempts to enforce federal laws within New York City, and any federal agents who worked for us might come across violations, leads, and contacts that could be pursued by their agencies once we were finished. The idea was, perhaps, harebrained, but we decided to give it a try. Otto, Paul, and I began canvassing all of the top agents with whom we had worked, or of whom we had heard, to see if any who had retired were interested in getting active again, and if any still employed might be persuaded to convince their bosses that our cause was not only just, but could be useful to their own efforts.

It was not going to be easy. First was the question of pay. The Commission had received funds sufficient to carry it through the end of 1970, and had only the mayor's promise that there would be money to carry us beyond that date. We were well aware that Lindsay's promise was no more than a pledge for him to use his influence with the City legislative bodies—only they had the actual authority to appropriate funds. So we could guarantee no more than a few months' work to any investigator we sought to hire. As for the agents we hoped to borrow, they would probably be involved in important cases of their own that they could not readily abandon. Also, most agencies would not permit agents on loan to us to carry firearms, a comfort many would be loath to forgo. Finally, many prospective agents might be uneasy about targeting fellow law enforcement officers.

With these formidable hiring obstacles, it never occurred to us to inquire whether we were governed by the growing network of regulations intended to insure impartiality in City hiring. We wouldn't be selecting from a pool of applicants. We were begging for help. So, we begged wherever it occurred to us to do so, and hired on the spot, with complete and innocent disregard for the substantial bureaucratic requirements that governed what we were doing—which, if followed, would probably have strangled our efforts by paperwork before we could begin.

Our problems were quickly demonstrated to me when I reached out to a particularly desirable prospect, an Internal Revenue Service special agent,

Marvin Sontag. Marvin specialized in going after organized crime figures, and the scalps on his belt were those of, among others, Johnny Dio, Jimmy "Blue Eyes" Plumeri, Carmine Lombardozzi, Aniello Dellacroce, Tommy Eboli, Gerardo "Jerry" Catani, "Bayonne Joe" Zicarelli, John "Peanuts" Manfredonia, Jiggs Furlano, and Ruby Stein, not to mention New Jersey congressman Cornelius Gallagher. Sontag was truly a legend in his own time. Twenty years a special agent concentrating on organized crime, he was now head of an organized crime task force operating, for the time being, in New Jersey. It undoubtedly would be impossible to tear him away from his current duties—chasing the mayor of Newark, New Jersey, and other highly placed miscreants—but it was worth the attempt.

Short, fat, and bald, in his late forties or early fifties, Marvin cut an unlikely figure as a super-agent. When I would introduce him as the "greatest detective since Sherlock Holmes," he would shrug, roll his eyes, and query in a distinctively Jewish accent, "Who's this guy Sherlock Holmes?" Marvin turned out to be, as I thought, too committed to the work he was doing to sign on with us. He did take the time to give me some advice. Squeaky clean himself, Marvin was realistic about the known propensities of many local cops. "Don't forget, Michael," Marvin warned, "the guys who have the balls to take the money are often the guys who have the balls to make the arrests." He also remarked that any agent who became known for helping our commission might not later get wholehearted cooperation from police officers whose brothers he had investigated. As Sontag put it, "If I am cornered in a phone booth with an angry mob trying to kill me—and I dial 911 . . . I don't want them to hang up on me." Marvin's warnings were intended only to give me perspective. He himself would have been happy to help were it not for the fact that he was currently involved in helping to lock up most of the city government of Newark, New Jersey.

We were astounded and delighted when not one but three agencies responded to our pleas to lend agents to us. The Internal Revenue Service lent us four agents, and the Bureau of Narcotics came up with another. All of these operatives were first-rate people whom we had targeted specifically. In each case, the deal was that we would have use of the agents for six months, and they would continue to be paid by the federal government. We would reimburse the agency for the agents' salaries while they were with us. I hoped that, if things were really hot when the six months were up, we might be able to wheedle some extensions.

In negotiating with the Postal Service for a particularly desirable agent named Frank Nemic, I ran into a stone wall. I persisted. Finally, his supervisor, tiring of my badgering, jokingly offered the agent's services for one month. "I'll take it," I said. Nemic wound up staying with us for almost a year.

Recent retirees were another source, and we signed three ex–FBI agents, a former Immigration officer, and a retired major from Army Intelligence.

We made two exceptions to our rule against hiring ex-cops. One was a former member of the detective squad in the Manhattan District Attorney's Office, a group sufficiently independent so as to be pretty well immune from the "code of silence" mentality. In the other case, we flatly violated our injunction against using police officers, because the individual was so outstanding on paper that we couldn't resist. We soon found out that we should have. Our agent-cop was discovered funneling information about our operations to police sources. He was dismissed.

The Commission could afford only a small support staff, and the first person we hired was a young woman by the name of Carol Ash, nicknamed "Flash," to be office manager for an office that did not yet exist. Some needs are basic. As Casey Stengel said in 1962 when choosing a catcher as his first pick in the expansion draft of the new New York Mets, "If you don't have a catcher, then the pitchers don't have anyone to throw the ball to." Analogously, the most immediate need for any new office is to have one. And that would be our office manager's first task. Bright, energetic, and, for her age, well connected, Carol had been one of the young campaign workers assisting Robert Kennedy in his quest for the presidency. Paul Rooney had worked with her, earlier that year, on Bob Morgenthau's unsuccessful campaign for governor. Paul suggested that she would be a good choice to help us find, and then run, our office. Whit and I interviewed her, agreed with Paul, and hired her.

She turned first to a potential landlord that had a stake in our enterprise—the City. 51 Chambers Street was an old, not fully used municipal building downtown near City Hall in which Flash had found an unused suite that no one else wanted. It consisted of a half-dozen rundown offices covering half a floor. At a level high enough—eleven stories—to avoid surveillance from the outside, and with no other tenants on our level, the place was adequate for our needs. The offices were appropriately grubby for an anti-corruption outfit; when one of the commissioners suggested they could be spruced up with a little paint and a few rugs on the floors, I respectfully answered that it was more consistent with our image to leave the place the way it was. We took the suite, and Flash set about equipping it with second-hand City furniture, a few typewriters, and some basic office supplies.

The City also supplied us with two ancient automobiles for use in surveillance work. One was a Ford and the other a Chevrolet. Both, at least in appearance, were absolute wrecks—most surveillances would take place in neighborhoods where a BMW or a Mercedes would have been somewhat conspicuous. We were not, however, supplied with parking facilities for our vehicles, so someone had to take them home each night when they were not in use. The duty to take a car home often fell to me. It was a good thing that neither my wife nor I had much of an inclination to "keep up with the Joneses," because the sight of one or the other of these miserable-looking vehicles repeatedly parked in front of our suburban home would not have been an aid to advancing our social position.

The Commission's support staff was completed with the hiring of an assistant for Flash named Anne Beane, who was quieter but just as intelligent; a secretary; and several other helpers, including Nettleton Wells, a very small and very feisty former receptionist at the U.S. Attorney's Office, who, among other things, took upon himself the jobs of keeping our press file up-to-date and seeing to it that everybody remained in good spirits. As a sort of volunteer law clerk, we also had the assistance of a family friend of Whit Knapp's, Elizabeth "Lisa" Barrett, a bright, attractive young woman who had just graduated summa cum laude from Columbia Law School. She helped in our investigations, did legal research, performed paralegal functions, and provided those of us who needed it with an understanding of the younger generation. The police department was rapidly filling up with young people, so it seemed sensible to have some understanding of their thought processes.

I in particular, at age thirty-nine, was somewhat out of touch with younger people who, in the 1960s and early 1970s, were undergoing considerable changes in attitudes and behavior—both of which had been greatly transformed since the time I was their age. Before, a man's speech in "mixed company" was more restrained, and his actions more attentive. On one occasion, Lisa Barrett summed up in one short sentence a lot of what I had to learn about changing mores and terms of expression. It was lunchtime and we went out for a hamburger, and when I automatically extended the courtesies that my parents had trained me were due a "lady"—opening doors, walking to the outside on the sidewalk, stepping back to allow her to proceed first, and finally, lightly taking her elbow to guide her as we walked across a street—she turned to me with a grin and said, "Oh, Michael, you're so fucking gallant."

Our secretarial needs were initially taken care of by a remarkable woman called Veri Sweete, her religious name as a follower of the Father Divine religious sect in Harlem. She had been assistant chief of the stenographic pool in the U.S. Attorney's Office when I was an assistant there, and I had lured her away to be my secretary when I returned to Cahill Gordon. Now she agreed to follow me to serve as the Commission's secretary. Her skill and efficiency was matched by her serene, authoritative good nature. When she first came to Cahill Gordon, other secretaries stationed near her complained that they couldn't concentrate on their work when she typed, because, using the mechanical typewriters of the time, she went so fast that she made a racket like a machine gun. A very religious person, she could not get used to the salty language used around the office, largely by our investigators. In a time when "sexual harassment in the workplace" was a concept as yet to be developed, she asked for a transfer, and became Whit Knapp's personal secretary at his law firm. She stayed with Knapp throughout her career.

In our proposed budget, we provided for two or three "neighborhood investigators," with the idea that we could take on people—presumably from the minority communities where police corruption was believed to be at its worst—who could help us by providing information about conditions in their neighborhoods. If, as we were constantly told, "any kid in Harlem" could give us an earful about cops on the take, why not hire a few such "kids" and put them to work? We had no really crisp notion of the kind of persons we were looking for, or how we would actually use them. In an attempt to explore what opportunities might exist, Knapp arranged a meeting with Livingston Wyngate, a prominent figure in Harlem who was, among other things, executive director of the New York Urban League. Whit was closely connected with the league. I was to become its pro-bono counsel, remaining in that post for thirty years. Whit, Milton Williams, and I met Wyngate for lunch. We had a pleasant meal at one of Whit's clubs, but it became apparent that Wyngate had agendas—quite worthwhile ones—of his own. If we gave him the opportunity of suggesting a few people for jobs, we would find ourselves enmeshed in practical politics in Harlem. It was not a good idea.

In the course of our search, Carol Ash said she had a friend, looking for work, who might be a good addition to our team. Paul Blitzblau was a "hippie." Extremely intelligent and personable, with a shock of curly hair, he really had little to offer in the way of neighborhood savvy, but he was bright, and we needed people. So he briefly became our first and, as it turned out, only "neighborhood investigator." It quickly became evident that we really didn't have much for Blitzblau to do. We had come up with the notion that street vendors might be a source of police payoffs, so Blitzblau was assigned to become one of them, and find out. He had even begun the process of getting himself a lunch wagon and a license to go with it when Otto Obermaier, the cool head among us, found out what was going on. With a smile, and a shake of his head, Otto came to me to put a firm end to the Blitzblau hot dog stand project, commenting that the Commission should be seen to have better things to do than proving that cops took free hot dogs. Shortly after that, Blitzblau came across a professional opportunity that suited his considerable talents better, and our experiment with "neighborhood investigators" was over.

Somewhere along the line we were joined by a motherly, soft-spoken, youngish woman by the name of Sue Johnson, who was pursuing her own academic efforts in the police field and agreed, as a volunteer, to share many of her thoughts with us. It quickly became apparent that Sue had perhaps the keenest mind in the organization. Her insights regarding all phases of what we were doing were enormously helpful. It was somewhat deflating for us to come to the realization that this unprepossessing female was also, without question, the best athlete in the outfit. She had been a member of a world record–holding swimming foursome. So much for appearances.

As the summer of 1970 drew to an end, we were rounding into shape. We had hired the attorneys and investigators who would be used in our investigation and most of them had joined us. We had offices and equipment. We were ready to make some progress. It was time to figure out exactly what we were going to do, and how we were going to go about it. Lacking any real idea of where to start, we made a list of all the "corruption hazards" we could think of: illegal activities that presented corruption opportunities, such as gambling, traffic infractions, loan-sharking, narcotics dealing, alcohol law violations, and prostitution; and businesses vulnerable to being shaken down, such as bars, construction sites, tow-truck operators, small grocery stores, hotels, and restaurants. Each attorney was assigned to one or more areas of concentration, and the investigators were broken into teams of two or three and assigned to an attorney. This would be the loosest of organizational structures, with the understanding that responsibilities would shift as opportunities arose.

Then, as we were beginning to pull everything together, a startling thing happened. On September 5, 1970, Police Commissioner Howard Leary announced that he was resigning, effective October 1. Leaving the job as strangely as he had performed it, Leary gave no advanced warning to anyone in City government, and refused to provide City Hall with a formal letter of resignation. Taking a job as head of security at a large corporation, Leary left the mayor to worry about a replacement, while we wondered what impact the change would have on our investigation.

Leary had been one indirect focus of the original charges by Serpico. As long as he remained in command of the police department, his responses to those charges and his testimony about future plans to deal with corruption were obvious areas of concern and interest to us. We continued to gather our resources and begin our work, conscious of the fact that the appointment of Leary's successor would have a great bearing on what it was we were supposed to do.

Within a few weeks, Mayor Lindsay named, as police commissioner, a former New York cop, then police chief in Detroit, Patrick Murphy. Murphy had served "on the job, in New York, for twenty years, rising from patrolman to the rank of inspector. He headed the Police Academy just before going to Detroit. A smallish man, with a droopy, sad face, Murphy had the reputation of being an intellectual rather than a street cop. He was well plugged in to the national network of police scholars that customarily gravitated to think-tank organizations such as the National Association of Police Chiefs. As such, he had accumulated a good deal of knowledge about how a police department should be organized. He also had an impeccable reputation for honesty. While in New York, he had never spent any time in a job that carried a high risk of corruption. The rumor was that he had briefly been assigned to plainclothes as a young cop and had asked to be transferred out, because of what he had seen going on around him. Murphy brought with him, as first deputy police commissioner, William Smith, a large friendly man who had served twenty-three years in the Department and then followed Murphy to Detroit. He was said to be more practical than Murphy, if less erudite. They seemed to be a good team.

Murphy's appointment, just as we were about to get going in earnest, created a real problem for us. Murphy was talking like a reform commissioner. He was making significant personnel changes, and was saying everything he could about the problem of corruption. Maybe we weren't needed anymore. Knapp, in particular, was disturbed by the idea that his commission might interfere with the ability of the new police commissioner to do his job. He and I met Murphy and Bill Smith and talked to them at some length about their plans. We realized that Murphy would have been within his rights to demand that we pack it in and let him run the Department as he saw fit. But he purported to have no problem with our continuing to function. He looked upon our investigation as something that would help him administer the Department. Or so he said. We had a friendly, disarming talk and left with the idea that we had been needlessly concerned.

When we reported on our meeting to the commissioners, it was agreed that we would stay in business. Murphy's replacement of Leary would, we thought, enable us to shift the focus of the investigation. Since we now appeared to have a very cooperative police commissioner and first deputy, we could actually count on some assistance from the Department. Things were going to be easier than we had thought.

We were to learn that it was not going to be so smooth going. Patrick Murphy liked to accomplish things by indirection. Not one to face a problem head on, his seeming acquiescence in the continuation of our work was apparently motivated by tactical considerations, not any confidence in our ability to accomplish something of value. In his book, published eleven years later, in 1981, Murphy told of his complaining to the mayor, as soon as he became police commissioner, about the existence of the Knapp Commission. He wanted the Commission ended—right away. Lindsay assuaged him by saying that the Knapp Commission would never get off the ground. It would run out of funds shortly after the turn of the year.

Lindsay must have been well aware, in late August of 1970, of something we were not sophisticated enough to appreciate. There was a growing fiscal crisis. By the end of the year, the City would be approaching bankruptcy. Newspaper editorials would be talking about laying off policemen and firemen. The corruption story that gave us birth would be old news. There wouldn't be a spare dime for such luxuries as renewed appropriations for the Knapp Commission. Lindsay must have known that he could fight manfully with the City Council and Board of Estimate, both packed with pro-cop politicians, for the additional funds that were necessary for our continued life, but that he would inevitably fail. We would go out of business for lack of money before we could really do anything. Lindsay would wind up getting credit for creating us and fighting for us, but he would not have to suffer the possible damage we could cause him if we did our job.

Whatever may have been John Lindsay's understanding of the political realities, they finally became obvious, even to us. By the end of 1970 we would run out of money, and the City's legislature would never give us additional funds. Besides, any small chance that we had to wheedle funds from the City would depend on our telling the City Council and Board of Estimate of our accomplishments to date. It would not be unreasonable of them to demand, before giving us any more, to know what we had done with the money they had already provided. But we could not give them information about our achievements—because as yet we really didn't have any.

We were beginning to get a pretty good idea of what conditions were in the Department. But despite a series of fits and starts leading pretty much nowhere, we had not yet come up with hard evidence—much less found the kind of testimony from corrupt policemen that we felt was necessary to prove what was going on. If our opponents in the City Council and Board of Estimate could point to six months of effort with nothing to show for the $325,000 we had already been given, it would be fruitless for us to ask for more.

If we could not look to the City for money, we would have to look else-where. Whit Knapp launched a fundraising effort among the various chari-table foundations with which he was connected. His social contacts stood us in good stead and we wound up, during the life of the Commission, raising $121,000 from twelve different foundations.

The president of one of the foundations Knapp approached happened to be, in the terminology of the day, a "lady." Whit decided that he and I would take her to lunch and urge upon her the importance of our work and the need for the generosity of private foundations, specifically hers. He se-lected one of the most impressive luncheon locations in the city, the Century Club on 43rd Street off Fifth Avenue. Whit was a "Centurian." The three of us met outside the club, and Whit graciously ushered us inside. We were confronted by a somewhat embarrassed club functionary. In those days the Century Club did not allow women, even as lunch guests. Whit had forgot-ten. Beating an awkward retreat, we found somewhere else to eat. The lady was indeed a lady, and held no grudge. She saw to it that her foundation contributed generously.

Nick Scoppetta came up with a major funding source that proved to be our salvation. Scoppetta had served in the District Attorney's Office with a lawyer named Marty Danziger, who had now gravitated to a job in the Justice Department with a newly formed branch, designated as the Law En-forcement Assistance Administration, or LEAA. The business of the LEAA was to dispense federal funds to local law enforcement agencies in aid of the latest "war against crime." Unhampered by local political concerns, Dan-ziger could direct the funds under his control to places where he felt it could really do some good: our commission, for instance.

Scoppetta and I met with Danziger and explained to him what the Knapp Commission was all about, and the political roadblocks that threatened to shut it down, for lack of funding. He agreed that our cause was worthwhile and our need dire. LEAA approved an initial grant of $215,000, which, with the private donations from foundations run by Whit Knapp's friends, would enable us to carry on for about an additional six months, without having to go to the City for money.

However, we faced one problem in accepting the LEAA funds. They came with strings attached. First, we were supposed to submit monthly reports on our progress. This task would be difficult at times when nothing was occur-ring in the investigations, and when something was occurring, we would be reluctant to tell anybody about it. Moreover, when we got busy, we simply didn't have time to prepare detailed reports of the kind required by federal agencies. We did our best.

Another problem was the fact that Danziger and I had a philosophical difference of opinion as to just what we were supposed to be doing. In his mind, we should concern ourselves more with academic analysis than investigations. He expected us to produce a report that would lay out the causes of corruption and offer recommendations to deal with them. We, on the other hand, thought our first job was to gather hard evidence that corruption existed, and identify the patterns it fell into. "You don't have to waste time investigating whether corruption exists in the police department," said Danziger. "Everyone knows it's there." "That may be," I answered, "but no one admits it or is willing to do anything about it." We felt we had to begin by proving, publicly, what everyone said they knew. To do that, we needed investigators on the street, not lawyers in libraries.

Mayor Lindsay was not told anything about our fundraising efforts, particularly our application for an LEAA grant, until the funds were promised. I never knew whether Lindsay really wanted us around or not, but with the foundation and federal money in our pocket, it didn't matter.

There was yet an additional hurdle to clear. The LEAA grant, fairly routinely, required us to have subpoena power in order to qualify as the kind of organization eligible for the funds we had been promised. The City Council bill authorizing us to issue subpoenas ran out on December 31, 1970. Unless the bill was renewed, we had no subpoena power and could not accept the LEAA money. Without those funds, we were out of business.

It became clear how futile it would have been to get the City Council to authorize the additional funds Lindsay had originally promised when, in a heated session on Christmas Eve, 1970, the council almost denied us even the opportunity to accept the federal funds. Pro-cop council members loudly, if somewhat inconsistently, complained that we hadn't done anything—and shouldn't be permitted to. Commissioner Murphy came strongly to our defense, giving a statement to the Council saying that the Knapp Commission "can perform a valuable service." He made it clear, however, that he expected us to undertake a "broad analysis" and avoid "building cases against individuals," views echoed by the police department's allies on the Council. Knapp gave the chairman of the City Council Committee a letter assuring him that such was our focus.

It was literally true that we were not intending to make cases against individuals, but it was equally true that we intended no bland general inquiry, and that we remained convinced that we could prove general patterns only by uncovering individual venality. If, as we strongly suspected, there was a good deal of corruption in the Department, the only way that fact could be brought home to the public would be through highly publicized "blockbuster" public hearings, at which the evidence of corruption would be presented in concrete terms by believable witnesses. We did not think it necessary to emphasize this distinction in the course of giving the City Council the assurances it required.

Our subpoena power was renewed in the City Council, by a narrow margin. The heated session went so late into the evening that only a drugstore remained open for some necessary last-minute Christmas shopping on my way home.

3

LURCHING INTO ACTION

We were beginning to grope about, starting to determine ways that a dozen investigators and a half a dozen lawyers could unravel the secrets of a gigantic municipal police department, when Otto Obermaier came into my office and closed the door behind him. "Mike," he said, "I know it seems a near impossible task to investigate a whole department with only twelve investigators, but we're going to have to do it with eleven. Otherwise you are going to jail." Otto had my attention.

His point was that, from an administrative standpoint, we were proceeding in an utterly haphazard fashion. Payroll checks for those employees who got them, reimbursement vouchers for agents on loan, equipment rental payments, expense vouchers, time records—all of the administrative elements that are part of any organization—were being shunted aside or completely ignored as we swept forward in pursuit of our mission. We were headed for trouble, and, as head of the organization, I would be held responsible when it turned out that some regulations had been violated or some money had gone astray. So one of our twelve, Pat Stokes, a retired FBI agent in his late fifties, with an accounting background, was given the almost full-time job of taking care of our administrative needs. After a few weeks, we actually began to look like a grownup operation.

Seeking some advice as to how to go about things, I reached out to a few people who I thought might be helpful. Among the first of these was Chief Sidney Cooper, then serving as head of the Department's Internal Affairs Division, which had principal jurisdiction in combating corruption. Understaffed and generally despised by the rank and file, Cooper's "shooflies" did not appear to have much impact on whatever corruption might be going on. Cooper was doing his best. Tall, brawny, and totally bald, Cooper looked a little like a TV cop of the time, Kojak, played by Telly Savalas. He had been "on the job" since 1941, with two years off for army service during World War II. His last seven years had been spent in anti-corruption work. A genuine Renaissance man, Cooper also had a law degree and was an accomplished artist. He used his formidable wit, which was aggressive yet often self-deprecating, as a weapon. It was he who originated the classification of corrupt police officers as "meat eaters" and "grass eaters."

Cooper had been Frank Serpico's mentor. Once the Department began investigating Serpico's charges, Cooper guided, cajoled, and threatened the rebel cop to follow through on what he had started when he first came forward with his accusations. Serpico had never been eager to take a leading role. His oft-stated position was that he had not signed on to be a "shoofly" and that it was up to the professionals to root out the rottenness to which he had pointed. "That's not my job," he complained when asked to wear a recording device. "I told you where to find it—now you go and do something about it." It had fallen to Cooper to see to it that Serpico kept going in the right direction. When it came time for Frank to testify in the grand jury, he refused. Cooper set him straight. "François," he snarled sweetly, "you are going to testify—either as a hero policeman or a suspended cop—take your choice—but you are going to testify." Sidney Cooper was a man whose will was difficult to resist. Serpico did his duty.

Paul Rooney and I arranged for a meeting to seek Cooper's advice, and found him more guarded than he would later be. He told us flat out that we might pick off a corrupt officer or two, but that we had no chance of effecting any significant overall change. We knew that Cooper spoke from long experience. The rumor was that when he was a sergeant, he would "steal a hot stove." Later on, when we were on friendly terms with him and slyly hinted at such rumors, Cooper would smile and say, "Thank God for the statute of limitations." He knew where the bodies would be buried, but had pretty much given up on being able to accomplish anything fundamental about digging them up. Paul and I came away from our talk with Cooper without much encouragement regarding the task that lay ahead of us. The best thing that came from our meeting was the fact that we got along well with Cooper and sensed that he would help us if he could, even if he obviously thought of us as a bunch of amateurs destined for failure.

Another source of advice came quickly to mind. One of the side benefits of my new position was the chance it gave me to consult with the legendary Judge Thomas Murphy. Now a federal district court judge, Murphy had served as police commissioner some years earlier. He had also been a federal prosecutor, counting among his scalps that of Alger Hiss, advisor to President Roosevelt, who was convicted of lying under oath about spying for the Soviet Union. Judge Murphy's wit and wisdom were known far and wide. Six feet five inches tall, with a handlebar moustache, he would gaze balefully over half-glasses as he skewered some victim with the latest of the thousand barbs for which he was famous. Among the lore celebrating Judge Murphy's humor was the tale of his response to a Black Muslim defendant, being arraigned before him, who loudly proclaimed, when Murphy asked if he had an attorney, "Allah is my lawyer!" "Yes, yes, I understand that," said Murphy, "and who is your local counsel?"

Murphy agreed to see me and, as we chatted, he focused in particular upon the Department's uncanny underground communications network. It was not, he said, until his last day of service as commissioner that he discovered that there was a hole in the ornate paneling of his office in the old Police Headquarters building on Centre Street. The hole was right at the ear level of the sergeant sitting at the desk outside. Murphy chuckled as he recalled the sergeant's flustered attempt to explain that he needed to know when Murphy's meetings were coming to an end, so he could plan for the next one.

The information network, said Murphy, did not depend on mere eavesdropping, however—it was far more sophisticated and mystical than that. "I would have an idea while shaving in the morning," he mused, "and, by the time I reached my desk, that thought would already have spread to the furthest reaches of the Bronx, Queens, and Staten Island." Even if Judge Murphy's anecdote was a bit exaggerated, it illustrated one of the basic problems we would face in trying to do our job discreetly.

As we brainstormed about sources, it occurred to us that the problem of police corruption must have been analyzed in academia. While this was not a major area of our inquiry, it didn't hurt for us to be educated in some of the accumulated learning regarding corruption. So we reached out to several academics, chief among whom was Herman Goldstein of the University of Wisconsin, who proved quite helpful in putting into context some of the behavior our investigations uncovered.

It seemed to me that police issues often break down on a liberal versus conservative basis, and that most of the academic world could best be described as liberal. So I reached out to one of the nation's foremost conservatives, William F. Buckley Jr., whom I knew slightly, to tell us if there was a particular conservative slant on the problem of police corruption and, if so, who could fill me in on it. Buckley was a prolific author, lecturer, magazine publisher, television personality, advisor to presidents, philosophical leader in the conservative movement, and former quixotic mayoral candidate (when asked what he would do were he to win, Buckley said, "Demand a recount"). As with Judge Murphy, this was an opportunity to spend some time with a fascinating person and, who knows, I might actually learn something relevant. After a delightful visit with Buckley, I came away with the understanding that there wasn't any political liberal–conservative difference in thinking on the subject of police corruption, that he knew of. Conservatives, like liberals, thought it was bad.

While we were still recruiting staff and investigators, Obermaier, Rooney, and Scoppetta started examining whatever documents might be available that related to our mission. In that pre-computer age, it would be expected that the files of the Department might not be maintained in crisp, orderly condition. In fact, they were a complete shambles. Little or no effort had been taken to collect and organize files in a way that might make them usable. Gathering information about an event or individual was a hit-or-miss project. A police officer did not even have a central personnel file. Relevant information about him would be scattered in precinct, division, borough, and specialized files, with no coordination among them or any index to indicate where a particular document might be. To make a thorough check on any particular cop, one had to examine a half-dozen files where information about him might be kept. We quickly realized that one of the Commission's ultimate recommendations for reform would be to put in place a sensible system for collecting and retaining documents relating to the various activities of the members of the Department.

As we rummaged through Department files, we came upon an extraordinary police officer who headed us in the right direction, for the first time. Captain Daniel McGowan was a decorated World War II veteran who had been on the job for twenty-three years. He had served in several anti-corruption units and was currently assigned in a supervisory capacity to the Intelligence Division. McGowan was smart, streetwise, and thoroughly honest, a trait that in recent years had instilled in him a certain fatalistic cynicism. The Intelligence Division, in which he worked, had become the last resting place of many corruption allegations and aborted investigations. Whenever something got too hot to handle, which was most of the time, it would be referred to Intelligence for further analysis. There it would stay, in disorganized files that no one ever really looked at.

McGowan, who had neither the manpower nor the authority to do anything about the information accumulated in the division of which he was a part, volunteered to tell us what it was all about.

Among the files buried in Intelligence was a report, made by federal investigators, of an investigation a few years earlier into corrupt federal narcotics officers who had allegedly coordinated their illegal activities with New York City narcotics cops. The file contained allegation after allegation of corrupt behavior on the part of police officers charged with narcotics enforcement. Specific names and incidents were set forth, sometimes in the form of second- or third-person hearsay, but often in a manner that could easily be followed up by any investigators who were serious about what they were doing. Apparently no one had thought it necessary to take action, and the file had been sent to Intelligence, where it languished. A memorandum from Chief of Personnel Joseph McGovern, dated February 1, 1969, made it pretty clear why the federal investigation got nowhere. McGovern wrote: "Get our people out of that. First Deputy Commissioner [John Walsh] doesn't want to help Feds lock up local police—let them arrest federal people."

Nick Scoppetta, whose special area of concentration for the Commission was narcotics, took it upon himself to analyze these allegations, to see if our investigators could do something to follow up on them.

Meanwhile, McGowan showed us other dead ends into which various allegations of corruption had been shunted. Otto Obermaier collected, with McGowan's help, various files, memoranda, and correspondence showing that the Department was not really interested in pursuing allegations of corruption, unless they were so public and compelling that there was no way to avoid dealing with them. It was not so much that the Department was conspiring to cover up for corrupt police officers, but rather that it was gripped by an institutional unwillingness to face evidence of corruption until that evidence was shoved in its collective face.

Everything was a matter of image. First Deputy Commissioner John Walsh, who allegedly had done nothing about Frank Serpico's charges of corruption, had a personal reputation of ferocious intolerance of corruption, once it was actually exposed—but only then. He was later to testify that if, in the course of a hypothetical major secret investigation of some serious crime such as the sale of narcotics, it was discovered that a police officer was involved in corrupt behavior, Walsh would order the immediate arrest of the cop, even at the cost of prematurely aborting the overall investigation. Regardless of the consequences, Walsh would not tolerate a corrupt police officer retaining his gun and badge—once Walsh actually knew the cop was bad. Of course, a preemptive strike of this kind would also have the side effect of protecting from exposure any other cops who might be involved but who were as yet undetected.

The police hierarchy's point seemed to be that the Department's reputation would be damaged if it did not deal swiftly and severely with corruption that became known, or inevitably would be known, but that same reputation was best maintained if allegations that were unlikely to see the light of day were quietly ignored.

It occurred to us that we might adopt some of the techniques used by the advertising agencies on Madison Avenue in order to stir up "business." So Lisa Barrett drafted, and we began to make arrangements to circulate, a sometimes broadly and sometimes pointedly-worded "Community Attitude Survey." The plan was to circulate the survey among a representative sample of the public, to find out what people thought of their police department. We would necessarily have to include a good deal of subjective assumptions in the questions we would ask. The PBA and Commissioner Murphy joined forces to argue the unfairness and unworkability of this scheme. This time what they said made a good deal of sense. The project was abandoned.

Employing a more direct advertising technique, we prepared a radio ad, simply urging the public to cooperate with the Commission. As a public interest advertisement, it was free, and would be inserted into normal programming, at the radio station's discretion, whenever there was an opening. That could have been, we realized, at 3:00 A.M. on some weekday, when no one would have been watching. We were amazed—and our police adversaries outraged—when the ad was run, locally of course, in the middle of the broadcasting of the 1971 Super Bowl.

While we developed our own investigative capability, Obermaier and Scoppetta, with McGowan's help, went through numbers of files looking for situations that were recent enough, and specific enough, for us to make them subjects of our own investigation. Ultimately, it turned out that the information was too stale, too vague, or required too much manpower to be of use. The general picture, however, emerged pretty clearly. There was plenty to look into, but the Department was concerned chiefly with its image, and viewed corruption as something to be dealt with only when absolutely necessary.

We had a powerful, if untested, weapon in our struggle to get started— our subpoena power. Anyone who refused to talk to us could be compelled to do so—under oath and in secret executive session. We got the City to give us another room, downstairs in our building, to use as a hearing room, where a commissioner would administer an oath and take testimony. Questioning would be conducted by one of our attorneys and a stenographer would make a record of the proceeding.

There was no precedent—or, indeed, legal authority—for these procedures. If, for instance, a witness had simply refused to testify or had demanded a copy of his transcript, we would have faced a long, time-consuming voyage through uncharted legal waters. It was clear that we would need a certain dexterity in dealing with procedural challenges, as they came up.

Commissioner Arnold Bauman exhibited this dexterity in the very first executive session we held. He was serving as the presiding commissioner, sitting behind a desk in our improvised hearing room, with the witness, his attorney beside him, seated at a small table facing him. Otto Obermaier, who was to ask the questions, sat to one side. The witness was sworn in, and Otto had hardly begun to ask his questions when the witness's attorney apparently did not like one of them. "Objection!" he proclaimed, somewhat hesitantly.

Objection? We hadn't really thought this one through. What, if any, rules of evidence, were we purporting to follow? What standard was there for whether a question was proper or not? Who was going to decide? What was supposed to happen if the lawyer simply instructed his client not to answer?

Bauman did not allow himself to be troubled by any of these questions. Bringing his open palm sharply down on the desk in front of him, he proclaimed, sternly and in a slightly raised voice, "Overruled!" Perhaps it was Bauman's naturally judicial demeanor—he was later to become a federal judge—or it may have been merely the inertia of the situation, but the witness's counsel meekly subsided and Otto went on with his questioning.

We had established a procedure. From then on, the commissioner presiding at an executive session was the equivalent of a judge.

Unfortunately, we were just beginning to use subpoenas to unearth information when the Sergeant's Benevolent Association, the labor union for the Department's sergeants, slapped another lawsuit on us, challenging the right of the City Council to give us subpoena power. The suit had no merit, but the proceedings dragged on and we could not free ourselves of them until May 1971, when we finally won the suit and again could use our subpoenas.

Obermaier returned one day from a visit to police headquarters with the wry observation that he thought he knew what was wrong with the Department. The old headquarters building was a monument of a structure located on Centre Street. Built in 1909, it was a massive stone Beaux-Arts building with thick walls and lofty ceilings. Obviously erected to impress with its majesty, it was hugely inefficient by modern standards, but still served the purpose of having an impact upon people. The police commissioner's office was in keeping with the general theme. Dark wooden paneling covered the walls. It had high ceilings, ornate windows, and the famous desk, seemingly the size of a football field, that had been used by Teddy Roosevelt when he was police commissioner. "I walked up the marble steps through the huge front door of this great building," Otto said, "and entered the reception hall. Opposite the desk of the police officer who greeted me was a huge poster depicting policemen in heroic poses. *The poster was covered in graffiti!*" Otto was aghast. "Can you imagine that? The Commissioner walks past that poster every day. How can he possibly assert leadership and pride in this outfit, when he can't even keep people from writing all over a poster in his own front hall?"

4

GABE

An obvious tactic in the identification of police corruption was to look for activities that were common, or even flourishing, despite the fact that they did so in open and obvious violation of the law. The absence of police interference with such illegal activities, we reasoned, was probably bought and paid for.

We began with a surveillance of a construction site. It was my idea. I recalled that when I was in college, working summer jobs as a construction laborer, policemen would often stop by the timekeeper's shack, and walk away, looking satisfied. Maybe if some of our new agents hung out at a large construction site, they might see something. This level of sophisticated thinking was properly rewarded when three or four days of watching a building under construction resulted in nothing other than a few hostile inquiries from laborers, wanting to know why we were lurking about. We would have to direct our energies elsewhere.

Another seemingly obvious source of police corruption were the small grocery stores that had proliferated in the Hispanic sections of town. These "bodegas" stayed open in violation of the then-prevalent Sunday closing laws and, in particular, continued to sell beer on Sundays. Nothing was ever done about such violations, and it seemed likely that, as usual, police forbearance had a price tag.

Logically enough, this investigation was supervised by the only Spanish-speaking attorney we had—Nick Figueroa. Our inquiries confirmed, from a number of sources, the fact that the bodegas regularly paid bribes in order to be left alone, but we never succeeded in persuading an owner to agree to testify about the payments he was making. Small wonder! It was quite obvious that one day we would move on, but the bodega owner had to face whatever retaliation the cops chose to administer. We would have to get testimony about these and other similar situations from the payees—the corrupt cops who were taking the money. At this point we had little prospect of obtaining such assistance.

Yet another potential target that we could not help noticing was one of the most obvious and open corruption hazards in the city—the raucous mélange of restaurants, bars, and late-night entertainment joints operating on the Upper East Side of Manhattan. Catering chiefly to the young, professional singles crowd, these establishments served minors, crammed many more patrons within their walls than the fire laws allowed, brought traffic to a crawl in the area by encouraging double parking, stayed open past the legal closing times, and openly violated just about every ordinance and regulation set up to control them. Where were the cops? This kind of thing could not go on unless the police officers who patrolled the area looked the other way. The question was whether police inattention was merely a result of laziness or a philosophy of laissez-faire, or was bought and paid for.

The heart of the East Side bar scene was located in the 19th Precinct, running from Fifth Avenue to the East River, between 57th and 86th streets. We set some of our agents the task of following the precinct's patrolmen and sergeants on their rounds. What our agents saw was a good deal of fraternization and drinking. Sergeants, in particular, spent a lot of time bellying up to various bars and engaging in chummy conversations with bartenders and patrons. It was a comfortable setting where, in the words of the theme song of *Cheers*, a TV sitcom about a bar that aired two decades later, "Everybody knows your name." All this lubricated conviviality was hardly consistent with aggressive police work, but that was not our concern. We wanted to know whether money was actually changing hands. We would never find out through simple surveillance operations.

As a way to get into the situation, we decided to examine the memo books of the officers assigned to bar duty in the 19th Precinct. New York City cops were required to enter "occurrences" on their tours in memo books they carried with them. We were certain that the cops would not write down many of the contacts we saw them making with owners, employees, customers, and suspicious characters. Questioning the cops, particularly sergeants, who were supposed to be supervising, about absent entries might be a way to get started. So, on the evening of November 2, 1970, our agents, under the direction of Paul Rooney and Milt Williams, were waiting in the 19th Precinct station house at midnight as the officers who had been working the "four to twelve" tour returned. Each sergeant was given a Commission subpoena and required to surrender his memo book, forthwith.

"Midnight raid," "Gestapo tactics," and "invasion of privacy" were only a few of the terms thrown around the next morning by the PBA and their sympathetic elements in the political world and the media. After a day of bitter public accusations, the PBA filed a lawsuit against us. They challenged us, in court, to show some reason for collecting the memo books. Forced to answer the lawsuit, I executed an affidavit giving some of the reasons prompting us to act. These included undocumented observations as well as theories and rumors about police payoffs in bars under the kinds of circumstances and pressures that made it likely to think that such payoffs occurred. Our response was, of necessity, speculative. We could never have made anything of the sort part of an actual allegation. But the PBA had demanded, in court—publicly—that we explain what had moved us to act. So we told them—publicly. Now they were really mad! The incident actually triggered a police strike that lasted several days.

This was the first serious publicity the Commission had gotten since the press conference in August announcing the beginning of our operations. We had resolved not to say anything publicly until we had something to say, and we had told the media that we would not comment on our investigations as they progressed. So far we had been successful in proceeding fairly quietly. Now we found ourselves catapulted into a situation where we were obliged to answer public charges against us.

I was invited to appear, live, on three television news shows on the same evening. It was to be a distinctively novel experience for me. I had never done this kind of thing before. The first show was the six o'clock news, on Channel 4, the local NBC station. I was to be interviewed by Gabe Pressman, who was locally well-known as a penetrating if sometimes shrill investigative reporter. On television, Pressman's appearance somehow went with his aggressive style. He was small, with eager piercing eyes, permanently black hair, and a greenish complexion. I did not expect to be comfortable under his questioning.

Appearing at the studio at the appointed time, I was ushered into a makeup room. Makeup! It was all very new, and I was nervously wondering what was going to happen, when Pressman came in and sat down to chat. I was surprised to find that he was not the abrasive, impersonal figure he presented himself to be on television. On the contrary, he was warm and friendly, doing his best to put me at ease. I asked him what, specifically, we would be talking about. He said not to worry. He just wanted me to talk about the investigation and the reasons that made the pickup of the memo books necessary. We talked easily about the work the Commission was trying to do.

Pressman professed to be knowledgeable about the police and disdainful of their attacks on us. He soothingly assured me that he agreed entirely both with our purpose in seeking memo books from the officers of the 19th Precinct and our method of going about getting them. When else, after all, could you pick up memo books other than when the men came off work? The PBA's characterization of the project as a "midnight raid" was pure demagoguery, he snorted.

After we chatted for a while, I again brought up the subject of the interview we were about to have. "Wouldn't it be a good idea," I ventured, "if I were to know a few of the questions you're going to ask?"

"No need," assured Pressman, smoothly, "we'll do exactly what we've been doing right here, I'll just ask you how the Commission responds to the charges, and you will say whatever you want. No problem."

My makeup complete, I followed Pressman into the studio. He pointed out two box-like podiums behind which he and I would stand. "When a camera is directed at you, and the little red light is on," he explained, "you're on. You just speak up and answer my questions. That's all there is to it. You'll do fine." It sounded simple.

Despite Pressman's kind reassurances, it was after all, my first real television appearance, and I was very nervous. We were given our cues to come on stage and, as we took our places, Gabe gave me one final friendly nod.

On the other side of the sound stage, the show's anchorman was on camera, giving the latest update with respect to the dispute between the PBA and the Commission. "And now," he concluded, "we have with us in the studio this evening—Michael Armstrong, Chief Counsel to the Knapp Commission, who will be interviewed by Gabe Pressman."

The red light glowed on the camera pointing at Pressman. "Good evening," he said, crisply, and turned to me. Gone was the genial friend of a few moments before. I now recognized the cold, almost malevolent glare that I associated with the investigative reporter I had often seen on television. This time the glare was directed at me. "Tell me, Mr. Armstrong, isn't it a fact that what you are doing is—MCCARTHYISM?"

McCarthyism? I was dumbfounded. What happened to my buddy? What's he doing to me? My red light was on, and I mumbled something in confused response. Pressman rolled on. Muttering defensively, I struggled through the interview.

Afterward, Pressman joined me, walking out of the studio. Putting a friendly hand on my shoulder, he said pleasantly. "Nice going. You were great. You guys sure are doing a terrific job and I wish you the best of luck."

It was part of my education in the ways of the media to learn that, like many other TV and radio reporters, Gabe Pressman's on-camera personality could be radically different from when he was off. As time went on, I learned to handle him, adequately, and I also came to like him. I found out, among other things, that however abrasive Pressman might occasionally be on the air, he was utterly trustworthy and professional in dealing with confidences or in avoiding breaches of agreed-upon security. I was to discover that not all of his sometimes more amiable brethren were as straightforward.

It was part of my job to learn whom in the media I could trust, and how to handle the ones I could not. Gabe Pressman was one of the good guys.

As for the East Side bar investigation, the PBA lawsuit quickly petered out and so did the investigation. We found little of value, other than to confirm our initial conclusions that cops did a good deal of on-duty drinking. If payoffs were going on, as they almost certainly were, it would take more than surveillances and examining memo books to unearth them.

My first foray into the television interview world, regardless of how it may have played among the general public, had one audience that needed only my mere appearance to give its approval. My three daughters, then ages eight, ten, and twelve, were absolutely thrilled when they heard their daddy was going to be on television. With my wife, all three waited eagerly for the six o'clock news. However, they did not count on the unexpected fact that Pressman's interview with me would be at the top of the show, so the youngest, Marnie, who was in later years to become a partner in a national law firm, had not quite finished her bath when I appeared. By the time she got to the TV, the segment was over. She was inconsolable. My wife, Joan, tried to soothe her: "Daddy will be on TV again." "I don't care," wailed Marnie. "This was the first time, and I missed it!" Indeed, Daddy appeared on television on many more occasions and for a time the children remained faithfully focused on whatever show I was on, even when it competed with, for instance, *The Brady Bunch*. After a while, though, it was *The Brady Bunch*, every time. *Sic transit . . .*

5

TEDDY AND XAVIERA

One of the most vital technical needs of any investigative outfit is electronic eavesdropping equipment. The Knapp Commission had no use for telephone wiretaps or hidden "bugs" because, not being a law enforcement agency, we could not legally employ them. Under federal and New York State law as it was then, only a law enforcement officer, with a warrant, could plant a listening device on a phone, or in a room, if no one taking part in the conversation knew the device was there.

What the law did allow us to do was equip our agents with concealed recorders or transmitters, to record conversation in which they personally took part. Paul Rooney said he knew just the fellow to supply us with the equipment we needed, a character named Teddy Ratnoff.

Ratnoff had cropped up during Paul's days as a prosecutor. He worked at home, manufacturing the most powerful body transmitters on the market. A pudgy, pasty-faced, bald little man with bright beady eyes, almost imperceptible eyebrows, and a weak fleshy mouth, he sweated profusely a good deal of the time. His glance darted nervously and constantly about, as if always on the lookout for an angle of some sort. In the shadowy world of informants and the information peddlers who customarily used his equipment, Teddy took an active personal role whenever the opportunity presented itself. By reputation, he was utterly without morals or loyalty and would sell himself or his wares to anyone to do anything—for a price.

Ratnoff's character aside, his equipment was indeed impressive. We were particularly interested in his concealable transmitters, which, although a little bulkier than some competitive models, worked marvelously. The batteries lasted for hours, and the transmitter would send a strong signal, through steel and concrete walls, as far as a city block. This was, in those days, a remarkable feat. Popular mythology of the time had it that electronic spying devices were so sophisticated and so compact that one could be secreted in a martini olive, where it would transmit for days over a distance of miles, without the aid of outside batteries. At that time, however, that kind of stuff existed only on TV. We actually checked with the Central Intelligence Agency, as well as military and police sources, and satisfied ourselves that nobody put out better equipment than Teddy Ratnoff.

After seemingly interminable haggling with Ratnoff over prices, we struck a deal whereby he supplied us with what in those days was highly sophisticated equipment. Each unit consisted of a transmitter about the size of a narrow cigarette package, together with a battery power pack that was slightly larger. These would be inserted into a cloth belt that tucked the unit into the small of an agent's back. A tiny microphone was taped to the agent's chest, under a sweater or inserted under his lapel or tie. Conversations were transmitted to a receiver, where they were monitored and recorded by other agents.

To augment Ratnoff's audio setup, we hoped to be able to film some of our operations, but that equipment, which had to be able to function in dim or fluctuating light conditions, was beyond Teddy's technological capabilities and our budget. So, we made a deal with both Channel 5, a local independent channel, and Channel 4, the local NBC outlet, whereby we would allow them to come along on certain surveillances. They would use sophisticated equipment, that we couldn't afford, to make surveillance films from considerable distances, even at night. The films would be kept by us and not used until our public hearings. Then the TV station could use all of the "outtakes," as well as the segments we chose to make public. Most of the time, however, we would rely simply on audio transmitters. After a few field tests, in which Ratnoff's equipment worked beautifully, we were ready to launch our investigations—if only we could find something to investigate.

We felt certain that if anyone paid off the cops, it was prostitutes who plied their trade openly in certain parts of the city, without much apparent interference from anyone in authority. So, we devised a scheme that we hoped would get one or more of these ladies of the evening to talk to us about the cost of doing business. Our agents would pose as out-of-town businessmen and strike up conversations with some of the high-priced hookers who operated in one of the better hotels. "We're too rushed now," our agents would say, "but how about setting something up for the next time we're in town." They would then call, supposedly from out of state, to make specific arrangements. Then we would confront the prostitutes with supposedly incriminating tapes that we would represent to be interstate. That, we would claim, made the conversations a violation of federal law. No more turnstile local justice. This would be a federal offense. We would threaten to turn the hookers over to the FBI unless they told us about the police we were sure they were paying. Hopefully, the unfamiliar prospect of federal prosecution would pressure some of the girls to talk to us. The plan was rather unsavory and very clumsy, but it was all we could think of at the time.

The agents who drew the assignment were Brian Bruh and Ralph Parente, two of the special agents on loan to us from the Internal Revenue Service. Both men had extensive experience in organized crime cases, if not a whole lot in undercover stings involving prostitutes. Bruh was Jewish, tall but inclined to be a little heavy, with a full face, thinning hair, and a friendly, eager grin. Bright, imaginative, and irrepressibly enthusiastic, he properly enjoyed a reputation as one of the best agents in the New York area. His partner, Ralph Parente, was equally renowned, if shorter, stockier, Italian American, and much quieter.

Bruh and Parente dressed themselves in slacks and colorful sports jackets, our idea of what a Midwestern businessman would wear. Armed with counterfeit drivers' licenses and credit cards identifying them as two guys from Chicago, they presented themselves one evening in the lounge of the Barclay Hotel, a relatively upper-crust establishment, then fairly well-known as a hangout for high-priced prostitutes. The agents were outfitted with the new equipment we had just bought from Teddy Ratnoff, and their conversations were transmitted across the street to a receiver and tape recorder manned by two other agents sitting in a parked car.

The only thing that worked in this operation was Teddy Ratnoff's equipment. The hookers' conversations turned out to be not explicit enough to provide the basis for meaningful threats. To make matters worse, unexpected complications arose as a result of the operation. The names used by Bruh and Parente were those of actual people, picked at random from the Chicago telephone book. Real names and addresses were used in case one of the girls got suspicious and checked with a Chicago information operator. But we did not anticipate the process being carried one step further. One of the prostitutes indeed reached a Chicago information operator a few days after meeting Bruh, got the home phone number of her new friend—and called it. The call was made not out of suspicion, but because she simply wanted to talk. The hooker reached the startled wife of a mystified and suddenly very defensive husband, whose marriage had to be straightened out at the cost of my breaching security by telling the couple more than we would have liked about our investigation.

The "hooker operation" was not a total loss. Ratnoff, whom we had allowed to come along on one of the surveillances in order to check out his equipment, had an idea. Schmoozing with prostitutes in hopes of getting information about corrupt cops was as good a place to start as any, he observed, unless there was a better way—and he knew of one. Her name was Xaviera Hollander. Ratnoff was then engaged in bugging the posh East Side apartment of an exclusive madam by that name. Xaviera was a twenty-nine year old self-proclaimed practitioner of the oldest profession, who brought a genuine enthusiasm to her work. She liked what she did, and she did it extremely well. Her hair was artificially blond, but her lush body, commanding eyes, and inviting smile were all real. So was her business sense. She had managed to organize her own efforts and those of a half-dozen of her "sisters" into a thriving operation, catering to the sometimes kinky whims of the well-heeled and, in a few cases, the politically well-known.

Ratnoff had planted his electronic listening devices throughout Xaviera's apartment. He was gathering information for the author of a book about her, to be called *The Happy Hooker*, destined to be a best-seller. It has never been quite clear the degree to which Xaviera consented to Ratnoff's eavesdropping. There is no question that he enjoyed a special relationship with her. Ratnoff claimed that he even had gone as far as to conceal a television camera in one of Xaviera's bedrooms. The camera was hooked to a transmitter that sent a signal to a receiver Ratnoff maintained in a nearby apartment. The technology of the time did not allow for easy tape-recording of transmitted visual images, and it may have been that the camera was as much for prurient viewing as for business "research." Ratnoff said that he had to remove it after it malfunctioned one evening. The signal was inadvertently intercepted on a local commercial frequency and beamed to a residential area just across the Hudson River. Xaviera's customers' goings-on were broadcast live, in prime time, throughout suburban New Jersey.

Offering to insinuate us into the world of Xaviera Hollander, Ratnoff claimed she was routinely paying off cops. Hollander was cautious. She kept careful records of her clients, who included prominent people, and new customers were accepted only by referral. Although she did not have regular police protection, she had had what she thought was an arrangement with one police sergeant that he would notify her if there was any threatening police action pending. Ratnoff said that Hollander's chauffeur also occasionally passed money from her to individual cops. On one occasion Hollander gave her sergeant five hundred dollars, which was to be forwarded to a Vice Squad lieutenant in order to avoid a planned arrest. She got arrested anyway. Now she had apparently gotten herself into a situation that required more certainty that she would get what she was paying for. She would like to regularize her payments. It was, said Teddy, a perfect opportunity for our Commission.

He, Ratnoff, could be the go-between—and record what was said. The idea was interesting, but dangerous. Ratnoff was wildly unreliable. After considerable hesitation, we decided to take the first step, and allow Teddy to introduce our agents to Xaviera and, perhaps, some of her friends.

As soon as we began using Ratnoff as more than a supplier of equipment, he began attempting to insinuate himself into our organization. He was invaluable in his technical role and as an informant, but he was constantly nosing around, seeking information about other investigations, and in general, attempting to make himself part of our operations, as if he were a regular. We realized that his desire to be recognized as one of our agents was not mere status-seeking. Anything Teddy did, he did for money. In this case, it was clear that if we let him look like a Knapp agent, he would use that pseudo-identity to con or pressure people into giving or loaning him payments of some sort. Indeed, despite our best efforts to make sure that he was never cloaked in apparent authority to do anything on our behalf, he engineered just such a swindle after he was "outed" during our public hearings. Now, at the outset of our investigation, we used him because . . . we needed him.

So, on Teddy Ratnoff's introduction, agents posing as businessmen presented themselves at Xaviera Hollander's penthouse establishment on 55th Street, off Third Avenue. The place consisted of a plushly furnished living room and several equally luxurious bedrooms. A maid served customers from a well-stocked bar. Everyone was very friendly. We instructed the agents to do no more than engage in preliminary conversations, with a promise to return later. Don't allow the transmitting equipment to "malfunction," they were told. Silence would bring backup agents, promptly.

Nothing of value came from the agents' initial visits but we persisted, broadening our focus to one or two of Xaviera's competitors operating in the area. Some of the agents' observations were extraordinary. On one occasion, while Brian Bruh conversed with a madam in her living room, a balding, paunchy, middle-aged customer scurried through the room on all fours, naked. He was followed by one of the girls, who was holding a leash, the end of which was tied tightly around the gentlemen's testicles. As he crawled spiritedly along, she would yank on the leash and he would bark like a dog. He seemed to be having fun.

On another occasion, one of the agents was shown a suit of armor, which was kept in a closet awaiting a special customer. The fellow would pay a handsome amount to be stripped, bathed, encased in the suit, and deposited in a dark closet, thereby satisfying some sexually-related claustrophobic urge. I always felt that Xaviera and her sisters actually performed a valuable function by providing outlets to these types, who otherwise might be satisfy their "needs" in ways directed at members of the general public.

Mere observations of creative perversity were not, of course, going to advance our cause. We needed to get involved with Xaviera's dealings with the police. It was clear that she was not happy with her current protection arrangements, and we hoped that her attempts to improve her situation could be turned to our benefit. Our agents bided their time. Threatening Xaviera did not seem a promising tactic. She was too tough. But the situation might lead to other opportunities.

6

THE GREAT MEAT ROBBERY

By mid-January 1971, the Knapp Commission had been in business for more than six months, and had been actually operating for a little over three. We had come up with absolutely nothing. It wasn't that we were finding the police department to be free of corruption. There was plenty of graft around alright, but we had simply been unable to find any proof of it. It was still early, but we were beginning to chafe under the taunts of the PBA as the cops slowly came to conclude they had nothing to fear from us.

It wasn't only the rank and file that seemed contemptuous of our efforts. The brass had been warily sizing us up and were undoubtedly heaving a collective sigh of relief as they concluded that we would probably not find anything to pin on them. Police Commissioner Murphy was at all times correct and polite in dealing with us, but it was perfectly clear that he was quite determined to do everything he could to make sure that any corruption in the Department was discovered and dealt with by the Department, not us.

Whit Knapp, always one to face his possible adversaries directly, had arranged for the police commissioner and his first deputy to join Whit and me, as Whit's guests, at the Yale Club for an informal breakfast every month. We sat around a table in friendly discussion, each side using the opportunity to discover what it could about the other. It was pretty clear, as of early 1971, that Murphy and Smith were becoming more and more convinced that our operation would not uncover anything serious to embarrass the Department.

Knapp agents Jim Donovan and Frank Nemic, snooping around on foot in the West Greenwich Village section of Manhattan after midnight on Sunday morning, January 24, 1971, did not really expect that they would find much to disprove the police commissioner's evaluation of our efforts. Donovan was a former agent of the Department of Immigration; wiry, blond, and energetic, he was thoroughly streetwise. Nemic was a postal inspector on loan to us, of medium height, conventionally good-looking; he was the agent whose formidable reputation led me to accept his supervisor's sarcastic offer to make him available for a month. Both men were topnotch agents. They had been focusing their attention on the West Village gay bars, whose flamboyant after-hours activities seemingly should have attracted the attention of the area's police.

The area was one of warehouses and garages, and nestled among them were a number of after-hours bars and homosexual prostitution hangouts, operating loudly and openly well past legal closing time. Donovan and Nemic hoped to find out what part, if any, the policemen from the 6th Precinct were playing in allowing these establishments to operate. So far they had come up with nothing directly showing that the cops' failure to do anything about the then-illegal but very open goings-on was the result of payoffs.

At about 3:00 A.M., the agents noticed two patrol cars parked halfway down Barrow, in front of a meat warehouse on West 13th Street, between Washington Street and Tenth Avenue. The warehouse had a sign on it, "Great Plains Packing Company, Inc."

As Donovan and Nemic watched, police officers emerged from their cars, and stealthily entered the dark warehouse. Before long they returned, with large packages in their arms, which they put in the trunks of their patrol cars. Then they went back for more. At this point, another patrol car pulled up.

Jotting down the numbers of the police cars, Donovan continued his surveillance while Nemic quickly went to a nearby phone booth (personal cell phones were a thing of the distant future) to call the 6th Precinct station house, six blocks away.

"I want to report a robbery," Nemic said to the desk officer.

"Oh, yeah? Gimme the details."

"It's going on right now at Great Plains Packing, on West 13th Street."

Pause. "Yeah, we just sent out a radio alarm about that one."

"Well, do you know that the guys who are committing the robbery are cops?"

Silence.

Without identifying himself, Nemic went on to give full details, including the patrol car numbers and the number of officers involved. The desk officer purported to take the information down and said that he "would notify the sergeant."

Nemic then rejoined Donovan in their surveillance. How quickly would the precinct deal with a report of nearby, ongoing thievery, by policemen?

Within a short period of time, a fourth patrol car pulled up to the scene, possibly in response to Nemic's phone call. Two officers got out of the car, spoke briefly to the policemen already there—and then joined their colleagues, loading packages into their own patrol car. As Nemic and Donovan watched, a sergeant's car pulled up and parked while the sergeant chatted with the patrolmen as they loaded the meat. The sergeant pulled away after a few minutes.

When the trunk of one of the patrol cars was finally filled, two of the officers got in the car and drove off. Nemic followed. Donovan maintained the surveillance.

The police car went straight to where a bronze late-model Buick Skylark was parked, at the corner of Hudson and West 10th Streets, a half-block from the 6th Precinct station house. The cops transferred the meat to the trunk of the Skylark and drove off in the patrol car. While Donovan watched as more meat was transferred to a blue Chevrolet, Nemic tried to call division and borough headquarters. Receiving no response, he called the offices of the police commissioner, the chief inspector, and Internal Affairs. Still no answer. A call to police information finally aroused a trainee, who, when asked for the identity of the ranking officer on duty, hung up.

Nemic then called back to the 6th Precinct and spoke to the sergeant on duty. It was 5:18 A.M., two hours since his first call.

"Hello, remember me?" said Nemic. "That robbery is still going on."

"Yeah, we have that one under investigation," replied the sergeant.

"Well, if you're interested in where they're taking the meat, some of it has just been put into cars parked about a half a block from you." Nemic then gave the locations, descriptions, and license plate numbers of the Skylark and the Chevrolet, and repeated the numbers of the four patrol cars. Nemic still gave no information as to who he was.

"Thanks, we'll look into it."

It happened that, at the same time, a successful jailbreak was underway at the Federal House of Detention at West Street, eight blocks away in the same sector. Three dangerous federal prisoners escaped down the outside of the building on a sheet rope, while the policemen who might have apprehended them were busy loading meat into their cars at the Great Plains Packing Company's warehouse.

When the cops finally finished removing meat and left, Nemic and Donovan followed one of them to the parked Skylark, the trunk of which had been filled earlier. One cop got out of the patrol car and drove off in the Skylark. Nemic and Donovan followed, but the trail was almost immediately lost when the police officer drove around a corner and apparently disappeared. The agents noted that the only possible place for him to have gone was a nearby police parking garage, the door of which had been open, but which was now closed.

Nemic and Donovan found a phone and, at 6:20 A.M., still without identifying themselves, called the 13th Precinct, located in the same building as division and borough headquarters. They reached a lieutenant, who said that he was covering for division headquarters. When informed of what was going on, the lieutenant suggested that Donovan and Nemic notify Internal Affairs when it opened on Monday. When the need for more immediate attention was pointed out to him, the lieutenant switched the call to a patrolman in borough headquarters, who said he would notify a superior.

Approximately one and a half hours later, the agents called back to the patrolman at borough headquarters, who said that he had reported the information to his duty captain immediately.

Someone finally sprang into action and, at 8:05 A.M., five hours after Nemic had first called the 6th Precinct, the area around the warehouse was swarming with patrol cars, this time with a purpose beyond that of picking up meat. The media came too.

News stories about the theft duly appeared in the next day's papers and, spurred by lively public attention, the Department undertook a prompt and efficient investigation of the incident. They had a good place to start. From Nemic's anonymous tips, they had received descriptions of all of the officers involved, together with car numbers and license plates. The Skylark and Chevrolet to which some of the meat had been transferred were found to belong to two of the officers assigned to patrol cars into which meat had been loaded. The cars were checked for traces of sawdust from the meat plant and all of the officers were questioned under oath. But, lacking the identity of the phantom telephone informant, the Department's investigation stalled.

We then held our own nonpublic hearings, ostensibly occasioned by public furor over the incident. In executive session, we carefully questioned the officers, under oath, on the basis of the facts as we knew them to be. Times, places, who was there, and what they did. All lied.

About five weeks after the incident, when media coverage had died down and the police investigation of the meat theft seemed going nowhere, I called up First Deputy Commissioner Bill Smith, saying that I had something fairly important to tell him. We made an appointment to meet in Smith's office that afternoon. Bill was a nice fellow, and I took no pleasure in causing him discomfort. But I was human enough to take a certain satisfaction in what I was about to do. Perhaps we weren't quite so inept after all.

After preliminary pleasantries, I turned the conversation to the meat theft investigation.

"How's it going?" I asked.

"Oh, we have a good deal of information, but no one has cracked and we have no eyewitnesses, so it looks like no case."

"Bill, there's something I have to tell you."

The commissioner's eyes narrowed and he seemed to brace himself.

"Oh, yeah? What?"

"Remember the guy who kept calling in to the precinct?"

"Yeah, of course. But he never identified himself. If we could find him, we'd have a case."

"Bill, he was one of our agents."

Smith received the news with about as much good grace as could be expected. He wanted to solve the case, but it was more than a little galling to have it broken by annoying "amateurs"—particularly us.

With the testimony of Nemic and Donovan, the investigation was pressed to a successful conclusion, and eight police officers were ultimately convicted for perjuring themselves in the grand jury and in our hearings. Other officers were disciplined.

As it turned out, there may not have been any theft at all. The warehouse was owned by one James Reardon, an ex-cop who himself had been convicted twenty years earlier in connection with the notorious Harry Gross scandal. He had maintained a close relationship with the police officers of the precinct and had put in a substantial insurance claim for a good deal more "stolen" meat than we had seen being removed from his warehouse. What we had stumbled upon may have been not a theft, but an insurance swindle. Either way, it told us a lot about the way cops investigated charges against other cops.

The episode did not reflect widespread or particularly serious corruption, and it rested not on the direct testimony of a corrupt cop, corroborated by tape recordings, or photographs, but entirely on our agents' testimony. Nevertheless, it was our first usable evidence for the public hearings we hoped to present. It was a start.

7

GEORGE

In 1960, some ten years prior to the creation of the Knapp Commission, the city had been rocked by a front-page scandal involving police payoffs by tow-truck operators. Reporters had exposed cops taking money to allow tow-truck drivers to haul away disabled vehicles. We were aware of this obvious corruption hazard and had begun some random questioning of tow-truck drivers when one of them walked into our office with just the information we were looking for.

George Burkert was twenty-three, of medium build, with sandy hair, bright gray eyes, a small beard and moustache, and a sometimes shy, sometimes raffish grin. His reason for coming to see us was to complain about being harassed by cops for not going along with the same kind of corruption uncovered by the press a decade earlier. He was also facing a number of traffic tickets, which, he said, had been given to him as part of a police shakedown. He wanted us to help him deal with the tickets. In order to spur us to action on his behalf, Burkert laid out, in specific and sometimes colorful detail, the situation as it currently existed, and his own experiences as a tow-truck driver over the last few years.

Whenever an accident took place, said Burkert, the police officer at the scene awarded the towing business, together with repair work that naturally followed, to one or more of the several tow trucks appearing at the scene. In some cases, the police car radio would even be used to clue a favored tow-truck driver. In return, the officer would later get in touch with the driver, or his boss, and arrange to pick up ten to a hundred dollars,[1] depending on the size of the repair job. The payoffs were routine, and a driver did not have the option of declining. Any driver, or tow-truck owner, who tried to make his way without police-directed business was hounded with spurious tickets. Burkert claimed to have refused to pay and been the victim of a campaign of harassment as a result.

Burkert told us that he had worked in the tow-truck business for six years. After a few months as a dispatcher, he had become a driver, responding to about ten–fifteen accidents each week. When he signed up his very first customer, he was approached by the police officer at the accident scene who asked him if he was going to "take care" of him. Burkert told the cop that he would talk to his boss about it and, when he did, discovered that the cop already had come directly to the shop, only to be told that the boss would not pay. A refusal like that came back to Burkert in the form of tickets.

Burkert told of working for several tow-truck garages over the next few years. Some went along, and some did not. The ones that refused were harassed on a regular basis, and Burkert told us in detail of the harassment he had experienced personally. For example, in one seven-month period, he said, he had received fifteen undeserved tickets. The cops giving them usually didn't say anything when they issued the summonses, but made it clear that his boss's refusal to pay off was the cause of his difficulty.

Some of the incidents Burkert described bordered on the bizarre. In particular, he told us of a cop who barred him from coming into Manhattan when he did not respond quickly enough to a request for a payment. In violation of this ban, Burkert later ventured into the 19th Precinct in Manhattan in his truck. He was seen by the cop, who stopped him, let him go, and then pulled him over again, this time at gunpoint. "Finding" a marijuana joint in the truck, the cop took him to the station house, where the cop and his partner wrote up thirteen tickets citing Burkert's going through successive lights every block or so while traveling across East 73rd Street and down Second Avenue. The tickets were problematic on their face. They reflected a wild, improbable dash through crowded Manhattan streets. Yet each of them was timed a minute or so from the last. Burkert said that he later got a telephone call from the cop saying to forget about the tickets. The summonses for them

---

1. The amounts of these payoffs, as well as those referred to elsewhere, must be viewed in the context of the times. In 1970, a dollar had at least ten times its present value. A loaf of bread, for example, cost twenty-six cents, a gallon of gasoline thirty-six cents, and a first-class stamp six cents. See www.1970sFlashback.com.

were eventually mailed to Burkert's mother, who didn't drive a car and who was instructed by the Department of Motor Vehicles to send them to Albany since there "obviously had been a mistake." According to Burkert, he had done absolutely nothing to warrant any ticket, much less thirteen of them.

We promised to look into his pending cases. We also were interested in using him to collect evidence. Would he agree to gather proof of the payoffs he described? Would he wear a wire? He said he'd think it over. Weeks went by. We met with Burkert a number of times to discuss his complaints about harassing cops and to urge him to work with us. Finally, he agreed.

Our agents schooled Burkert in the use of surveillance equipment and what to say, so the tape would be clear and intelligible. Then we waited until the next time he was approached. We didn't have long to wait. In a few days, Burkert called and reported that he had shown up at an accident scene where a cop made it clear that the privilege of towing a damaged car depended upon an agreement to pay something. When George indicated that his boss would probably go along, the cop let him tow away one of the cars. Later, the cop telephoned George and set his price—thirty dollars. George said his boss had OK'd the payment, and they arranged to meet that evening.

Burkert hurried down to our office to prepare for the meeting. A transmitter and a battery pack were taped to his body under his shirt and a microphone was concealed in his shirt collar. He was told what to say and how to make sure that the conversation clearly identified what was going on. Then George left for his appointment, trailed by two agents.

The meeting was an utter bust. George paid the thirty dollars, but was so flustered that he forgot to say anything to reflect the fact that money was changing hands:

POLICEMAN: How you doing, you stiff? You remembered, huh?

BURKERT: Yeah, I didn't forget.

POLICEMAN: We forgot. We just came through the plaza and I thought a fucking cab was wrapped around a girder, but he was giving a guy a jump. And I say, "Hey, shit, we was supposed to meet the guy."

BURKERT: Oh.

POLICEMAN: How'd you make out?

BURKERT: All right.

POLICEMAN: Good. Beautiful. [*pause*] What are you going to do, right? You know, what Donald [*Burkert's boss*], uh, Ronald, oh what's his name, Donald, gave you?

BURKERT: Yeah.

POLICEMAN: I know, he's a little fucking stiff. What's, uh, your name?

BURKERT: George.

POLICEMAN: Your last name?

BURKERT: Burkert.

POLICEMAN: Burkey?

BURKERT: Yeah.

POLICEMAN: Burkey, Burkey, Burkey?

BURKERT: I used to work for, uh, Neal.

POLICEMAN: I'm looking at you. I know you from somewhere. I can't figure out . . .

BURKERT: I used to work for Donald a long time ago.

POLICEMAN: Oh, yeah, how's he doing over there, Donald?

BURKERT: Doing all right.

POLICEMAN: Uh, huh.

BURKERT: It's kind of slow lately.

POLICEMAN: Yeah, well, that's the first one we've had in God knows how long.

BURKERT: Yeah [*name omitted*], and the rest of the guys are all down here like hot. Yeah, they got a lot of trucks.

POLICEMAN: Oh yeah.

BURKERT: Okay.

POLICEMAN: All right, Burkey.

The record of the conversation contained no reference to the fact that money had changed hands. The agents observed George and the cop talking. They knew that the money had been paid because, as part of the surveillance routine, they had carefully searched George before and after the meet and he never got out of their sight. Since the money was gone, it must have been given to the cop. It was probably enough evidence to arrest the cop, if our agents were willing to blow George's cover. But we weren't after arrests. We wanted tapes we could use at a hearing. This one was useless. Besides, our purpose was to show patterns, not individual behavior, and we hardly wanted to unmask George after his first encounter. He had lots of work to do.

We were sensitive to the fact that George was anything but a professional undercover agent. Anyone in his situation would be nervous and likely to forget his lines. So we chalked the first meeting up to lack of experience and went back to working with him to see that the next effort would be more successful.

But George couldn't seem to get the hang of what he was supposed to do. Several times he set up meetings to pay cops, only to flub his lines. He seemingly could not keep in his mind the fact that money changing hands does not get recorded on a tape, and an operation is worthless unless you say something to the cop like, "Here's the bread, thanks for the job." As a matter of fact, in one instance, the recording equipment actually picked up the rustle of the money being counted. But Burkert couldn't get the cop to identify what was going on and didn't know enough to refer to it himself. It was frustrating.

We gave Burkert a crash refresher course on how to handle recording equipment and how to follow a "script." When another opportunity arose we hoped that he was now ready. This opportunity arose when a cop tried to collect an old debt. Burkert had gotten a tow job at the Bridge Plaza North and a cop had let him know that he wanted to be taken care of. For one reason or another, the payment had never been made, and then, three months later, the cop ran into Burkert again and gave him a twenty-five-dollar ticket for supposedly running a red light. The word was passed, through a mutual acquaintance, that the cop wanted twenty-five for the original Bridge Plaza job and an additional one hundred dollars "to be friends." He would "let bygones be bygones" and do what he could to fix the ticket.

Wearing a wire, Burkert went looking for the cop, with our agents following. When he found him, Burkert complained about being harassed, saying that his boss never gave him any money on the Plaza job in the first place. The cop purported to believe him, and settled for the twenty-five dollars for the car. He also said that he would try to fix the ticket, but wasn't guaranteeing anything. The conversation was recorded:

POLICEMAN: Yeah?

BURKERT: Listen, what's the story? I can't have you keep bothering me for something I didn't do.

POLICEMAN: Well, you know why, it's all right.

BURKERT: Huh?

POLICEMAN: You know what it's for.

BURKERT: Oh, for the car at the plaza.

POLICEMAN: Yeah.

BURKERT: So, it wasn't my fault, you know what I mean, I was just working for the guy. He didn't give me nothing to give to you, you know what I mean.

POLICEMAN: He didn't give you anything.

BURKERT: No, he didn't give me nothing to give to you. If you want I'll give it to you myself—I don't care—but if you keep giving me tickets forget about it, they'll take my license away, you know what I mean.

POLICEMAN: Get the twenty for us, I don't know if it's from Neil. Go back to him. Whatever you want to do.

BURKERT: Well, I'll tell you what I'll do, I'll give you a quarter, what can you do about the ticket? You know, that will put hurt into me, you know what I mean?

POLICEMAN: Well, alright, let me put it this way.

BURKERT: No, I'll give it to you myself, you know.

POLICEMAN: Well, that's that—something different.

BURKERT: The ticket is something completely different—all right?

POLICEMAN: Alright, listen, plead not guilty.

BURKERT: Yeah.

POLICEMAN: I'll see what I can do—I can't guarantee, I don't want anything now. I can't guarantee what I'm going to be able to do. It's according to who you know, right? If I can beat it, well, you'll take care of me.

BURKERT: It's not a judge anymore, right.

POLICEMAN: No, it's a referee, I think I can beat it. I'll tell him you rolled through it. I'm not positive. It's according to the judge again. You'll take care of me, I'm sure.

BURKERT: Right, right.

POLICEMAN: Alright, George.

A few weeks later, the same cop let it be known that he wanted fifty dollars more from the other driver who was present when Burkert had gotten the twenty-five-dollar ticket. The meeting was arranged and the cop tore up the tickets in exchange for fifty dollars. Again, the event was recorded by surveilling Commission agents.

George had gotten the hang of it. He continued to undertake undercover meetings for us from time to time, collecting tapes that we considered to be useful for our prospective hearings.

This was the first such material we had gathered. It would add considerably to our public hearings, but it still did not represent the kind of stuff on which a hearing could center. We were dealing with a relatively minor area of corruption that had already been fully explored in the press some years earlier. We were making progress, but we would need much more.

8

SOME ROUGH SPOTS

Sometimes things did not go well. On February 3, 1971, we got the shocking news that Frank Serpico had been shot! Temporarily working with a plain-clothes unit, he was shot in the face while trying to force his way into a suspect's apartment. He survived, albeit with a loss of hearing in one ear.

We were not having much contact with Frank at this point. His sole real involvement with the Knapp Commission had been to give it life. Our investigation focused on what was going on in the Department currently, a subject Frank could not help us with very much, since he was too well-known. Nevertheless, we kept in touch. He would drop by our offices every so often to chat. It was a real jolt to hear of his almost being killed.

Rumors and speculation have suggested that Frank was set up by the cops in an attempt to exact revenge for his turning on his comrades. Frank never made any such claim. He faulted the cops who were with him for not being quicker in coming to his aid, but he firmly denied the suggestion, made in the later book and movie about his exploits, that he had been deliberately put in harm's way.[1]

Moving from the near tragic to the trivial, I ran into some criticism from friends for an incident that was considered by certain of my colleagues to be treachery. One day, a number of us were working in the Commission's offices

---

1. At that time, Frank generally groused about the minor inaccuracies he said abounded, particularly in the movie.

on the eleventh floor of 51 Chambers Street. Suddenly, one of our agents, former Army Counterintelligence Agent Mark Hanson, called out from a back
room for everyone to come and look at something.

Hanson had been sitting on the back windowsill of Paul Rooney's office,
cleaning some binoculars. The window looked down on a narrow alley. On
the other side of the alley were the rear entrances to a row of buildings. One
of them was to a restaurant named Gasner's.

A block from the federal and state courthouses, Gasner's was the only
restaurant in the vicinity that made any pretense at even a semblance of
elegance. It was a hangout for better-off defense lawyers when they found
themselves having business in court. An appropriately expensive meal was
served in surroundings that at least approached Midtown sophistication. Adjoining the restaurant's dining room was a comfortable bar, presided over by
a particularly jovial and personable bartender called "Gunner," that served
drinks at quite reasonable prices. The bar was a traditional gathering place
for federal prosecutors, whose offices were then in the Federal Courthouse.

Jack Gasner, the establishment's long-standing proprietor, undoubtedly
reasoned that inexpensive drinks for young prosecutors represented an in-
vestment. Many would later turn out to be affluent defenders of affluent,
accused wrongdoers, and would then be able to afford Gasner's wine and
meals, as well as its bargain-day drinks. Every Friday in particular, current
and former federal prosecutors would gather at Gasner's bar, some for a
drink before heading home and some for an evening of more extensive conviviality. In the more than five years I served as a federal prosecutor, I spent
my share of time at Gasner's.

As we gathered around the window, Hanson pointed to a patrol car
parked in the alley eleven stories below, directly underneath our window. The
car was planted right next to Gasner's back door. We watched as a Gasner's
waiter, in his professional attire, served what appeared to be a sumptuous
lunch to the two officers in the car. Napkin over his arm, the waiter presented the food on trays. A peek through the binoculars that Hanson had been
cleaning revealed that the officers had been provided with Gasner's china,
silverware, and linen. Two glasses, apparently containing alcoholic refresh-
ment, sat on the dashboard.

The waiter came and went several times, tending to the needs of the officers and, after dessert and coffee, removed the used dishes. The patrol car
drove off. No one had been presented with a bill.

The Commission had its first free meal case, whether we liked it or not.
We had always trumpeted the seriousness of our purpose and insisted that
we were not interested in spending our time doing things like spying on po-

lice officers mooching free meals. But what were we to do if they did it literally under our noses? Moreover, the meal at Gasner's was apparently a regular event. We made a minor point of checking the back window each day at lunchtime. Every day, at the same time, whatever patrol car was on duty would pull up, and the officers would be served their lunch. Our "surveillance" became a running joke and one day we even took movies of the festivities. After a while, the novelty wore off and we stopped paying attention.

In our written report, we commented briefly upon a number of the less serious problems with which we had not been principally concerned, including free meals. We described, generally, the incident of free meal-taking that had been thrust upon us. Still later, when our work was finished and the Department's Internal Affairs Division routinely reviewed our allegations, they asked us for the details of what we had seen.

While not serious from our point of view, the incident still constituted a violation of police regulations. Department investigators, careful to be meticulous about anything we uncovered, felt obliged to follow through. Minor disciplinary charges were brought against the officers involved and, most significantly from my point of view, the people at Gasner's were directly confronted with what we had observed. Technically, they were violating the law by wining and dining cops. No charges were brought. But the incident caused considerable embarrassment.

Some of my former colleagues said they were aghast at what I had done. How could I "rat" on an institution like Gasner's? It took me years to live down the fact that I had betrayed the local office watering hole.

Another incident that involved a genuine screw-up was initiated by an informant who at first appeared to have promising information. He was a gypsy, one of the large community in New York City that, like so many of the city's ethnic and national groups, had a very defined society in which its members operated. In the case of the gypsies, we were told, there was a very precisely organized hierarchy of social status, culminating in a "king" who ran just about everything within his community. Traditional gypsy activities—like fortune telling, palm reading, wearing and selling colorful costumes, and giving dance performances—were allegedly augmented by the also-traditional con games and thievery practiced by some.

Our new informant presented himself as being well plugged in to the gypsy hierarchy. He said he had become disaffected by the illegal behavior of his brethren, and by the organized conspiracy of protection afforded them by the police. He described thieves and con men operating openly in the gypsy community, while policemen who were supposed to control them were being paid to look the other way.

We were given the names of the members of the illegal gypsy governing hierarchy, right up to the "king" himself. This organization operated in secret. It asserted its authority by means of threats, and its members exacted tribute for allowing others to do business. As described, it seemed little different from some of the organizations of Italian gangsters, which were more familiar to the general public. Our interest, of course, was in the effect this operation had on the police, but in order to develop that information, we had first to unveil the structure itself. So we set our agents to the task of investigating the activities of the individuals named for us by our informant as the key members of the gypsy mafia.

Then, as we were getting underway with our new investigation, we had a rude and public awakening. Channel 5, one of the local television stations with which we had a special "sharing" arrangement on surveillance films, had a gypsy informant of their own, with whom they had been working for some time. They learned of our investigation and, knowing a good deal more about the gypsy community than we did, came out with an exclusive television exposé of . . . the Knapp Commission. Never mind the fact that we had a special relationship with Channel 5. Under these circumstances, when it came to a scoop, all bets were off.

What we had not known, until it was revealed to us on television, was the fact that there was not one "king" of the gypsies, but two. One of them was our informant. He had been using us in an attempt to unseat his rival. So we had blundered into the middle of a power struggle, unknowingly allying ourselves with one side. When confronted, our informant freely admitted what he had been up to. This was played out in glorious color on a Channel 5 News Special. There was little to do but pull in our horns and be as quiet as possible about the incident.

All in all, things were not going very well. Despite a few minor successes, our investigations were turning up little that we could use in our hoped-for public hearings. Having self-righteously announced at the outset that we would not get involved with the media until we had completed our work, there had already been two occasions when we emerged, involuntarily and unflatteringly, into the public arena: the memo books incident in the 19th Precinct and now our ill-fated gypsy investigation. An objective observer might well have found some truth in the sneering evaluation of our work by the president of the Patrolmen's Benevolent Association, "Those guys couldn't find an elephant in a phone booth."

9

LEUCI

In the fall of 1970, when our investigations were just beginning, we had been introduced to a narcotics cop named Bob Leuci. Leuci had somehow gotten to know Frank Serpico, whose experiences had led to the creation of the Knapp Commission, and David Durk, Serpico's friend who had guided him to notoriety. Leuci had led Serpico and Durk to believe that he had a pretty thorough knowledge of the workings of corruption in the New York City Police Department, particularly in the Narcotics Division. Durk followed through, eagerly pressing Leuci for more information. But Leuci gave nothing of significance. Instead, he tantalized Durk with hearsay, generalities, and speculation—all having a very authentic ring.

Leuci was a member of the elite Special Investigations Unit (SIU) of the Narcotics Division. SIU consisted of seventy-five hand-picked narcotics detectives who were charged with investigating important narcotics cases and, in particular, organized crime's involvement in the drug trade. The unit was one of the most prestigious in the Department, and presumably above suspicion.

Leuci did not tell Durk that he had any information that his own unit was in any way tainted, but said that he had general information about openly conducted gambling, loan sharking, and drug peddling in the Pleasant Avenue section of East Harlem. This was a relatively small enclave centering on Pleasant Avenue, between 110th and 120th Streets, where the neighborhood retained its Italian character in the face of the general domination of the area by African Americans and Puerto Ricans. It was from this location that most of the numbers rackets in the rest of Harlem were directed. Those who ran and participated in the various illegal activities did so with an openness that might lead one naturally to wonder why the police did not move in. Leuci's information consisted of little more than speculation along these lines, based on facts everyone knew. Nevertheless, David Durk was impressed.

Durk trotted Leuci around to every law enforcement outfit in town. When it got to be our turn, Paul Rooney was given the task of seeing what Leuci had to offer. Rooney conducted a couple of interviews with Leuci, accompanied by Durk, and it became apparent that Leuci had no information of value that he was willing to share. The same thing happened at the offices of the Manhattan district attorney, the U.S. attorney for the Southern District of New York, and other law enforcement agencies having an interest in anti-corruption activities. All came to the same conclusion—Leuci was a big nothing.

We later found out that Leuci was a self-styled double agent. He deliberately set Durk up to arrange these meetings, seeing them as opportunities to find out about the status of investigations that might involve him or his friends in SIU. The elite outfit was, it later turned out, not what it appeared to be.

For his part, Durk could not understand why none of the anti-corruption organizations had any interest in Leuci's information. He kept bothering, among others, Whitman Knapp, whom he ran into on a number of occasions when they both were traveling to Nantucket on weekends. Durk, convinced that Leuci's information had great value, kept pressuring Knapp to interview Leuci again. Knapp, in turn, pressed me to go through the formality of talking to Leuci, so Knapp could get Durk off his back. I had better things to do, and simply didn't get around to it. Finally, early in 1971, I asked Nick Scoppetta to take on the task. Then, every time Knapp bugged me, I bugged Scoppetta.

Scoppetta, like Rooney and Obermaier, was an experienced prosecutor. He had the additional advantage of having done his prosecutorial service as an assistant district attorney in the office of Manhattan District Attorney Frank Hogan. He knew cops and had worked with them. He also knew a good deal about the practical side of life in New York City, having come from a poor family and having grown up in foster homes.

Scoppetta had been assigned the specific job of looking into narcotics corruption. Assisting him were George Carros and Sy Newman, who were two of the agents on loan from the Internal Revenue Service. Carros was heavily built, muscular, and seasoned; Newman was slender and relatively new to his work. Both were sharp and dedicated. Part of their work had been to review the file, previously looked into by Otto Obermaier, that had been

went back to Nick's place and began to talk. The conversation was tape-recorded—openly. We explained that we wanted a tape only for our convenience, so that we could be accurate and not be troubled with taking notes. With that understanding, Leuci agreed to let us put a tape recorder on the coffee table. He had two conditions—that no copies be made of the tape, and that he could have it if he ever wanted it. We agreed.

Starting at the beginning, Leuci told us about his childhood, in Bensonhurst, an Italian section of Brooklyn, and about the contacts that he made with so many people who seemed destined to become either cops or mobsters. He told of his family life and how his brother had died of a narcotics overdose and how he developed a revulsion for drugs. He spoke of joining the New York City Police Department with the usual idealism, and of the familiar process of disillusionment that overtook him in the first few years. He spoke of the common run-of-the-mill corruption that he had observed and sometimes participated in during the time when he was a patrolman.

Then Leuci turned to the subject of his being appointed to SIU. Each new man in this handpicked outfit had to be interviewed, personally, by its commander, Captain Daniel Tange, a rugged gray-haired veteran of the narcotics wars. Leuci's interview had gone along standard lines, covering his background, experience, and emotional fitness for the difficult and dangerous job of being a top-level narcotics detective. Then Tange's questioning had taken on deeper significance. What would Leuci do if he learned that one of his comrades in SIU was corrupt? Would he turn him in? Without a flicker of hesitation, Leuci said that he would, under no circumstances, turn in a fellow cop. Tange pressed him, hitting hard on his obligation as a law enforcement officer, the seriousness of narcotics enforcement, and the evils of corruption. Leuci remained steadfast, despite an increasing awareness that Tange was viewing this conversation as a test. Leuci was convinced that he was flunking—badly. When the interview was over, Tange looked stern and disappointed. Leuci left, dispirited.

The next day Tange called him to say that he had been accepted in SIU. He had not flunked the test; he had passed it with flying colors.

Leuci elaborated for us on his experiences in SIU. The unit handled only the biggest, most important narcotics investigations. It was detectives in SIU who were responsible for taking on the big drug dealers in organized crime. They took them on all right—for money. Leuci told of "scores" in the tens and even hundreds of thousands of dollars. The SIU cops would use their considerable skill to uncover information about an upcoming narcotics sale of large proportions. Working the case professionally, they would swoop down on the buyer and seller just as the money and drugs were changing hands. It was perfect timing for making an ironclad arrest. It was also perfect timing for making a lot of money. The SIU cops invariably opted for profit. The narcotics dealers would go free and the police officers would pocket both the money and the narcotics. The cash would be divided and the narcotics would be used to pay off informants or, sometimes, sold.

A refinement of this operation, calculated to remove the hit-or-miss element, involved the use of illegal wiretaps. Knowing that somebody is a major drug dealer is not enough to justify a court to allow the mobster's phone to be tapped. But such niceties are irrelevant to someone whose purpose is profit rather than evidence-gathering. SIU cops secretly tapped the phones of known narcotics dealers to learn the times and locations of planned drug deals. Then the SIU would show up to take its cut.

What Leuci said dovetailed nicely with the federal task force reports reviewed by Obermaier and Scoppetta, which had wound up buried in the Department's Intelligence Division. Leuci's name had been included, along with most of the other detectives in SIU. Prominently mentioned in those files had been some detectives who went on to achieve considerable publicity, even to the extent of being featured in books and movies. Leuci confirmed that, as far as he knew, every one of the detectives at SIU was corrupt.

Leuci's revelations were particularly important because they put to rest whatever lingered of the notion that narcotics was "out of bounds" for policemen taking illegal payoffs. Previously, cops had traditionally looked upon narcotics graft as "dirty money." A generation raised before and during World War II shared with the general public a revulsion for narcotics. That was something for people in the ghettos. Many police officers, particularly the older ones, still reflected the attitude of a society in which narcotics were only for the very rich and very poor, not for the respectable middle and working classes. But times changed, and, as marijuana, cocaine, and even heroin became more acceptable to the general public, some policemen relaxed their scruples about taking money to allow the drug trade to continue. In SIU, where the rewards for looking the other way could be so immediate and so enormous, the cultural transformation had been complete. Everyone in the unit took graft.

We talked until 3:00 A.M. Leuci's story was spectacular. His potential for undercover work was mind-boggling. The Commission was going to be not just a success, but a sensation. We said goodnight to Leuci and began planning the operation in which he was to star. Leuci himself didn't want to be a star and stated that he had no interest in testifying at any public hearings. That's OK, we thought. If we get the investigation deeply underway, he'll change his mind.

We had promised that the tape we made of Leuci's revelations would be kept in absolute security. Having no access to a safe, I took the tape home and hid it behind what I thought was a well-camouflaged wall panel, under the family television set. I arrived home one evening, weeks later, to find my youngest daughter, Marnie, eight, merrily bouncing the tape up and down, from hand to hand, as she watched TV. There were times when we could have used the accoutrements of a more conventional outfit—like a wall safe.

It was apparent that security would be of vital importance in any venture involving Leuci. To guard against a slip, we decided to run the operation out of a new office. Scoppetta and the two agents with whom he had been working, Carros and Newman, moved into a small, previously empty suite, two floors below our main office. The other agents wondered what was going on, but accepted the arrangement without much question.

Over the next few weeks, Leuci moved smoothly into his role as an undercover operative. He set up a number of monitored conversations in which he recorded SIU police officers discussing the kinds of corrupt activities about which he had told us. He even managed to arrange a golf game with Captain Tange but, for once, Teddy Ratnoff's electronic surveillance equipment malfunctioned. Nevertheless, things began to go about as well as we could have hoped. Leuci was able to insinuate himself into situations involving police officers and mobsters that promised to yield returns far beyond our most optimistic dreams.

But it quickly became clear that Bob Leuci was, literally, too good to be true. We assumed that Leuci would wind up as a central witness in our hearings, even though he expressed no enthusiasm for such a role. Then, as Leuci's potential became clear to us, we began to realize that using, or even referring to him, in the prospective public hearings would mean that his work would have to come to an end, just when it should be beginning. Leuci was capable, we thought, of working undercover for a year or more, during which time he would be able to gather evidence against scores of drug pushers, gangsters, and corrupt police officers. Used properly, Leuci could break the back of serious corruption in the police department's Narcotics Division. But he could not do this if his cover was blown in a few months by our telling the world about him in our public hearings—then anticipated to begin in June 1971.

Whit Knapp, Scoppetta, and I went over and over the choices available to us and finally came to the conclusion that the only thing we could do was forgo using Leuci in our hearings and instead turn him over to federal authorities. He could work for them, as an undercover agent, for as long as he was needed to make cases.

It was, to say the least, very difficult to turn away the only significant corrupt police officer we had been able to persuade to work with us. Had it involved anything other than narcotics, we might not have been so altruistic. But when the question was put to the full Commission, everyone agreed that, however painful it might be, Leuci would remain undercover—as a Fed.

We felt that the circumstances were special enough to require dealing at the top level in the Justice Department. So Scoppetta and I flew to Washington to meet with Will Wilson, chief of the Justice Department's criminal division, for the purpose of offering to turn Leuci over to him. Wilson gratefully accepted, and we set about making arrangements. In a private room at one of Whit's clubs, Scoppetta and I met with Whitney North "Mike" Seymour Jr., who had replaced Bob Morgenthau as U.S. attorney for the Southern District of New York, to tell him about Leuci and what we proposed doing with him. Needless to say, Seymour was delighted.

It remained to cut a deal with Leuci. Although he trusted Scoppetta implicitly, Leuci insisted that he had to have assurance from a source high in the Justice Department that he would receive immunity for his own actions and that he would get help in working things out with the police department. The matter was considered to be of such importance that Wilson flew up from Washington to meet with Scoppetta, Leuci, and me. We gathered in a room in the Waldorf-Astoria Hotel, where Leuci received his assurances, firsthand. Assuming Leuci made the cases we all expected, he would get federal immunity for past misdeeds, the Justice Department would work things out with local prosecutors, we would try to save his job, and, if necessary, he would be relocated in the Federal Witness Protection Program. Leuci agreed.

Our good deed turned out to cost us a lot more than the services of Bob Leuci. Because of Scoppetta's special relationship with Leuci, it was essential to the success of the operation that he and his two agents, Carros and Newman, continue their roles. So we had to lose all three. Scoppetta would become a Special Assistant U.S. Attorney, and the two agents would work with him. Seymour would devote as much of his office's resources as he could spare to help with the investigation. They would operate under the direction of Edward "Mike" Shaw, a contemporary of mine in the U.S. Attorneys' Office, who still worked there and now headed a unit devoted to investigating police corruption.

In partial return for our sacrifice of Scoppetta, Carros, and Newman, the Justice Department assigned to us two young lawyers, John Sweeney and Stephen Stein. Stein was later replaced by another beginning attorney, David Ritchie. The intelligence of these bright young men was matched by their eagerness, but they hardly made up for the experience we had lost by surrendering the team working with Leuci.

It was felt that the security in our offices was better than would be possible if Scoppetta's operation was run out of the U.S. Attorney's Office or the Federal Bureau of Narcotics, where frequent contact with the cops was unavoidable. So Scoppetta, Carros, and Newman were to remain in their suite in our building, even after they stopped working for us.

The arrangement was perfect for Scoppetta. He had the resources and support of the government and the informality, ease of operation, and freedom from bureaucracy that went with working for a commission only loosely tied to government agencies. We also helped, from time to time, in whatever way we could. We arranged, for instance, to wire a rental car for Leuci's use when it turned out that bureaucratic federal agency requirements made it almost impossible for the U.S. Attorney to get the job done without a lot of people finding out about it.

One constant irritant and potential source of difficulty was David Durk. Durk did not know that Leuci was working for "the good guys" in an undercover capacity. Nor did he know anything about the information that Leuci had given us involving corruption in the SIU. All Durk knew was the original false cover story that Leuci had told in order to ingratiate himself in anticorruption circles, a story that no one swallowed but Durk. Nevertheless, Durk was convinced that Leuci's information, as he knew it, was extremely valuable and he was intent upon seeing to it that he was the one who caused that information to be acted upon.

Whit Knapp's observation about Durk pithily summed up the trait that led Durk so desperately, and often annoyingly, to pursue his vision. "David," said Knapp, "simply cannot understand why the world resists his efforts to reform it."

This time, Durk's efforts at reform represented a real threat to Leuci's cover. Realizing that something was afoot, but not knowing what it was, Durk was determined to be part of the action. His tack was to try to persuade Leuci that he needed a direct meeting with the police commissioner. On his own, Durk tried to approach Commissioner Murphy to suggest such a meeting.

Leuci, by this time, was actively working undercover for the Feds, but of course the police department did not know it. The federal investigators wanted to keep it that way. Leuci told Scoppetta about Durk's overtures to arrange a meeting with the police commissioner. It was decided that Durk would have to be told something. Scoppetta gave Durk broad hints as to Leuci's cooperation, along with instructions to stop meddling. Durk was not to be put off so easily. He pressed his requests of Leuci and actually spoke to Commissioner Murphy about arranging a meeting.

Durk was not finally headed off until Scoppetta, at the top of his voice, told him that if he did not "get lost" he would be indicted for obstructing a federal investigation. That finally did it. Durk faded into the background and Leuci continued his work, undisclosed and undisturbed.

Leuci's work as a federal agent was just getting underway when it hit a significant snag—he was routinely transferred out of SIU. It was essential to get him transferred back, and to make it look as though his transfer had been an administrative mix-up, so no suspicion would be aroused. This kind of maneuvering could only be accomplished from the top. Pat Murphy had to be told what was going on.

It would be risky, since once Murphy knew, others would have to know. Once again, the need for security for our operation had to be weighed against the more fundamental need of seeing to it that the operation was carried out. As before, it seemed to us that Murphy's full cooperation could more easily be obtained if he could be subjected to some meaningful pressure. Once again, the best source of that pressure appeared to be the Justice Department. Since Leuci's efforts were now under the direction of Justice, it now had a significant stake in the success of his efforts. That meant that the attorney general of the United States was potentially available to put pressure on Murphy. A meeting was arranged with the police commissioner, his first deputy, U.S. Attorney Mike Seymour, and Deputy Attorney General Will Wilson to explain the need for Leuci's quick transfer back to SIU. Even more vital was the need for complete secrecy. To drive the point home, Wilson arranged that the meeting be preceded by a personal phone call from Attorney General John Mitchell to Murphy, explaining the importance of what we were going to talk to him about.

Murphy agreed to cooperate. Leuci was duly returned to SIU and, for the time, security was maintained.

As Leuci began to work for the Feds in earnest, the rest of us, still concentrating on the business of the Commission, had less and less to do with Scoppetta, although Nick kept me generally informed. It was understood that if Leuci's cover was blown or the federal investigation ended, for some other reason, the Commission would then be free to use in its hearings or in its report, or both, whatever information about patterns of corruption had emerged in the course of Scoppetta's investigation. We had to be content with the satisfaction of having done a good deed and the hope that somehow, some day, we would be able to use some of the information Leuci was collecting.[1]

For now, we were right back in the position of having not much to offer for public hearings, which were then still tentatively scheduled for late spring 1971, just a few months off. In addition, our strength had been depleted by one attorney and two agents. We had lost Scoppetta, Carros, and Newman. Things were not looking up.

---

1. The Commission never got to use Leuci's information, because he turned out to be as useful to the Feds as could be hoped. In an eighteen-month investigation, lasting long after our hearings were over, Leuci participated in dozens of undercover operations and was an invaluable source of information, making numerous important criminal cases. Unfortunately, his efforts were ultimately brought to a premature end. The *New York Times* got wind of the operation and, despite an urgent personal request from U.S. Attorney Seymour to hold off for a few weeks so Leuci could complete his work, the *Times* printed a front-page story, on June 15, 1972, identifying him as a secret agent.

10

TOODY AND MULDOON

On May 12, 1971, we arranged to monitor, film, and record one of tow-truck driver George Burkert's meetings. A police officer had sent him some business and had stopped by to collect what was owed, but Burkert was not at his garage. We had George arrange to meet the officer, and then we called Mark Monsky, the news director at Channel 5, with whom we had made a deal to allow filming. On this occasion, Monsky himself showed up at the scene, in a panel truck equipped with a night camera.

At about seven o'clock in the evening, following the cop's directions, Burkert parked his tow truck at the appointed meeting place, Lexington Avenue just north of 67th Street, one half-block from the 19th Precinct station house. Monsky pulled up and parked across the street in a small, nondescript commercial van, used by Channel 5 for secretive filming of their own. A slot had been cut in each of the three sides of the van's cargo area, through which Monsky could aim his camera. The surveilling agents were in another nearby car with their recording equipment.

A police car pulled up and double-parked next to Burkert:

COP: Hi, there, we just turned out.
GEORGE: Oh, all right. . . . So where do you want me to give it to you, right here?
COP: Yeah—just drop the money in the car.
GEORGE: Huh?
COP: Just drop it in the car and you know what happens to it. That's all.

GEORGE: I laid thirty bucks on it because it's a 1969.

George dropped the money into the car and the cops drove off down Lexington Avenue. Monsky's van, with Monsky and his camera concealed in the back, pulled out into traffic and followed. Both vehicles, traveled about half a block, where they came to a red light. The cop stopped for the light, and Monsky's van eased up next to him. The cars sat, side-by-side, waiting for the signal to change.

Monsky thought it would be a terrific idea to get a close-up picture of the police officers sitting in the patrol car. He poked his camera through the peep hole in the side of his truck, and began to film the driver of the car, sitting a few feet away, relaxed and bored, waiting for the light to change. Casually, the cop looked around—and found himself staring directly into a camera lens. For a split second what he saw did not register and he looked forward again. Then, he did a horrified, classic double-take, staring back into the camera just as the light turned green, and Monsky's panel truck dashed away.

The police car, snapping on its siren and overhead light, took off in hot pursuit, as Monsky's camera continued to grind away, through the rear window.

The van was quickly overtaken and ordered to pull over to the curb. Monsky hopped out. He showed the police officers his Channel 5 identification, and explained that he was doing some anonymous "street scenes" for a human interest special on his news program. The officer looked skeptical but ultimately let him go.

The next day, in panic, one of the cops telephoned George Burkert. The cop had told his precinct captain and PBA delegate what had happened and they had instructions for George, telling him what to say in case he was questioned. George was prepared for the call. So were our agents, who listened—and recorded:

GEORGE: Hello.
COP: Yeah, how you doing George? Al.
GEORGE: Al?
COP: Yeah, how you doing?
GEORGE: I'm worried about this thing here a little bit. Yeah, well, I guess
    they seen me, like, hand you the money, right?
COP: Yeah.
GEORGE: They got a picture of it?
COP: Well, that's it. We were talking about that. That's why we spoke it
    over with the PBA delegate, you know, and the captain before, you

know. We told them exactly what happened, you know, especially after
it was so obvious, you know . . .

GEORGE: Yeah.

COP: But that's why the only thing to do is to continue to deny it.

GEORGE: Right.

COP: You know, that's what they told us, you know. I had originally
thought, you know, to say that I know you and I had lent it to you the
night before, you know, and that you had just met me to pay it back.

GEORGE: Right.

COP: But it's not going to go over. It's going to go over like a lead balloon
they felt. That's what they feel. First of all they told us it's very hard,
very hard to photograph at night and even harder to photograph money.

GEORGE: Right.

COP: You know, it could have been, you know, like they say it could be
interpreted that you were counting your own money.

GEORGE: Yeah.

COP: You know what I mean. Like I'm saying, we're hoping and we're
praying that nothing really is even going to come from it, but just in
case it did, that's why I figure we all have the same story.

GEORGE: Right.

* * *

COP: So they can say anything they want, I mean they can intimidate, they
can threaten, they can do anything they want to do, but as long as you
stick to your story . . .

* * *

GEORGE: Yeah, but wasn't that kind of, you know, that was kind of a bad
spot for you to tell me to meet you in the first place.

COP: What, over there?

GEORGE: By the precinct, where there's cops all over the place?

COP: The cops are nothing. You know what we should have done? We
should have taken you right into the station house.

GEORGE: The cops are nothing?

COP: Well, that's the easiest. Cops you never worry about.

By this time Burkert had become pretty adept at channeling recorded conversations. He prodded the cop:

GEORGE: Well, who are they, they're cops?

COP: No, no, no, no. It's that Knapp Commission. Lindsay appointed this
commission.

GEORGE: Oh.

COP: To look into the police department.

GEORGE: Knapp Commission, yeah.

COP: Yeah, that's the one . . .

GEORGE: I heard it on TV.

COP: Right, you probably heard about it, right.

GEORGE: Yeah.

COP: That's how it is. They really have no power.

GEORGE: They have no power?

COP: None at all, all they can do is recommend to the police department. In other words, say here . . . they end next month. The end of June they end. That's the end of it.

GEORGE: They end next month?

COP: Yeah, the end of June they run out of money. They were allocated three-quarters of a million dollars, you know, and now, at the end of June, they're over.

We set up a few more recorded telephone conversations between Burkert and the cop, in which the event and its possible consequences were rehashed over and over. Then Brian Bruh and Ralph Parente took the tapes, and a portable tape machine, to the cop's home.

His name was Alfonso Jannotta and he lived with his wife in a modest house in Queens. Once the agents identified themselves, he meekly invited them in. He knew what was coming. Bruh, Parente, Jannotta, and his wife sat down in the living room. Bruh said that he wanted to play a tape for Jannotta, but that perhaps their business should be discussed in private and he might wish his wife not to be there. No, said Jannotta, he had nothing to hide from his wife, and he preferred that she be present. Bruh played the tape. Jannotta broke down in tears.

This was no swaggering high roller. Jannotta was a terrified little man struggling with the awareness that his life was shattered. He readily agreed to answer questions. Jannotta's interrogation was one of the most difficult things Bruh and Parente had done. His tale was pathetic, and he told it in sobs. His wife was seriously ill and insurance did not cover the medical bills. In order to make ends meet, he moonlighted by working evenings as a laborer, sanding floors. Jannotta indulged in the kind of low-level graft that was tolerated in the Department at that time, but he certainly was not getting rich on corruption. He got a few dollars from tow-truck operators like George Burkert, took his share when he rode in a sector car that had pickups from construction sites or bars, and occasionally made a small score on a traffic violation. Nothing big. Nothing sensational, but helpful to us in getting a full picture of what was going on in the Department.

We were glad to have what we thought was our first live police witness for public hearings, but Alfonso Jannotta was a very small fish. A real "grass eater." We did our best to figure out a way that he could work for us, to get more information and to help himself out by making cases against others. We tried ineffectually to set up conversations with the captain and the PBA delegate with whom Jannotta had previously discussed the false testimony he was supposed to give in the event he was questioned by authorities. They became suspicious, and he got nowhere. He also tried to develop other contacts, but the simple fact was that Jannotta didn't know anybody important enough to be a target. Finally, in desperation, he offered to wear a wire and set up his partner. Even that was a nonstarter. His partner was as insignificant as he was.

Jannotta was the victim of a system, the criminal justice system, that necessarily rewards the bad guy. Someone with valuable contacts—garnered during a life of crime—can trade information about those contacts for consideration, perhaps even his own freedom. But a fellow like Jannotta, who is only a little bit crooked, has nothing of value to offer.

We felt sorry for Jannotta, and tried our best to help him. But it was hopeless. All he wanted was to keep his job, and we knew we could not save it for him. Among ourselves, we took to calling him and his partner "Toody and Muldoon" after the inept cop heroes of a then-current TV comedy series, *Car 54, Where Are You?*

Then one day we were informed that Jannotta and his partner, in attempting to make an arrest, had been injured, and Jannotta was in the hospital. I assumed that, in misfortune, Jannotta had finally managed to accomplish something for which he could claim credit. A police officer who is hurt in the line of duty is considered a hero, and Jannotta and his partner at last seemed to have earned some recognition, which could be turned to their benefit in meeting the charges that were bound to be brought against them once our hearings were finished, and we turned our information over to the Department and the district attorney.

No such luck. "Toody" had not been shot by a bank robber or injured while trying to save someone in distress. He had been driving on patrol when he noticed what seemed to him to be a suspicious individual walking on the sidewalk on the other side of the street. He called for the individual to stop, but the fellow took off running, never to be seen again. Jannotta pulled the car over and he and his partner jumped out to give chase. Unfortunately, Jannotta's partner, in his haste, tripped over his own feet and fell headlong in the street. Jannotta, close behind him, tripped over his partner and cracked his head on the pavement, hurting himself rather seriously. Toody and Muldoon, it seemed, could not even get themselves injured without appearing foolish in the process.

The pressure, added to his miserable situation at home, proved too much for Jannotta. He began to deteriorate emotionally, and it became clear to us that he simply was not up to testifying as a witness in our hearings. He would fall apart. Besides, he was a small, unimpressive witness. It would have been too cruel to try to put him through the ordeal of a televised public confession. We had the tapes and film, plus George Burkert's testimony. That would have to be enough.

We were moving forward, but we were still without any "inside" witness.

11

BATMAN AND ROBIN

There were a few police officers who, for one reason or another, had "gotten a bit of a name for themselves." In a department rife with rumors regarding just about everything, scuttlebutt abounded about graft among the high-ranking and the well-known. A borough commander, a chief, a couple of high-profile narcotics detectives, of whom a laudatory movie had been made, a top-level PBA official, and a number of others had reputations within the rank and file of the Department that, fairly or not, were so well established that one need only mention their names to evoke a raised eyebrow and a smirk from people who thought of themselves as being "in the know." The rumored proclivities of one high-ranking officer were so openly accepted that he allegedly received, as a "going-away" gift, upon changing commands, a suitcase—to put money in.

Of course, we were interested in any cop with a public image of being corrupt. But we needed better evidence than smirks and raised eyebrows. We eagerly attempted to zero in on any high-profile alleged malefactor, whenever we were given the chance. Among the most prominent of this group was a pair of patrolmen nicknamed "Batman and Robin."

Robert Hantz and David Greenberg, during a mere three years "on the job," had earned their nicknames by making a show of doing things their way. Flamboyantly violating departmental procedures, they justified themselves by making a good many arrests—the validity of which were often in serious question—and the publicity they aroused made them more-or-less invulnerable to a timid departmental disciplinary apparatus. They were later to record their supposed exploits in a book, followed by a movie, each modestly entitled *Super Cops*. Also, they supposedly were the inspiration for a popular movie and television series, each named *Starsky and Hutch*, about two renegade cops waging a lonely war against crime and departmental bureaucracy.

I first became aware of this "dynamic duo" from an African American police officer named Lenny Weir, who was introduced to me by David Burnham, the *New York Times* reporter whose story about Frank Serpico had started everything. Weir was slight of build, quiet, and very intense. Most black police officers did not feel welcome in the traditionally Irish American police culture; perhaps as a consequence, they generally seemed not to participate in the widespread rough-and-ready corruption that predominated. Blacks may have had their own avenues for illegal moneymaking, but we never discovered them, and Lenny Weir certainly did not take part.

I met Weir for lunch, with David Burnham, at a health food diner of his choice. He was a Black Muslim, and shortly thereafter he changed his name to Humza al-Hafeez. He was intelligent, serious, and deeply focused on doing whatever he could to help people in general, and his own people in particular. I liked him a lot and in the years after the Knapp Commission, we became good friends.

At our first lunch, and in meetings thereafter, Weir enlightened me considerably about the lives and problems of police officers, particularly African Americans. One of his chief preoccupations was his resentment of the ravages of Batman and Robin. As Weir described them, the two detectives preyed in particular on the black community, bullying, arresting, and shaking down all kinds of people in all kinds of circumstances. For example, he said, the two would regularly stop as many as a dozen young blacks, line them up against a wall, smack them around pretty much at will, and confiscate any contraband. They also took any money they might find. Anyone who protested got arrested, and the rest were released for another day. In this and other ways, said Weir, Hantz and Greenberg terrorized the African American community, earning themselves the derisive appellations "Batman and Robin." Apparently missing the intended irony, Hantz and Greenberg took no offense at their nicknames, but gloried in them. The reckless abandon of the "dynamic duo" was not seen by them as contrary to police regulations, but rather as a hero's cloak for whatever they wanted to do.

It was not only blacks who saw themselves as being victimized by Batman and Robin. One complainant with whom we spoke had come forward to Department authorities, alleging that Greenberg had stolen some gargoyle statues from a construction site. The complainant, an accountant working for the City, said that he was brutally beaten for his trouble. He originally charged that Greenberg had administered the beating, but then withdrew his charges, leaving no basis to go forward with the matter.

The suppositions about Hantz and Greenberg did not stop at thievery—petty or otherwise. The Brooklyn District Attorney's office had amassed evidence—not sufficient for indictment—that led the prosecutors to believe that the two were guilty of a double murder. Just before midnight on November 18, 1969, two minor drug dealers had been shot to death. They were in an automobile with Greenberg, who later claimed that he was attempting to get information from them when they turned on him, one with a knife, the other with a gun. Supposedly, Hantz rushed to his partner's aid and together they killed both of the "attackers."

As later chronicled in the book *Super Cops* (1973, authored by L. H. Whittemore), the incident took on the attributes of a heroic fantasy. Supposedly, the victims were major drug dealers, who would lead Hantz and Greenberg

> to the top leaders of an international drug ring. [Hantz and Greenberg] would explode the entire worldwide operation. Two young guys from Coney Island, on the police force for only a year and nine months, would be responsible for winning the war on heroin.   (242)

Further, according to the book, the Brooklyn District Attorney's office ostensibly orchestrated the meeting, in coordination with an impressive law enforcement array:

> Dave figured that at least twenty agents had been assigned to the case. And the FBI was probably involved as well. Maybe even the Secret Service and the CIA.

Greenberg was supposedly told that the D.A.'s office only had one recording device to give him ("the rest are out of order" [241]) and that he should conceal it in an attaché case for his meeting with the two disreputable drug dealers (the device somehow never worked, so no record was made of what went on).

As the story set forth in the book proceeded, Greenberg got in the drug dealers' car while Hantz watched from another car behind him. Then Greenburg was allegedly taken on a wild ride, with sudden U-turns across traffic, 70 mile per hour spurts, dashes the wrong way up one-way streets, and other maneuvers worthy of a fantastic spy movie. Hantz managed, somehow, to follow, unseen. After winding up in Brooklyn, in a deserted section of Coney

Island, the drug dealers found the recording device in the attaché case, forced Greenberg to raise his hands in surrender, and attacked him with a knife and a gun. But Hantz, seeing what was happening through the rear window of the car, rushed to the aid of his partner, who then pulled his own gun from its ankle holster. The drug pushers were dispatched in a well-deserved fusillade of bullets.

The story told by Hantz and Greenberg simply did not add up. To begin with, the pushers' car was a beaten-up 1953 Dodge convertible with a translucent plastic rear window, through which Greenberg could never have seen what was going on in the back seat. The bullet wound in one pusher's head was on the wrong side for him to have been shot in the manner claimed. Other details of the shooting, as told by Hantz and Greenberg, did not check out. The local precinct reported that, just prior to the alleged time of the shooting, Greenberg had shooed away the patrol car in the sector, saying that there was an operation going down. Some cops in patrol cars had been cruising in the area anyway, but they heard no shots. Perhaps the pushers had been shot elsewhere and driven to the area, where Batman and Robin could claim they killed them as part of an undercover operation.

Brooklyn District Attorney Eugene Gold conducted an investigation into the incident, coming up with considerable evidence that what had occurred was murder. There wasn't enough, however, to level any charges. Gold kept his file open.

We got what we could from Gold's files, and two of our agents undertook our own investigation. One of them, an African American named Gordon White, was on loan to us from the Bureau of Narcotics, where he specialized in organized crime cases. Quiet and extremely capable, he knew the law enforcement business. He was the only one of our agents-on-loan whose agency permitted him to carry his weapon while working for us. Fortunately, he was never called upon to use it. White was later to become an attorney, with a flourishing practice in his native Houston, Texas. The other agent, Jim Rogers, was newly retired from the FBI. Reserved and formal in demeanor, Rogers was adept not only at street work, but in the area of document analysis.

The two agents reviewed Gold's records and interviewed those witnesses who were still available. Among others, they interviewed the girlfriend of one of the dead junkies, who told them that the two had been paying protection money to Hantz and Greenberg; on the day they were killed they left saying they were going to meet the two cops. She never saw them again. On the basis of White's and Rogers's investigation, we concluded that Gold had ample basis for his suspicions, but agreed with him that he didn't have enough to do anything about them. Neither did we.

In a more general way, Lenny Weir attempted to educate me in the ways of the underground power structure in Harlem. For example, he pointed out that the most influential periodical was not the prominent *Amsterdam News*, but a primitively reproduced newsletter distributed in Harlem, hand-to-hand. He also arranged to introduce us to a man whom he described as one of the most powerful men in Harlem.

Milt Williams, the African American ex-cop who served as one of our assistant counsels, and I met with this man one afternoon in the back of a store on 125th Street. Tall and powerful, with a gleaming bald head, he was dressed in white robes and wore a fez. He had recently been released from prison, after doing hard time for what we were told were several narcotics offenses. Looking at us with a suspicious attitude that was mostly disdain, he let us know that his primary interest was not in corruption, but in police violence directed against blacks. He was, however, willing to listen to us because, as he said, "the dudes that are taking the brothers' money are the dudes that are breaking the brothers' heads."

We tried to persuade him to cooperate with us and to give us information about police corruption in the black community. Here was one predominantly white outfit, we argued, doing work that actually benefited his people. We even suggested that he might provide someone who would work with us in undercover operations. Although he said he would consider it, he ultimately turned us down. I think that he found the prospect of working with the "white establishment" just a little too much. We spoke to him for several hours, however, and got some valuable insights into relationships between police officers and some elements of the Harlem population.

Weir continued to be helpful, introducing us to members of a small association made up of Black Muslim cops. I was able to attend some of their meetings and spoke with them about their perceptions. For whatever reasons—distrust on their part, or the fact that they were sufficiently out of the mainstream that they didn't know much about the graft that was going on—they had little to add.

All-in-all, we did not get the kind of outpouring of information about corrupt cops that I expected from the minority communities. It was clear that the brunt of police shakedowns was felt by minorities. I would have thought that we would experience a flood of minority complaints—some justified, some perhaps not. It was not the case. Probably, like the formidable ex-con in the fez, people simply did not trust us, and preferred to suck it up and suffer the likes of Batman and Robin in silence.

12

WAVERLY LOGAN

Information about a particular source of narcotics corruption in the minority communities came to us through local Channel 5 television producer Mark Monsky. Monsky, who had provided us with surveillance cameras for the memorable filming of "Toody and Muldoon," discovered a troubled thirty-year-old African American ex-cop by the name of Waverly Logan who had just been suspended from the force for taking a hundred-dollar bribe and was ready to talk. Logan had been a member of yet another supposedly elite outfit, the PEP (Prevention Enforcement Patrol) Squad. This was a unit of black and Hispanic police officers formed to deal with the narcotics problem in Harlem and other minority neighborhoods in the city.

Monsky was intent, of course, on preserving his news scoop, so he told us nothing of his find until just before putting Logan on the air. Then Monsky asked us to listen to what Logan had to say and to give our opinion of his story. We found Logan to be believable. So did Monsky. He and Logan went on in prime time for a series of three exclusive interviews. Logan did not come across too well on TV. Monsky did not have the time or the inclination to prepare him in depth for his appearance. Anyway, all Monsky needed was a few sensational "news bites." So Logan told a somewhat sketchy, confusing story and looked like a bitter, disgraced ex-cop trying to shift blame by making charges that sounded as improbable as they were sensational.

We were convinced that Logan was telling the truth and, if we invested some hard work preparing him properly, he could look that way on the witness stand at any hearings that we might conduct. We asked him to work with us after his TV stint was over. He agreed. It was a difficult task to get Logan to tell us everything he knew, and to teach him how to tell his story convincingly. Shy and defensive, he was suspicious of everyone. "You guys are full of ideals now," he told us, "but if you stay in business for five years, you'll be as corrupt as everyone else." This attitude, coupled with a reluctance to cooperate developed during his police days, meant that we had to spend hour after hour working with Logan to make his expected testimony complete, accurate, and believable.

The account Logan gave was typical, in a number of ways, of many we had already heard. He was of local origin—Laurelton, Queens—and began his six years on the force with a feeling of dedication and idealism. Then he was gradually introduced to traditional graft and, little by little, got used to the idea that picking up payments from merchants and petty crooks was a natural thing to do.

Logan had been a taxi driver with a wife and two children when he joined the New York City Police Department in 1966. He had served in the Army Airborne and Reserves and was employed as a hospital worker until he entered the Department's Cadet Training Program, designed to help underprivileged people from the ghetto to become cops. He passed the course in 1967, while earning a high school equivalency diploma, and was appointed to the Department in June 1968. After a ten-day crash course in the Police Academy, Logan was assigned for two months to the TPF Unit (Tactical Patrol Force), known throughout the Department as tough—maybe brutal—but not corrupt. His training had been cut short because of the extra manpower needs that arose because of community unrest following Dr. Martin Luther King's assassination. Police in the TPF knew about corruption in the rest of the Department and deliberately tried to break protection contracts when they could by arresting people they knew to be on someone's "pad." Logan said the only graft the TPF cops accepted were occasional free meals.

In February 1969 Logan and about seven hundred other rookies returned to the Academy to finish their training. Graft was openly discussed and joked about, and the instructors ignored it, never offering any guidance on how to handle corruption on the street. There was a basic lack of respect for the instructors, since the men already had personal experience with how different real police work was from the picture painted in the classroom.

After graduation, Logan was sent to the 73rd Precinct in Brooklyn, a particularly high-crime area. Police were rarely assigned to foot patrol, especially on the 12 A.M. to 8 A.M. shift, and, if one was assigned to work during the night, he usually spent his shift "cooping" (hiding) in his own home or in the basement of the station house. On Logan's first night, he and another rookie were sent out in a car, with no training or guidance. They got lost. The next week, he started his first day on a daytime shift by going out for his sergeant, to pick up some free beer from a bodega. Later that week, a call came in about a suspicious character outside a supermarket. When he and his veteran partner responded, it turned out that the owner just wanted to be escorted on a trip to the bank, for which he paid them each five dollars.

Logan responded once to a burglary at a men's clothing store and saw cops all over the place stuffing clothes down their pants and up their shirts. The sergeant never came in because, as one cop told Logan, the owner would take care of him later. Logan took one shirt, but felt so guilty that he never wore it. "It wasn't even my size," he told us. On a later date, Logan took a shirt and a pair of pants at the scene of a kid's store break-in where, again, many policemen were helping themselves. In that case the sergeant hadn't been called yet and the men were taking what they could before he arrived. Although there was not much "contract" money to be made at the 73rd, there were many such instances during Logan's time that involved scrambling for small amounts.

Once, while riding with an experienced cop, Logan pulled up across from a dice game and the gamblers stopped playing. When the cops drove away, the game started again. After driving a bit, the cops returned and one of the gamblers came to the car and gave the cops five dollars to split. Another experienced cop took Logan to a beer wholesale warehouse, where he loaded twelve cases of beer into the squad car.

After he had become inured to the idea that taking money was part of the job, Logan was assigned to duty with the PEP Squad. Made up of twenty African American and Hispanic officers, the PEP Squad had been established three years earlier for the purpose of operating as a mobile strike force to combat narcotics traffic in the minority communities. This special, hand-picked group of police officers presumably disdained taking the petty graft so commonly collected by cops. Logan found that the PEP Squad indeed did not get involved with petty graft. It was into the big time.

Logan told us that the cops assigned to the PEP Squad regularly shook down those they arrested. The take was divided up, on the basis of seniority, much as it was in the plainclothes divisions, except that money was divided not equally, but on an informal merit basis. It was pretty much "eat what you kill." Each cop kept his own scores. A relatively inactive young cop, like Logan, got $1,500 a month. Others got as much as $3,000 a month. The commander of the PEP Squad, according to Logan, got $5,000 a month. It was a story of deliberate graft by a group of highly respected police officers whose responsibilities covered the most serious and sensitive area of law enforcement in the city.

Logan said that he never came across a large policy operation—through which the numbers racket was administered—that was not paying off the police on a regular basis. This made it complicated for him and the other PEP Squad members to score policy spots, since the proprietors would complain to their "protectors," who didn't take too kindly to other cops horning in on their territory.

Logan considered himself a light scorer, since he didn't go looking for money; he just accepted it when it came along. We were later to hear such cops described as "dunces" by their more opportunistic brethren. Other cops hustled for extra cash. In one instance, community complaints about drug pushers on 114th Street led to a PEP Squad operation to clean the street up. Logan and his partner arrested a man in a Buick who was dealing drugs dressed up as a woman. When they took him to the station, other cops searched the car, removing a fur coat and some 8-track tapes, and put them in their own cars. Logan moved on to 116th Street, and arrested a man he saw sniffing some drugs. The suspect removed two bundles of money, totaling $1,500, from his pockets, gave them to Logan and fled.

Another time, Logan and three other cops went to 116th Street with an informant to make a drug buy. The informant and one cop made the buy and left. Logan and the others then raided the suspect's apartment, finding him with a gun, 105 "decks" (glassine envelopes) of heroin, and cash in the amount of around $1,500. They called the 28th Precinct for help, and the officers who arrived began helping themselves to items in the apartment, such as jewelry and other valuable portables. Logan arrested the suspect, vouchered the gun and eighty-five decks of heroin, but kept all the money except two hundred dollars. He gave ten decks of heroin to the informant, kept ten decks for himself, and let the officer who made the buy keep what he bought. It was later rumored that this officer was himself a junkie.

On another day Logan, another patrolman, and a lieutenant went to 114th Street to arrest a known dealer called "Heavy." While searching the apartment, Logan found twenty-eight bundles of a hundred dollars each as well as some other money, which he showed the lieutenant, not knowing whether he was straight. The lieutenant talked to the suspect and eventually gave him eight hundred dollars back, keeping at least a thousand for himself and giving five hundred each to Logan and his partner. Logan felt that he had not been treated fairly by the lieutenant and apparently neither did the drug dealer, since he complained that the cops were stealing his money. Nothing came of his complaint and he was in due course convicted of dealing drugs.

This type of "score" was not unusual. Once Logan and some other patrolmen were called to assist on an arrest in which the suspect and his wife were screaming about their money being stolen by the cops, one of whom was a lieutenant. Logan later saw a suitcase of money in the squad room, and, since no money was vouchered on that arrest, he assumed it had once belonged to the suspect.

After one big arrest, Logan and his partner were offered $2,000 to let the suspect go but Logan was suspicious that it might be a setup since the lieutenant had asked him if any of the drugs were missing. He told his partner to let the arrest stick, but he scored the suspect for four hundred on the way to court.

Perhaps the most significant thing Logan told us was that, in the course of his being cashiered for taking a bribe, no one asked him anything about his knowledge of corruption in the Department. As First Deputy Police Commissioner John Walsh was later to all but acknowledge in his testimony, Department policy was swiftly to fire anyone actually caught in a corrupt act—but not to ask about what was going on.

Logan's usefulness to us as a street operative was pretty well eliminated by the notoriety he had gained by appearing on TV. Moreover, we had no way of checking out what he told us. The confused and sometimes contradictory story he had told on TV was considerably cleared up in our conversations with him, but we could not be sure that he wasn't telling us what he knew we wanted to hear. On the other hand, everything he said was consistent with what we were learning elsewhere, and we didn't catch him in any major inconsistencies, so we felt he could add something to the picture we intended to present. We couldn't use him as an operative, but he could have use as a witness, albeit secondhand—assuming we ever held public hearings.

13

SUPER THIEF

We were beginning to wonder if we would ever be able to gather enough live testimony for public hearings. It wouldn't be long before we would be out of money and our lend-lease agents would have to return to their regular jobs. We still did not have enough to warrant going public in the way we felt was needed to make enough of an impression to do some good.

Then we found what we had been so earnestly seeking. His name was William R. Phillips.

Phillips was a patrolman assigned to the 25th Precinct in Harlem. Athletic in a dissolute sort of way, he moved as smoothly as he talked. He was 6 feet tall and 190 pounds. A mischievous grin usually played across his Irish American face and he was totally at home in the ranks of police officers, with whom he had served for thirteen years. During that time, he had been a sector car and foot patrolman, a gold-shield detective, a member of the youth squad, and a plainclothesman. In one way or another he had been assigned to or had contact with just about every precinct in the city. He had received five commendations, including one for shooting a man to death in Harlem late one night. He reported the incident as an act of self-defense.

For virtually his entire career as a New York City police officer, Phillips had been thoroughly corrupt.

Among those from whom Phillips was extracting payoffs was the "Happy Hooker" herself, Xaviera Hollander. She told our informant, Teddy Ratnoff, about Phillips, and Ratnoff told us. Phillips had offered to arrange to put Xaviera on the pad, purporting to be able to insure her against being bothered by any of the police units that might normally have an interest in the business operations of a high-priced prostitute. In addition, Xaviera was involved in a court case, following her arrest by a cop named John Ryder, on a charge of prostitution. The case was in its preliminary stages and presented more than the usual threat because Xaviera's immigration status was precarious and she faced deportation for even a minor morals conviction. Xaviera was not happy with the haphazard protection provided in return for the payments she had been making to various cops. She was looking for a way to centralize her bribes and to take care of the pending case against her as well. Phillips claimed to be able to handle both.

Ratnoff convinced us that he could persuade Xaviera to let him become the liaison between Phillips and her. Wearing his own equipment, he would obtain for us direct proof of police corruption in progress.

Here was an opportunity to plunge into the middle of some real ongoing corruption. If we could gather evidence—on tape or even film—of what Ratnoff described to us, we would finally have firsthand material that might justify holding public hearings. One problem was that we would have to use Ratnoff as our undercover agent. We knew him to be not merely unreliable, but potentially treacherous. Anything he learned about our operations he felt entitled to use for whatever purposes—nefarious or otherwise—he might dream up. But we had no choice. If we were to take advantage of the opportunity, we had to trust Ratnoff and hope that he would find his interests enough aligned with ours to keep him from betraying us.

Agents Brian Bruh and Ralph Parente were assigned to be the principal operatives on the matter, but this was so important to us that all of our other agents, sometimes four or five at a time, became involved at one point or another.

So Ratnoff persuaded Xaviera that she needed a go-between to deal with Phillips and that he, Ratnoff, was her man. With that understanding, Ratnoff began to meet with Phillips. We did not wire Ratnoff right away. Phillips must be given time to get to know him, and we wanted to avoid the possibility of Phillips patting him down. Phillips was no ordinary target. We had to be particularly careful. For a while, Phillips was crisp and demanding, but then he began to relax a bit, so the time came when we equipped Ratnoff with one of his transmitters in time for a meeting at Xaviera's apartment, attended by Teddy, Phillips, Xaviera, and Xaviera's boyfriend, Larry Dreyfus. They discussed Xaviera's going on the pad to protect herself from any more arrests. Phillips explained that there were several levels of cops that had to be taken care of. Teddy asked whether Phillips could handle all levels, even the inspector who commanded the precinct or division:

PHILLIPS: If I were a full inspector, I wouldn't even sit down and talk to you, believe me. I wouldn't.

RATNOFF: Yeah.

PHILLIPS: I'd have somebody else do it. Who needs this bullshit aggravation. They don't do this.

RATNOFF: Yeah.

PHILLIPS: Your conception of what's to take place—what happens—is off somewhere in the blue.

RATNOFF: Listen, we don't know . . . we're asking you.

* * *

PHILLIPS: All I gotta do is say, "Listen, I got a friend of friend of mine . . . I got a operation . . . they want to go on. What do you want to do?" I'll tell him what the operation is. He'll say, "Okay, how much?" I'll give him a figure. He may give me a figure up in the sky. I'll say, "No deal."

RATNOFF: "No deal." What . . . what are we working on?

DREYFUS: But when you speak you won't mention any location or names?

PHILLIPS: No . . . no names at all.

RATNOFF: What are we talking about in figures . . . approximately?

* * *

PHILLIPS: Yeah, well, I don't think the division is going to take two hundred. I really don't think so.

RATNOFF: Well, how's it work . . . division, borough, and precinct?

PHILLIPS: And precinct, yeah.

* * *

PHILLIPS: I think . . . I think . . . you could wrap the whole thing up for between eight hundred and a thousand.

RATNOFF: Eight hundred and a thou . . .

PHILLIPS: But I gotta have a little bit to work with.

RATNOFF: Yeah. Look, you gotta have a little for yourself. We appreciate that.

PHILLIPS: Well, listen, she said I got a hundred dollars a month for myself, right?

RATNOFF: Right.

Phillips also referred to his second task, contacting Officer Ryder to arrange dismissal of the case against Hollander:

PHILLIPS: Now wait, I will try to get to Ryder. I don't know how successful I'll be. I can't tell you. But I'll try to get someone who knows him, and we'll sit down and talk—"Listen, we want the case thrown out—what do you want?"

RATNOFF: Alright, yeah, for dollars and cents, not . . . not nothing else.

PHILLIPS: Yeah, right. You want to take the contract. That's all we can do.

Then, under the constant surveillance of two of our agents, who listened in and recorded everything, Ratnoff engaged in a series of meetings with Phillips. Chief among the items of business between Xaviera, represented by Ratnoff, and Phillips was the task of putting her on the pad. Of first concern in this regard was the extent of her "coverage":

RATNOFF: Now, *define* the other deal, we're going to get protected from the precinct—no, we, she . . .

PHILLIPS: Division. Division, borough, *and* precinct. Listen, you give me the money, you have any problems—you ain't going to have—you're not going to have any problems, I'm telling you right now, you're not going to have any fucking problems. . . . The only thing that won't happen is the Chief, something like that, the PC—that I can't control.

RATNOFF: The chief of what?

PHILLIPS: The Chief Inspector.

RATNOFF: Yeah.

PHILLIPS: And the Police Commissioner—I can't control him.

Then came the cost of her coverage. How much would she have to pay?

RATNOFF: That's eleven hundred a month.

PHILLIPS: Right.

RATNOFF: That's a hundred for you and two—what was it?

PHILLIPS: No, it's uh, five—five—three and two.

RATNOFF: Right.

In a rare lapse of his normally infallible self-protective instincts, Phillips had gotten to trust Ratnoff. He carefully set things up so he would deal only with Ratnoff, avoiding the presumably unreliable Xaviera:

RATNOFF: No, look, here's what she wants to do . . .

PHILLIPS: Right.

RATNOFF: She'll go on the pad and that's what she's going to do.

PHILLIPS: Right.

RATNOFF: On a monthly basis. You're going to come, see me or see her or see . . .

PHILLIPS: I'm not going to see her, I'm going to see you.

RATNOFF: Alright, you see me. . . . That's OK.

PHILLIPS: I'm not going near her.

RATNOFF: OK, you see me every month.

PHILLIPS: Right.

RATNOFF: We have to make a date and a time.

PHILLIPS: I'll just call Larry [Dreyfus]. "Hey, Larry, I want to see Teddy" . . . between the first and the fifth—whatever your convenience.

Another detail to be attended to was the mechanism for warning Xaviera if something went wrong. Phillips said that if an arrest was threatened, Xaviera would get a phone call from a "Mr. White":

RATNOFF: She's gonna get, she's gonna get a call like you said, the man, from Mr. White.

PHILLIPS: Mr. White from Chicago.

RATNOFF: "Mr. White from Chicago is in town." Close it right up.

PHILLIPS: Close the fucking doors. Forget about it.

Some of these meetings were not only taped, but recorded on film. Under our arrangement with TV Channel 4 and Channel 5 we accumulated some good footage, including a segment where Ratnoff could be seen handing over an envelope, the contents of which, several hundred dollars in cash, were described in the accompanying tape-recorded conversation. Over the course of three weeks, we watched—and recorded—as Ratnoff passed on to Phillips a total of about $8,000 of Xaviera's money. The tapes of Ratnoff's meetings with Phillips were not merely useful, but entertaining as well. Phillips had a natural gift of gab. As he got to know Ratnoff, his discourse became more and more laced with anecdotes. Good ones. He was a marvelous raconteur, and obviously enjoyed illustrating whatever point he was making with some colorful tale.

The venue for most of the meetings between Ratnoff and Phillips was Phillips's "office"—the bar at P. J. Clarke's restaurant, famous as a speakeasy-like eatery in a ramshackle two-floor building, whose owners refused to sell out to the gigantic office building that was eventually built next to it on the corner of 55th Street and Third Avenue. Phillips considered the public telephone booth at the end of the bar at P. J.'s to be his office phone.

In paying Phillips his share, Ratnoff did his best to draw him out about the cops who were to receive the balance.

RATNOFF: Okay, okay. Okay now, she said she didn't have much cash in the house. I'm going to give you five today . . .

PHILLIPS: Alright.

RATNOFF: And I'll give you the balance on Friday.

PHILLIPS: Okay, but meet me here like five o'clock Friday, because I've got to meet them at five thirty.

RATNOFF: You wouldn't mind if I watched that, would you? Or is that . . .

PHILLIPS: Yeah, you can watch it. I wish you were here to watch it. Okay, you be here at five o'clock, okay? I'm going to meet these guys here at five thirty. I'm going to give the guy an envelope. You can watch. I'll be right here, by the bar.

RATNOFF: Now, you're going to give me the third name on Friday, right?

PHILLIPS: Right.

RATNOFF: Are you going to meet the three guys, or just one?

PHILLIPS: I'm going to meet one, uh two, I'm going to meet two guys there Friday. I'll give, I'm gonna give them a white envelope.

RATNOFF: So, I'll have to meet you with the rest of the money before then?

PHILLIPS: Yeah. But you'll be at the bar. I'll give the guy the envelope. I'm going to be right at the end of the fucking bar, and you can sit at a table, whatever you want to do. You can see the transaction.

* * *

RATNOFF: Okay, look, there's five in there.

PHILLIPS: Here's a pound, right?

RATNOFF: A pound, that's five hundred dollars. You want to make sure . . . here, I'll hold your drink.

PHILLIPS: You say it's five hundred, here's the kind of guy I am. It's five hundred.

RATNOFF: Okay, you got five hundred dollars.

PHILLIPS: If there's four hundred there I lose a hundred, but I don't think you'll do that because I don't count money, right?

RATNOFF: There's fifties and hundreds, so there's no problem.

PHILLIPS: Now.

RATNOFF: You got five, we owe you six. I'll pay you Friday six, I'll be here early enough.

Negotiations with Officer Ryder—to get him to recant key testimony in the case against Xaviera—turned out to be more protracted than expected. Ryder had heard that Xaviera had paid a large sum for another prostitute's "book," so he figured she must be doing well, and he knew about her problems with Immigration. It added up, he told Phillips, to big money. Phillips passed the news on to Ratnoff:

PHILLIPS: Okay. It's a "going to devastate you" day.

RATNOFF: Oh—oh.

PHILLIPS: The kid knows what he's got. He knows what he's got. He knows if she goes, she's out of business.

RATNOFF: Who's that?

PHILLIPS: If he convicts her, he knows she's going out of the country. He talked to Immigration about her.

RATNOFF: Who did? You did?

PHILLIPS: No, no.

RATNOFF: Ryder did?

PHILLIPS: Yeah—Immigration was up to speak to him about the case. They got a case against her. The kid's no dope.

PHILLIPS: He knows that she bought the books off the other broad for $10,000.

RATNOFF: You didn't know that, 'cause I never told you.

PHILLIPS: I didn't know it. Well, how'd I find out?

RATNOFF: Well, maybe she told Ryder.

PHILLIPS: Well, he busted the other broad too. The one she got the books from.

After explaining Ryder's position generally, Phillips hit Ratnoff with the specifics: the cop wanted $10,000 or he would testify to the truth, consistent with his arrest report.

RATNOFF: You ready?

PHILLIPS: Let's have a drink first, then I'll be ready. Our man wants ten.

RATNOFF: Ten what?

PHILLIPS: Ten big ones. I'm telling you I almost fell off the fuckin' chair. I said, "Waddaya kidding me?" I says, "When I tell this guy I got" . . . Sit and have a drink. I was drinking a soda and he says, "What you want?"

RATNOFF: Ryder wants ten thousand?

PHILLIPS: Yeah.

RATNOFF: She wouldn't buy that.

PHILLIPS: Huh?

RATNOFF: She wouldn't buy that.

PHILLIPS: She's out of the country then. Let her run here as long as she can, then she's finished.

RATNOFF: He wants $10,000 to change his testimony?

PHILLIPS: That's right. He knows what he's got. If she goes, the whole operation goes, right? He knows what he's got. . . . He says, "I don't do it very often. When I get a case that's good, I want to get paid."

RATNOFF: Now, assuming she does it.

PHILLIPS: She walks. And he'll throw the other broad in as a gift.

Appearing to be astounded, Teddy dug for more information about the threat from the Immigration authorities:

RATNOFF: He said he went to Immigration already—and reported it?

PHILLIPS: Immigration came to him. Immigration picked up the case when the fingerprints went downtown as an alien, right? So they come up to him, "What do you got?" So, "I got this, I got this . . . I got this."

RATNOFF: Oh, I see. I see.

PHILLIPS: So, when she's convicted, she's gone, she is gone guaranteed.

RATNOFF: An automatic deportation.

Phillips sneered at Xaviera's attempt to get by with a few hundred dollars:

PHILLIPS: You know what, she gave me a figure yesterday. Go from two or three hundred.

RATNOFF: Yeah, right.

PHILLIPS: I wonder if she thinks she's got a fucking boy scout out there. This guy's not a boy scout.

RATNOFF: What kind of assurance do we get? That's a lot of money.

PHILLIPS: You get a guarantee. You get a guarantee. I'll hold the money until the case is over. And if she don't walk, you get the money back. Is that good enough?

RATNOFF: Uh, huh.

Ratnoff took the news of Ryder's $10,000 demand back to Xaviera. She was incredulous. Meeting again with Phillips, Ratnoff told him that Xaviera wouldn't pay. The haggling that resulted was recorded:

PHILLIPS: Now, about Ryder. He's got, he's got her by the balls. He's got her by the fucking balls. Give me a figure. Jew him down. He asked me for ten.

RATNOFF: You jew him down, I can't. I mean, you know, she, she almost fell off the bed.

PHILLIPS: Give me a number . . . offer him seven, eight, what can I tell you? He'll bend it. Listen, it's like I say, when you buy a car, "I want ten thousand for the car." "Okay, give me eight, give me seven, give me a number." . . . All right? Sure, we can bend him, but she's gotta know this is a big fucking number, 'cause she's in big trouble. Let her talk to her lawyer. She wants to go to trial. But the golden goose is gone.

RATNOFF: The golden goose is gone. Right.

PHILLIPS: That's the golden goose. He goes on the stand. I'll bet you. I'll tell you what I'll do. I'll bet you a thousand dollars of my own money that if he goes on the stand, she goes out of the country. My own money.

RATNOFF: See him again. See what you can do. Because ten thousand she's not going for. I can tell you.

PHILLIPS: Teddy, money is only money. You can make money. You can't make for her time. You can't make time.

RATNOFF: She's not going to the can. All she's gonna do is leave the country, that's all.

PHILLIPS: Yeah, but what happens to the business?

RATNOFF: True, true.

PHILLIPS: The golden goose is gone. You lose, I lose, we're all out of the fucking business, right? I don't want to see her go; I hate to see her go. I want to make a few dollars on the fucking deal. But I guarantee you a thousand of my own money that if he goes on the stand she's out of the country.

Ratnoff went back to Xaviera, who raised her offer to $2,500. Ratnoff resumed the bargaining:

PHILLIPS: Teddy, believe me, he's going to bury her, I know it.

RATNOFF: I believe you. Look, will you try twenty-five?

PHILLIPS: I couldn't even go back to him with that figure.

RATNOFF: Try. All he can do is say more, right?

PHILLIPS: If you say, maybe, thirty-five, I'd say okay, maybe you have a shot.

RATNOFF: Why thirty-five, what, it's only a thousand bucks.

PHILLIPS: I know, but I say give me thirty-five, right, you give me twenty-five. It's the rock bottom. I'm on the bottom of the deck now. He's going to say, "Well . . . So long buddy, nice seeing you." He's going to laugh at me, he's going to say, "What, are you kidding?"

The deal was closed at a price of $3,500. In the course of the negotiations over details, Ratnoff tried, unsuccessfully, to get an introduction to Ryder:

PHILLIPS: So we got a deal.

RATNOFF: What's the deal now?

PHILLIPS: $3,500.

RATNOFF: $3,500?

PHILLIPS: I could have squeezed another five hundred out of you, I'll tell you the truth, if I wanted to break balls, right?

RATNOFF: Yeah.

PHILLIPS: . . . told me you got a deal for thirty-five you got a deal for thirty-five.

RATNOFF: Okay. Now, what is it you're going to do and how do I ascertain it, and all that? You know.

PHILLIPS: Well, I'm going to hold the money, he's not going to get a dime until the thing's over with, until when he walks out of court, he's got the dough, that's the deal. No, no, uh, walk-off, no money, he knows this. In other words, if he says he's got a deal and he gets all fucked up and she goes down the drain, there's no money.

RATNOFF: Yeah, but we got to have more assurance than that.

PHILLIPS: We've got a guarantee, she's not going to get fucked up. He's going to walk in and he's gonna say he went to the apartment, she said she was going to get him a girl.

RATNOFF: Yeah.

PHILLIPS: There's no sex, no sex talk about you're going to get laid, fucked, etc., none of that bullshit. We're going to say where she had a fee or something like that, like an escort bureau. She's going to walk.

RATNOFF: He won't meet with me, I take it. That's what. That's what he's afraid of me.

PHILLIPS: Meet with you? Forget about it.

PHILLIPS: Huh.

PHILLIPS: Forget about it, he's not going to meet with you.

RATNOFF: Why, I mean . . .

PHILLIPS: You want to meet him?

RATNOFF: I, look . . .

PHILLIPS: He's not gonna meet you.

Another point to cover was making sure Xaviera's courtroom lawyer understood the deal. It would not do for him to light into Ryder on cross-examination, probing for inconsistencies in testimony that was already fixed:

PHILLIPS: Yeah, you've got it. She's got a walk-off at $3,500.

RATNOFF: Now he's going to get on the stand, he's not going to incriminate her in any way.

PHILLIPS: All you've got to do is tell her lawyer. Say, okay, listen. He's on our side. That's all you've got to tell her lawyer, so her lawyer doesn't fucking hammer away like he's going to play Clarence Darrow and really break the guy's balls. She'll walk on it. She'll walk on it.

Next came the ticklish question of how much, if any, money had to be paid up front. It was agreed that $1,500 would be given to Phillips to hold until Ryder testified. Then the rest of the $3,500 would be paid to Phillips, who would turn it all over to Ryder, who would then give Phillips his cut.

RATNOFF: Yeah. Uh, huh. What if I get the money, I hold it, I show it to you, and then as soon as you get the deal, you get the money.

PHILLIPS: Give me half, how's that? So I can show him, okay? We have half the bread now we . . .

RATNOFF: I'll have, I'll have all of it. I'm not going to Jap you for $3,500.

PHILLIPS: He ain't gonna go for that.

RATNOFF: Huh?

PHILLIPS: Listen, he wants to see something. He don't know who the hell you are.

RATNOFF: Well, we made a deal already. You've got to have some faith.

PHILLIPS: You made a deal with who? With Ryder?

RATNOFF: No, we made a deal. You see that you get the money, you see that.

PHILLIPS: Oh, I have faith in you, but what am I going to tell him? Tell him, "Listen, I've got a nice big envelope here with nothing in it so everything is fine"?

RATNOFF: No, no, you'll get it, you'll get it, you'll get it, as soon as she walks.

PHILLIPS: I've got to have something to show him though. Give me $1,500, and I can say, "Look, I've got fifteen in my pocket. When she walks, we get the rest of the money." That's all. Is that hard? I'm not going to hurt your money. I don't want your fucking money. I'm not going to run away with it.

RATNOFF: Yeah, I'll put up fifteen hundred and the balance when she walks.

PHILLIPS: Fine, that's a decent deal.

RATNOFF: Now you've got to check that out with him, I guess.

PHILLIPS: I've already spoken to him. I said we'll have half the money out front. When she walks you've got the rest of the money. He knows he's not going to get anything until she walks. So I say, "Look, I've got $1,500 in my pocket, here we are, go do your thing. When the thing is over you get the rest of the money."

RATNOFF: See, now, I've worked deals before . . .

PHILLIPS: You ain't up there for your health, so stop the bullshit, right. I mean this running all around in the middle of the fucking night. You ain't doing this because you're a good-time Charlie. Listen, we're all making a few dollars off the fucking thing, right? Fuck, we aren't going to fuck the golden goose, right. Never fuck the golden goose and never squeeze anybody.

As all this was going on, a new opportunity presented itself. Xaviera's boyfriend, Larry Dreyfus, was arrested on a charge of being in possession of a phony check—for $250,000. Phillips charged to the rescue, with us right behind him, listening in:

PHILLIPS: How's Larry doin'?

RATNOFF: Okay, he's crying a bit. He's got a charge against him you know.

* * *

PHILLIPS: Oh, yeah?

RATNOFF: Yeah, he was indicted.

PHILLIPS: For what?

RATNOFF: He had a $250,000 bogus check in his possession.

PHILLIPS: Yeah?

RATNOFF: Yeah, total accident, he says, anyway.

PHILLIPS: Two hundred and fifty thousand!

RATNOFF: Well, I mean, if you're going to deal, you might as well deal big, right?

PHILLIPS: Don't fool around with pennies, right?

RATNOFF: [laughs] They were going to try to get that fixed too, but . . .

PHILLIPS: Listen, if you get to the right people, you can fix anything, believe me.

RATNOFF: That's what they say.

PHILLIPS: This is no lie. I'm a judge to it, believe me, I know what can be done.

Phillips began by arranging to fix the detective assigned to the case. Then he determined that this matter was too heavy to be fixed at the cop level. He told Ratnoff that there was a different way. Fix not only the detective, but the judge.

The case was pending before Justice Mitchell Schweitzer, a senior Manhattan trial judge of considerable notoriety. Phillips claimed to Ratnoff that a lawyer by the name of Irwin Germaise had boasted about being able to bribe Schweitzer on Xaviera's behalf. If Phillips was right—and if we could get the whole thing on tape or, better yet, film—we would have a sensational cornerstone for the Commission's public hearings and report: a corrupt cop acting through a corrupt lawyer to fix a case involving a prostitute's paramour, before a corrupt judge.

Then suddenly the whole setup threatened to come apart. Xaviera decided not to pay Ryder to fix the case against her. When finally told she had to come up with $1,500 down payment, and a total of $3,500, Xaviera flatly refused. She had already paid Phillips more than $8,000. She would take her chances.

When Ratnoff told us of Xaviera's backing down, we huddled frantically, trying to find some way to keep things going by making the first $1,500 payment—which was due that night. As for the rest of the money, we would worry about that later. Our hope was to keep the deal alive long enough to get direct evidence on Ryder and, hopefully, Germaise and Schweitzer as well.

But Ratnoff's usefulness might come to a quick end if the money for the first payment in Ryder's case was not forthcoming. Phillips was jittery to begin with, and any sign that money was slow in coming might make him suspicious enough to stop having anything to do with Teddy. The stinginess of law enforcement agencies was well known, and Phillips was aware that in those days no undercover agent would actually pay out any substantial amount of money under circumstances where he might not get it back. So far we had been making payments with Xaviera Hollander's money. Now, in order to keep things moving, we would have to hand over at least $1,500. It was a sum with which no law enforcement agency in those days was prepared to part.

But while government law enforcement agencies were stingy, we were penniless. There was simply no money to make the payment.

In desperation, I called Jerry McKenna, a former member of the Manhattan District Attorney's Office, now counsel to the New York State Senate Joint Legislative Committee on Crime; his office was in the state capital, Albany. This committee, chaired by State Senator John Hughes, had been active in looking into corruption, and we had exchanged some information with them in the past. McKenna knew, generally, that we had a police officer under direct surveillance in a corruption situation. We thought it might be possible that McKenna's committee had funds available that it would be prepared to risk losing in an attempt to get information about a crooked cop, a crooked lawyer, and a crooked judge. I asked McKenna. He was interested. The money would buy him a foot in the door to share some possibly spectacular publicity down the road. Acting quickly, McKenna got $1,500 in cash out of the Committee's bank account in Albany. We were told that the money was to be put in a package and given to the pilot of an Allegheny Airlines plane flying from Albany to New York late that afternoon.

Somebody goofed. Instead of giving the package containing the money to the pilot, the committee staff decided at the last minute to send a messenger with it. But they neglected to tell us of the change. So, while our agent was aggressively questioning a mystified pilot about a supposedly missing package of money, the committee messenger was making his own way from Albany to New York. When our agent called in from the airport to say that the money had not arrived, we called McKenna, and learned for the first time that it had been sent by messenger.

It was Sunday. The time for the payoff meeting loomed. It was scheduled for 8:00 P.M. and it was already after six. Apparently the messenger had taken a wrong flight, or was lost or stuck in traffic somewhere. We had no way of knowing when he would arrive and, in those pre-cell phone days, no way to contact him. At six on a Sunday evening, there were not too many places where we could quickly get our hands on $1,500 in cash. ATMs were years in the future. We pooled what we each had and what we could find around the office. It came to about five hundred dollars. Ratnoff hurried off to Germaise's office, at 717 Fifth Avenue, with the five hundred dollars we had collected, to keep Phillips at bay.

RATNOFF: Here. It was slow. So you know, there's only five in there right now. It's gonna be a while.

PHILLIPS: There's only five hundred in there? You gotta be kidding me.

RATNOFF: I'm sorry. She ain't got—

PHILLIPS: Oh, for Christ's sake.

RATNOFF: You gotta wait another hour or so, 'cause she's got checks and she's got somebody coming over with cash.

PHILLIPS: Tell you what, I'll meet you at eleven o'clock, 'cause I gotta be to work at eleven thirty.

RATNOFF: I thought you were going to meet the guy.

PHILLIPS: I gotta, huh. At twelve I gotta meet him.

RATNOFF: And you gotta go be at work? I can meet you later. I can meet you any time. It doesn't make any difference. You see, the thing is, here's what happened; she gets uh, a lot of checks in . . .

PHILLIPS: Yeah.

RATNOFF: And she anticipates two, three thousand dollars easy by now.

PHILLIPS: Yeah.

RATNOFF: And she's got a lot of checks in, and then do you know until the guy comes over and gives her the cash for the checks. This is just the cash money she took in.

PHILLIPS: Yeah, well, let's see.

RATNOFF: Well, you got five bills in there. I grabbed it fast. Make sure it's five when you get a chance . . .

PHILLIPS: I'll meet you at eleven o'clock.

RATNOFF: Where's that now?

PHILLIPS: Right over near the corner.

RATNOFF: Beautiful.

Now we had until 11:00 P.M. to come up with $1,000. All I could think of was the office safe at the law firm from whence I had come, Cahill Gordon Reindel & Ohl. As a relatively junior partner who had been on leave of absence for a year, I didn't swing too much weight in the partnership, but I knew the support staff. Mary Forcelon, the office manager, was a good friend, and she had the combination to the firm's safe. Fortunately, she happened to be putting in some weekend overtime at the office. I called her up. How would she like to go into the safe and lend me $1,000 out of petty cash? I promised it would be back in the morning. It took a little persuasion, but she agreed. We promised each other not to say anything to anyone.

Ratnoff used the money from the law firm safe to pay the remaining $1,000 to Phillips:

RATNOFF: You want to do it here, is that all right?

PHILLIPS: Yeah.

RATNOFF: Okay, there's a G in there.

PHILLIPS: Beautiful.

RATNOFF: And it's in some small bills and stuff.

PHILLIPS: Okay, fine. Teddy, thanks a million, you got me off the hook.

RATNOFF: We're all straight now, right?

PHILLIPS: We're all square. And then, uh, I'm going to meet Ryder at one o'clock, uh, two o'clock.

RATNOFF: Now you're going to meet him at two o'clock tonight?

Once the money was paid, they lapsed into small talk, Phillips bragging about killing three people (he in fact had killed one) and repeating instructions about what to do about the lawyers:

RATNOFF: You got decorations too. What's that?

PHILLIPS: Oh, yeah, I killed three fucks up here.

RATNOFF: Killed three fucks, yeah?

PHILLIPS: Oh, yeah. I blow them up like they're fucking nothing. After you get outta court, oh, before I forget, two important things: Remember, talk to the lawyer, tell him the cop's on your side. And when you go down there, like a lot of guys go, don't be friendly.

RATNOFF: Don't be friendly?

PHILLIPS: Don't be friendly. And don't talk to him, because you don't know who the fuck is watching him. With the Knapp Commission and everything else. Just walk in like nobody knows nothing, right?

RATNOFF: Right.

PHILLIPS: And the same with the lawyer. Don't have any conversations with him in the hallway or any of that bullshit, because you never know who the hell is watching you.

Fortunately for my relationship with my law partners—and Mary Furcelon's job—McKenna's messenger finally showed up that evening. By the start of business the next day, the money was back in Cahill Gordon's safe, with no one the wiser. Although the episode ended without disaster, I would later regret having to reveal the facts about Phillips's operation to McKenna and his committee.

After all the maneuvering, Xaviera's lawyer got to court before Ratnoff, who never had a chance to tell him what was going on. Ignorant of the arrangement, the lawyer made a perfectly legitimate deal with the prosecutor to settle the case and let Xaviera off. For us, it was a satisfactory ending. We had gathered a good deal of evidence about Ryder, even if Teddy had been unable to meet him and, more importantly, we did not have to produce the balance of the $3,500—which would have been an impossible task. Teddy was now free to pursue his efforts to gather evidence about Judge Schweitzer and Irwin Germaise in the case against her boyfriend, Larry Dreyfus.

Mitchell Schweitzer was not just any ordinary judge—he was one of the most notorious jurists on the prestigious Manhattan trial bench, specializing in criminal cases, particularly highly visible ones. In his twenty-five years, he had developed a reputation for being brilliant, well-versed in the law, flamboyant, and pro-prosecution. He had a practical, shoot-from-the-hip style and those in the anti-corruption business felt that there was a certain aura about him that made Phillips's claims believable. Indeed, three years after the Knapp Commission ended its work, a full-page headline on page one of the *New York Daily News* quoted a U.S. Senator, Charles Percy from Michigan, as identifying Schweitzer in a Senate hearing as "The Best Judge Money Can Buy." Percy's comment was gratuitously injected into the testimony of one of those hooded informants who regularly testify before congressional committees about the current "inside" story of organized crime, and Percy appears to have had little basis for the charge other than rumor. Nevertheless, whether fair or not, Schweitzer's reputation was such as to make us, even several years earlier, willing to take seriously a charge that he was susceptible of taking a bribe.

Irwin Germaise, the lawyer through whom Phillips said he could reach Schweitzer, was a dapper, successful practitioner with a twenty-man law office and a varied practice. He appeared regularly in federal as well as state court to defend all sorts of individuals, including mob figures. I remembered him, from my days in the U.S. Attorney's Office, as a personable and proficient lawyer about whom a charge of corruption was not particularly surprising.

Phillips informed Ratnoff that he had "gotten" Germaise, who would arrange matters with Schweitzer, through a certain bail-bondsman who was close to the judge:

RATNOFF: All right. Just tell me quick what the deal is with the guy.

PHILLIPS: Okay, I, I—He's gotta go see—Irwin Germaise is his new lawyer.

RATNOFF: Yeah.

PHILLIPS: Him and the bondsman are like that. He'll walk through that and he's got the detective on the hook, the whole bit, the whole thing's set. I'm all day with this fucking thing. He's gotta—he's gotta go see Irwin Germaise. That's the lawyer, his new lawyer, and this guy and the bondsman are buddies, they're friends, forget about it. It's going to cost her money but he'll walk. What, I don't know. You gave me the contract with the cop, right? I got the contract with the cop. The cop's not going to bury him, but he needs help because he's got a broad, a witness, and he signed for the check.

RATNOFF: A witness signed for the . . .

PHILLIPS: That's his hang-up. But when he puts the juice into with the bondsman and the other guy—he'll take care of the whole thing. He'll walk. You're going to fuck around, chintz nickels and dimes, you're going to go to—he's going to go.

RATNOFF: Now, we got the detective in the picture, the guy can't guarantee, we gotta get a lawyer involved.

PHILLIPS: Okay, I will tell you—the way we'll do it. Fuck the squad. Right? I'll tell 'em, "No deal," and let's just go with the bondsman. And, and, uh, Germaise. Don't give 'em nothing.

RATNOFF: Don't give who nothing? The detective nothing?

PHILLIPS: Nothing. Let's work the other way. Let's . . .

RATNOFF: Now, we need that too. Why can't we do both things?

PHILLIPS: No, let's put the juice in the other—it's going to cost a lot of fucking money.

Ratnoff next had Phillips introduce him to Germaise, with whom Ratnoff, using the pseudonym "Randell," had several telephone conversations, setting things up. Again, the trick was to drag things out as long as possible before any real cash had actually to change hands, and hope that Xaviera would be willing to come up with it:

RECEPTION: Germaise and Quinn, good afternoon.

RATNOFF: Mr. Germaise, please.

RECEPTION: Who's calling?

RATNOFF: Mr. Randall.

GERMAISE: Hello.

RATNOFF: Hello, sorry to bother you again.

GERMAISE: Yeah, Ted.

RATNOFF: Listen, uh, I know I got to do a little running tonight, what can we use as a starter here 'cause I can get it all together by trial date.

GERMAISE: You can get it all together—I didn't hear you, Teddy, I'm sorry.

RATNOFF: I can get all the dough together in time for the trial date.

GERMAISE: In time for the trial?

RATNOFF: Right, but how much can we give you as a starter?

GERMAISE: Well, you got to do the best you can so I can do what I have to do 'cause I've already, you know, pledged it, you know what I mean? I've done some things.

RATNOFF: Yeah, I understand that.

GERMAISE: So you got to help me fulfill my obligation.

RATNOFF: Well, you know, listen, I'm on your side.

GERMAISE: Ah, Teddy, I know that, I mean don't be silly, I am not . . .

RATNOFF: I mean it's just that, you know, she's impossible . . .

GERMAISE: I know you're dealing with people that you have no control over.

RATNOFF: Right.

GERMAISE: Well, what have you got your hands on now?

RATNOFF: A couple of thou.

GERMAISE: Well, let's get started with that. At least I can go and do what I promised people I would do.

RATNOFF: Yeah.

GERMAISE: And then as you get it you'll bring it, you know.

RATNOFF: Right. Are we pretty sure on this Irwin?

GERMAISE: Yeah.

RATNOFF: Huh.

GERMAISE: Yeah.

RATNOFF: Okay, I mean you . . .

GERMAISE: I'll say this, Teddy: as sure as you can be.

RATNOFF: For future reference . . .

GERMAISE: Teddy, sure as we can be. There's always, you know, that outside chance that it's not going to work because no one can guarantee God, you know.

RATNOFF: Uh huh.

GERMAISE: But I say, "As sure as anybody could possibly be, we are here."

RATNOFF: Uh huh.

GERMAISE: Which I guess is as good as it could be, you know.

RATNOFF: Okay, well, Bill has something to do yet anyway, you know.

GERMAISE: Yeah, I know all about that. I know 'cause he'll be here today at four.

RATNOFF: Great, so he'll let you know.

GERMAISE: Yeah, I'm going to see Billy.

RATNOFF: Okay.

GERMAISE: Yeah, I know what he's doing.

RATNOFF: Okay. You see, he knows the problem I have in getting dough for him.

GERMAISE: Yeah.

RATNOFF: You know that.

GERMAISE: Well, do you have your hands on anything?

RATNOFF: Yeah, two.

GERMAISE: Well, bring that up.

RATNOFF: Well, let me see what else I can do today, okay?

GERMAISE: All right.

RATNOFF: And I'll definitely see you tomorrow without fail.

GERMAISE: OK, I'll be here tomorrow all day.

RATNOFF: Okay.

GERMAISE: Right.

RATNOFF: Thank you, bye, bye.

GERMAISE: Bye, bye.

Then Ratnoff recorded conversations among the three which left no doubt that Phillips had accurately stated what Germaise said he could do.

We had a crooked cop and a crooked lawyer, but no actual connection had yet been made to the judge himself. While a prosecutor, I had learned that it was common for a certain type of defense counsel to tell a client that he could bribe a public official to do something that the official was probably going to do anyway. The lawyer then put the supposed bribe money in his own pocket. When a lawyer like this attempted to make friendly conversations with a prosecutor during a break in court proceedings, the routine response was a noncommittal nod. Better to risk hurting an attorney's feelings than to give him the opportunity of claiming to his watching client that he had arranged some illegal accommodation. In one instance, our surveilling agents observed a meeting between Germaise and Judge Schweitzer in a restaurant. Germaise told Phillips that he discussed bribing the judge, but we had no way of knowing actually what was said.

Our plan was for Ratnoff to keep feeding Xaviera's money to Germaise, through Phillips, and hope we would get lucky when and if the payment to Schweitzer was made. Maybe we would be able to monitor the meeting between Germaise and Schweitzer, and observe something that would corroborate the corrupt arrangement.

However, we had a major problem. As we had already learned in the Ryder case, Xaviera was getting increasingly reluctant to part with any large sums of cash. This posed a real obstacle, because Phillips had a way of requiring payment as we went along. It would be too bad if, just as we were finally getting close to getting something concrete on Schweitzer, we were stymied by a lack of cash. We continued to have no money of our own, McKenna was tapped out and I couldn't very well take any more from Cahill Gordon's safe, having no way of putting it back. We had no choice but to play things "by ear" and string the operation out as long as we could.

On June 2, 1971, Teddy called Germaise to arrange a meeting in Germaise's Midtown office, for the purpose of giving Germaise some money. There was none to give, but we hoped to stall, somehow:

RECEPTION: Germaise and Quinn, good morning.
RATNOFF: Mr. Germaise, please.
RECEPTION: Who's calling?
RATNOFF: Mr. Randell?
RECEPTION: Randell?
RATNOFF: Uh huh.
RECEPTION: Thank you.
GERMAISE: Hello!
RATNOFF: Hi, how are you?

GERMAISE: Hiya, Teddy. Good.

RATNOFF: Good. Listen, I'm stuck downtown a little bit. I'll come up in the early afternoon.

GERMAISE: All right, I'll be here all day.

RATNOFF: Okay, is Bill around?

GERMAISE: Bill Phillips?

RATNOFF: Yeah.

GERMAISE: No, he'll be here at four.

RATNOFF: He will be there at four.

GERMAISE: Yeah.

RATNOFF: Okay, 'cause I got to talk to him about something.

GERMAISE: Where's that other guy, that, uh, Larry?

RATNOFF: Oh, I've got it. I've got it. I'll give it to you.

GERMAISE: Oh, you got the money?

RATNOFF: Yeah.

GERMAISE: Did he give you the money?

RATNOFF: Yeah, I got a check.

Our thought was that by promising, or even using, checks, we could stretch things out. It doesn't take money in the bank to write a check, and there are all sorts of explanations for why one bounces. Teddy was instructed to keep promising, and explaining, as long as possible.

GERMAISE: You got a check?

RATNOFF: Yeah.

GERMAISE: What good's a check I've got to pass out – well, that's all right. Okay, I didn't want to put it through the account but . . .

RATNOFF: Well, you have to have cash?

GERMAISE: No.

RATNOFF: Tell me. I can arrange it.

GERMAISE: How can you arrange it?

RATNOFF: I'll cash it for you.

GERMAISE: How big is it, what have you got?

RATNOFF: Twenty-five.

GERMAISE: Uh, because I want to pass it out and do what I have to do. I don't want it to go through my account if I don't have to.

RATNOFF: Well, if you have to have cash I'll have to get cash.

GERMAISE: Well, will you have it when you come here?

RATNOFF: Huh?

GERMAISE: Will you have it cashed when you come here?

RATNOFF: Well, then I'll have to come a little later. I want to take care of
   Bill too today.

GERMAISE: Yeah.

RATNOFF: So I'd like to meet him at four o'clock there.

GERMAISE: He'll be here at four o'clock.

RATNOFF: Great. So I'll take care of him at four.

GERMAISE: But don't give him any check.

RATNOFF: No. Hey, what's the matter, you think I'm stupid?

GERMAISE: No, I don't at all.

RATNOFF: Okay.

GERMAISE: All right, come at four.

RATNOFF: Okay.

GERMAISE: Do what you have to do . . .

RATNOFF: Okay. I'll get some cash.

GERMAISE: Okay, Teddy.

RATNOFF: Right-o. Thank you. Bye-bye.

Ratnoff showed up, as planned, at Germaise's office. As usual, he was wearing a transmitter, which was monitored by Brian Bruh and Gordon White, sitting in a parked car on the street below, listening and recording. Ratnoff routinely introduced himself to the support people in the Germaise's outer office, and was announced:

RATNOFF: Anybody here? Mr. Germaise in?

RECEPTION: Do you have an appointment with him?

RATNOFF: Yes I do, if he got back from court.

RECEPTION: He's here, yes, OK you can go right in.

RATNOFF: Yeah.

But, things were about to come to an end. Unknown to Ratnoff, Germaise had gotten nervous about him and instructed Phillips to pat him down.

"Come in," said Phillips, "How are you, how you doing, kid?" Phillips's customarily friendly greeting was accompanied by a casual but obviously deliberate pat on Ratnoff's back. Skillfully, without apparent purpose, Phillips let his hand drop, until it came to rest on the belt containing the transmitting equipment. Ratnoff froze.

RATNOFF: O.K., what's the matter?

PHILLIPS: He's loaded. Irwin, the man is loaded.

RATNOFF: With what? Money?

PHILLIPS: I'm not kidding!

PHILLIPS: What do you got there? You wired?

RATNOFF: You're crazy.

Ratnoff began to pour sweat. He knew the game was over. What he had to do now was stall long enough for Bruh and White, listening below, to come to his rescue. The agents were on their way, stopping long enough to get help from a uniformed police officer who happened to be giving a ticket to a peddler a few doors down from the entrance to Germaise's building. White, mustering as much authority and urgency as he could, identified himself and persuaded the officer to come along. They might need back-up. With the cop in tow, Bruh and White raced to a building elevator and headed for Germaise's eighth-floor office. The tape machine in the car kept recording.

Upstairs, Phillips ripped Ratnoff's jacket and shirt from his back, leaving the fat little man sweating and quivering with fright, the transmitter and battery pack clearly exposed.

GERMAISE: What is that?

RATNOFF: It's a transmitter.

GERMAISE: What is that?

RATNOFF: It's a paging system.

PHILLIPS: Yeah? Take it off.

[*sounds of activity*]

RATNOFF: [*indistinct*] Pick up the telephone. I'll show you it's a page. It's a paging system.

PHILLIPS: Take it off!

Enraged, Phillips tore the equipment from Ratnoff's body and threw it outside the room, slamming the door. In a tribute to Ratnoff's workmanship, the transmitter continued to function, picking up the conversation, albeit less distinctly, right through the closed door.

RATNOFF: It's a paging system.

GERMAISE: What do you page?

PHILLIPS: Well, how come you're so shaky now?

GERMAISE: What do you page?

RATNOFF: It's a paging system.

GERMAISE: What do you page?

RATNOFF: Huh? I'll show you. I'll pick up the phone and I'll page somebody.

GERMAISE: Alright, good.

PHILLIPS: I'll tell you what. If this is what I think it is, you know what you are?

Desperately trying, until help arrived, to keep alive the fantasy that they were dealing only with a simple paging device, Ratnoff retrieved the equipment and offered to give a demonstration.

RATNOFF: Can I put the thing on?

GERMAISE: Here, I want to hear it page [*static*]

RATNOFF: . . . through and then I tell . . .

GERMAISE: Well, go tell them to page you. Go tell them to page you. I want to hear you paged.

RATNOFF: Look what you did to the fucking thing, Billy.

PHILLIPS: What did I do to it? What do you think I was supposed to do with the thing. I didn't do nothing to the fucking thing. You come in here, you look like a fucking electronic robot here walking in the door. Listen, you . . . [*static*]

GERMAISE: I want to hear you paged.

RATNOFF: [*Fumbling with the telephone*] How do I get a dial tone on this thing?

GERMAISE: Just press the middle thing, you'll get a dial tone right outta here.

RATNOFF: When it pages there's a beep that comes out of the thing.

GERMAISE: Yeah, I know, then you answer and you call it. I know all about it. I know all . . . I seen nurses have these paging systems. They're little walkie talkies.

PHILLIPS: And you can talk through this? You answer this?

RATNOFF: I can answer the page and say call me back on such a number.

GERMAISE: Yeah, good.

PHILLIPS: Through this?

GERMAISE: I want to see him do it 'cause I've seen hundreds of pagers— never one like this.

PHILLIPS: I want to hear you talk through here and tell them to call you back at this number.

RATNOFF: Right.

At this point, there was a pounding on the door. They all wheeled around to face the noise. Phillips and Germaise were as startled as Ratnoff was relieved. There was a pause, then two men burst into the room. It was Bruh and White, their commandeered cop following behind:

BRUH: We want him, and we want him out of here.

GERMAISE: Wait a minute, wait a minute, cop—wait—wait.

BRUH: I think you oughta sit here a minute too.

COP: Come on, get over there. Please, they called me in here. Now.

BRUH: We want him out of here.

GERMAISE: Who are you, sir?

BRUH: I'm with the Knapp Commission.

Phillips and Germaise had no intention of making trouble. They stood silently as Bruh reached out a protective hand for the shivering, half-naked Ratnoff, who was standing, bathed in sweat, still partly paralyzed with fear. "He's coming with us," said Bruh. Then turning his attention to the transmitting equipment, now lying on the floor, he asked Germaise and Phillips, "Does that stuff belong to you?"

They shook their heads.

"Good," said Bruh, "because it's mine, and I'm taking it with me."

With that, Bruh and White scooped up the equipment, and Ratnoff's jacket and torn shirt. They whisked Ratnoff out of the office to the elevator, leaving behind a devastated pair of conspirators. The borrowed patrolman followed.

When the agents arrived back at the Commission offices at 51 Chambers Street, we sent Ratnoff on his way and discussed what to do. Obviously, the Schweitzer operation was blown. Teddy would be of no further use. He had been exposed and anyway he was terrified out of his wits. Xaviera Hollander presumably would be warned by Phillips. We had not gotten what we had hoped for—proof of a corrupt link between a cop and a judge. Still, we had a lot of good tape and film for a public hearing. Although the recorded tale was mostly limited to the activities of one crooked patrolman, the conversations clearly implicated many others and reflected the existence of widespread systemic graft.

We tried, over the next few days, to locate Phillips, but didn't find him at his usual haunts. It turned out he had simply gone home and taken a few days off. We didn't try too hard to find him because we thought it would be alright to give Phillips and Germaise a little time to think about what had happened. Neither of them, we reasoned, was going anywhere.

We turned out to be right as to Phillips, but very wrong about Germaise. After making a nervous phone call to me, in which I responded to his inquiries noncommittally, Germaise was subpoenaed to appear forthwith, to testify in executive session. He took the Fifth. Then he loaded everything from his apartment and his office into a truck, late one night, and simply disappeared. We later found out that he had fled to Israel. Apparently, he has never returned.

Phillips, on the other hand, was fatalistic. Not only that, he had nowhere to go. Two days after the incident in Germaise's office, he resumed his normal rounds. Then, one afternoon, a day or two later, he was sitting having lunch in P. J. Clarke's with an old friend, former middle-weight boxing champion Rocky Graziano, when Bruh and Parente confronted him. Phillips appeared to be expecting them.

Bruh and Parente asked Phillips if he would mind stepping away from the table. When he did, Bruh said to him, "We have you in stereo." He replied simply, "I know."

On the ride downtown, Phillips made no attempt to dissemble. "You guys did a great job," he said to the agents. He had no hard feelings toward them. His animus was reserved for Teddy Ratnoff. To him, Ratnoff was not a professional, like Bruh and White, but a stool pigeon. He made no bones about what he would do to "the fat little prick" if he ever got his hands on him.

When Phillips arrived at the office, he was introduced to Paul Rooney. We felt that there really was little hope of getting any information or cooperation from an obviously hardened veteran. The mythology of the "blue wall of silence" was well accepted among all knowledgeable professionals. Cops like Phillips didn't talk. When I had first considered accepting Whit Knapp's offer to be counsel to the Commission, I was repeatedly told by experienced friends that it would be foolish to take the job because the only way to find out about corruption in the police department was to get a cop to talk about it and, even when caught in the act themselves, police officers never—never—talked! Bob Leuci, a volunteer acting on his impetus, not ours, was really not much of an exception to this supposedly iron rule. Nor was poor, terrified Jannotta. We had no reason to expect a tough guy like Phillips to say anything to us. It was one thing for him passively to admit the obvious, as he had done on the ride to the office. It would be quite another for him to "sing."

Nevertheless, we felt it couldn't hurt to try. Our rather unimaginative plan was to use the hoary "Mutt and Jeff," "good cop–bad cop" approach. Paul was to come on strong with dire threats as to what would happen to Phillips if he did not help us. Then I, as the "nice guy," was to join the group with an offer of a cigarette and a little friendly advice about the benefits of cooperating. We really had no hope at all that this tired technique would be effective with a hard case like Phillips, but we couldn't think of anything else to do other than simply to let him go, without even trying to obtain his cooperation. If we turned him over to the authorities now, we risked blowing our whole operation. So, we gave "Mutt and Jeff" a try.

Rooney had been talking to Phillips for less than a minute when the intercom on my desk buzzed. "Come on in," said Paul. "He wants to cooperate." Astounded, I hurried into the room. Rooney had hardly begun talking before Phillips had offered—in exchange for our intercession on his behalf with the authorities—to "turn" and work with us in our investigation.

I sat down opposite Phillips and, in my most stern and professional manner, began to lecture him on the need for full cooperation. I started giving him the usual admonitions about being on "one side of the fence or the other," and not being a "little bit pregnant." He stopped me. "Mr. Armstrong," he said, with a faint smile, "I've had people sitting where I'm sitting—and I've sat where you're sitting—I know what I've got to do."

The next day, Bill Phillips, wearing a wire under the surveillance of Commission agents, made cases against five organized crime members. Going from spot to spot in northeast Manhattan, he met with mob-connected gamblers who customarily made payments of protection money. Chatting easily with them about paying off cops and about various other criminal activities, he obviously could do the same with cops themselves.

We had finally hit real pay dirt.

14

THE FRESHMAN

Finally, things seemed to be going our way. While the investigation of Phillips was in progress, we came upon another very different but nevertheless promising target: patrolman Edward Droge. Twenty-five years old, from Bay Ridge, Brooklyn, Droge had a wife and three children, decorations for valor, and ambitions to go to college and law school. He had been on the job for four years, leaving the telephone company on his twenty-first birthday—the first day he was eligible—to become a cop. Initially he had been stationed in the 80th Precinct, in the Crown Heights section of central Brooklyn. Now, in the late summer of 1971, Droge had been accepted for the fall term as an undergraduate freshman at the University of California at Los Angeles. He wanted to be a lawyer. His plan was to take a leave of absence from the police department, begin his studies as a full-time student at UCLA, and then notify the Department that he was resigning. His family was to stay in New York with his mother and father until he could see his way clear to have them join him in California, as soon as feasible. Assuming things went as planned, he could get a part-time job and arrange for his wife to work as well. After UCLA would be law school.

Earlier, in the spring of 1971, Droge had made an arrest of a minor drug dealer on a relatively insignificant misdemeanor charge. Typically, the case had dragged on in court for months, with one adjournment after another. Then a trial date was finally set, and the defendant reached out to Droge with a not-too-unusual offer—money in exchange for altered testimony, or no testimony at all. The timing was perfect. The trial was scheduled for a date in

September. By that time Droge planned to be in California, with no prospect of returning to New York any time soon, if at all. Without his testimony, the case would routinely be dismissed. Droge could get a few bucks for doing what he intended to do anyway—not show up at the trial. He agreed to a payment of three hundred dollars.

The defendant then told his lawyer about the deal, and the lawyer came to see us. It was a smart move. His client had been caught dead to rights and stood little chance of avoiding a jail term unless he could give up, in trade for his freedom, someone more important than himself—the cop who arrested him. While the Commission had no power to grant immunity, I assured the defendant's lawyer that a strong recommendation from us to the district attorney would accomplish the same thing, assuming that we gathered evidence against a corrupt cop that could later be turned over to the district attorney.

Moving quickly, we wired up the defendant, and taped a telephone conversation between him and Droge, setting up a face-to-face meeting. A few days later, we watched and listened while the defendant gave Droge two hundred of the three hundred dollars that had been agreed upon. Then we staged a few follow up telephone calls between the defendant and Droge in which Droge openly discussed what had happened. We were delighted to have had a situation like this drop into our lap. It was a small-time transaction, but the fact that it involved a narcotics deal, however minor, made it of particular interest.

But we did not know of Droge's imminent plans to go to California. By the time we transcribed our tapes, selected the most forceful ones with which to confront Droge, and arranged to call on him at his home, he was gone. When agent Jim Donovan and ex–FBI agent Ralph Cipriani dropped by at his home, on the pretext of being acquaintances who happened to be in the neighborhood, they were informed by Droge's wife that he had left, on September 1, for Los Angeles, and would not be back in the foreseeable future.

Droge was now three thousand miles away, across the country. We had neither the manpower nor the money to chase him. We would turn the evidence over to the district attorney when we were finished with our work, but it didn't look as if we were going to get anything out of it for ourselves. The situation was rankling. Not that we thought we had much hope of repeating our success with Bill Phillips by making an agent out of Droge—he obviously didn't have Phillips's connections or background—but it was galling not to at least be able to try.

Then I happened to learn that a friend, who was a former colleague of mine at Cahill Gordon, had just gone to California for a few weeks to work on a case. I got an idea. My friend, whose name was Joe Foley, had been an assistant district attorney in Frank Hogan's office. Maybe he could find time to assist us with Droge. As an experienced prosecutor, he could be trusted to handle things. I called Joe in California. He agreed to help.

By courier, I sent Foley a tape of one of the incriminating telephone conversations between Droge and the drug dealer, from whom he had taken the two hundred dollars. On September 15, 1971, upon receiving the cassette, Foley called Droge. He indicated that what he had to say was important—and told him to call a man named Armstrong in New York. Droge did so. I told him I was with the Knapp Commission and Foley had a tape I wanted Droge to hear. I suggested that he should arrange to meet Foley—right away.

Droge agreed, inviting Foley to his new apartment. That day, Droge had enrolled in UCLA, put down his deposit for his tuition and moved into the bare flat that was to have been his home, perhaps for the next four years. He sensed, with dread, what was coming. Foley quickly put to rest whatever doubts, or rather hopes, Droge might have had. He had a tape for Droge to hear. Then he played, on a machine he had rented for the purpose, the tape of Droge and the drug-pusher, discussing their payoff on the phone.

Droge was devastated. He couldn't seem to comprehend that an indiscretion he hardly remembered was shattering his plans for his life and family. "What do I do?" asked Droge, numbly.

"Call Armstrong," said Foley.

Droge called. I did my best to make it clear to him the spot he was in, and how he might help himself. The tapes were damning. Droge stood little or no chance of successfully defending himself at trial against a bribery charge. If he did not cooperate with us, we would simply turn the information over to the Department. He would be dismissed, indicted, and undoubtedly convicted. By cooperating, he stood at least some chance of salvaging something of his future. I could promise him nothing other than a good faith assurance that if he worked with us, we would do everything we could for him. I explained that the Commission was interested in his telling us—truthfully—everything he knew about corruption in the police department. Law enforcement authorities did not as yet know about what he had done. If he worked with us, we would go to bat for him with the police department and the prosecutors. It all depended upon how valuable his information was and whether it could be translated into actual cases for the local or federal authorities.

"When do you want me to come back?" he said.

"As soon as possible."

"Tomorrow morning?" he asked, almost sarcastically.

"I think that would be a good idea," I said.

"I don't have very much money," he said. "I just paid my tuition today, I'm not sure I have enough for the price of a round-trip ticket from California to New York."

"Well . . . ," I paused.

There was a long silence on his end of the phone. Then, weakly, "I guess what you're telling me is that I won't need a round-trip ticket."

"No, I really don't think you will."

Droge came in on the plane the next day. I met him at the Cahill Gordon offices and we talked for several hours. He was a tall, mild-looking man of medium build. His story was very different from that told by Phillips. This was not the saga of a predatory rogue cop, but the fairly ordinary tale of a basically decent, even heroic one who had been molded by pressures in the Department to the point of routinely, almost mindlessly, taking the kind of low-level graft that virtually all his buddies took. His testimony would be particularly relevant to our task because he spoke not for the relatively few aberrant criminals like Phillips, but for the great majority of police officers in the Department—the 80 percent who, according to Frank Serpico's analysis, wished they were honest.

Droge told of his first act of corruption as though it was the fall of Adam. It was a sad and typical story. He was a fresh-faced young patrolman, eager to do good and fight crime, assigned, with an old "hairbag," to night foot patrol in Brooklyn. As the two were walking late at night in a quiet neighborhood, a drunk careened past them in an automobile, the car coming to rest with a jolt against a telephone pole about two blocks away. Droge ran the entire two blocks at top speed in order to be able to render assistance. As he arrived, puffing, at the accident scene, his partner also pulled up, having been driven the two blocks in a passing car that he had commandeered.

The drunk was not injured and the car was not seriously damaged. Before the officers had much of a chance to say anything, the driver took ten dollars out of his wallet, handed it to the older cop, and suggested, blearily, that he be allowed to drive home without a ticket. Droge's partner pocketed the ten dollars and waived the driver on. "Take off, pal."

As the drunk went on his way and the two cops returned to their beat, Droge's partner said nothing. He just reached in his pocket, took out a five-dollar bill, and handed it to Droge. For a split second, Droge hesitated. He didn't want the five dollars. He didn't like it that his partner had taken the ten dollars in the first place. He thought they should have locked up the drunk, for his own protection if for no other reason. But what was a rookie like him going to say to a grizzled veteran? He put the five dollars in his pocket.

As Droge saw it, he lost his innocence at that point. Like almost all his comrades, he grew cynically to accept a certain level of corrupt income, which he considered to be his due. Droge became, under Sidney Cooper's definition, a typical "grass eater." He took his share.

Droge described his time at the 80th Precinct. He said that all but two of the seventy or eighty men he knew personally, out of the one hundred fifty to one hundred seventy-five patrolmen in the precinct, participated, to some extent, in the kind of routine graft in which he was involved. He described one of the two as a "priest type" who was always organizing charities and retreats, and the other as a near fanatic who would stop his car on the way to court in order to ticket an illegally parked car, even one in a precinct other than his own. Save these two, everyone else in the precinct was "on."

Corruption in the 80th Precinct was a matter of routine. Payments were taken from tow-truck businesses, supermarkets, check cashiers, bodegas, bars, afterhours spots, liquor stores, and any other establishment that wanted to escape the kind of technical violations that could be pinned on just about anyone for operating outside the law—or even on its edge. Droge also told us of referral money from local attorneys whom cops would recommend to those they arrested. Police escort services, at a price, would be provided for payrolls, bank deposits, or other cash transactions by local merchants. Low-level illegal operations, tolerated by the general public, were natural targets. Droge told us of a particular illegal card game conducted in a second-floor apartment. Each night the patrol car assigned to cover the area would pull up on the street in front of the apartment and honk the horn. Someone would throw a ten-dollar bill out the window. Local groceries and small-item factories would regularly let the police, in uniform, help themselves to merchandise and, if such an establishment was subject to a break-in, cops would race to beat the owner to the scene, so they could receive five dollars in "appreciation." If the cops got there first by a substantial amount of time, they would simply pillage the place.

Droge also told of his service in the 90th Precinct, in the Williamsburg section of Brooklyn. The neighborhood was then a high-crime area, a fact that might be gleaned from the nickname of its main thoroughfare, Myrtle Avenue, which was commonly called "Murder Avenue." He had arrested a man for felonious assault (possession of a pistol and a loaded shotgun). Precinct veterans all agreed that he was crazy to have arrested the individual, since the pistol was a valuable antique that could have been traded for its owner's freedom. Another time, he was approached by a man asking directions who, as he walked away, dropped an illegal switchblade knife. Droge picked it up, turned down the man's offer of twenty dollars to give it back, and started his own knife collection.

Commenting on a tour in a traffic safety unit in lower Manhattan, Droge said that he was often offered money by motorists he stopped, but never took any, since to do so carried too many risks. Occasionally cops would take money from a driver who was unlikely to be a cop—a woman, or "a small man wearing glasses." Those were the days when one had to be a husky male in order to be a policeman. But you never knew when someone might be related to a cop or a federal law enforcement officer. So it was risky.

Gambling, of all sorts, provided the largest and steadiest source of outside income. The most prominent gambling operation in Droge's area was run by three brothers. They were all well known to the police. Indeed, they were listed in Department files as "Known Gamblers." But they never were arrested. A common method of payment by the brothers to patrolling sector cars was simply to bunch up some bills and throw them in the open car window. Droge told of one occasion when the payment went through one open window and out the other onto the street.

Droge had dealings with other, less powerful, gamblers in the 80th Precinct, like "Patty," who ran a candy store that was open for business until 2:00 A.M. Droge originally thought he might be dealing narcotics and sent an informant to check him out. Patty admitted that he was involved, not with drugs, but gambling. He was working with the three brothers. "Cheech," another "Known Gambler," ran a lucrative card game Wednesday, Friday, Saturday, and Sunday in the factory district. The radio car on each shift of those nights would pull up outside the game and wait until someone brought ten dollars. If the money didn't come fast enough the cops would honk to improve the service. Even though this game was painfully obvious, Cheech was only arrested once (by Borough Command) in the entire time Droge was at the 80th. Another card game, run out of a barber shop from Friday to Sunday, would net the cops ten dollars a day, and a bookie named Sal, who worked out of a plumbing store—which curiously had no plumbing supplies in it—would pay five dollars per day per sector car. When the cars pulled up to collect their money they would write the visit up as an investigation, noting that no illegal activity was observed. Once, when driving in another sector, Droge encountered a man named Cully (aka Stetson) who came to the car and gave him fifteen dollars, apologizing for missing the week before. Droge didn't know him, or even know what he was paying to protect, but he returned once a month, collecting ten dollars each month.

Droge told of a strong feeling among the uniformed cops against taking money in narcotics cases. For one thing, there was an incentive to make narcotics arrests: after every arrest the patrolman got a day off, which was supposed to compensate for the added paperwork and trips to the lab involved in a narcotics arrest. He also spoke of the traditional feeling that narcotics graft was "dirty money." Droge concentrated a large part of his work in the narcotics area and stated that he never took money to let a suspect go. However, narcotics enforcement was hardly handled "by the book." Often cops would keep some confiscated drugs when a large arrest was made in order to use the drugs for "flaking"—planting drugs on—arrested suspects who didn't have drugs on them, or for adding weight to the amount of narcotics taken in an arrest that was just shy of the minimum for a felony count. Informants were customarily allowed to keep some of the narcotics confiscated during arrests in which they participated. Otherwise, at the uniform level, narcotics enforcement was relatively straight. One woman Droge arrested complained that she was paying one hundred dollars a week for protection against arrest, a payment that would have gone to the Narcotics Division or to the Brooklyn North Narcotics District. Droge's response was that she wasn't paying him, so the arrest would stand.

Overall Droge received about sixty to a hundred dollars a month in illegal income, which, he said, was pretty typical. Christmas graft was supposed to net about two hundred fifty more, but that never materialized for Droge. His first year he got nothing. Since he was new to the sector, he only received twenty dollars and three bottles of booze on his second Christmas. By his third Christmas the Knapp Commission had put a damper on seasonal gifts so he only received a hundred dollars and a couple of bottles of liquor.

Just about all of the patrolmen in the 80th Precinct behaved much the way Droge did. In fact, honest cops were ostracized, and one's judgment of whether a man was a good cop never involved whether or not he took money. There was little fear of reprisals for corrupt activities, and of the ten to fifteen sergeants in the 80th Precinct, Droge knew for certain that two took money themselves.

Droge later wrote about his feelings as a "grass eater":

I was taking money as routinely as a bus driver accepting a fare. Not a lot of money. It would not make me wealthy. Pin money, spent superficially. And that made it all the worse; there was no dire need. It was just there. Mostly, the people offered and everybody took. . . . I had become cruel and ruthless, slithering in the gutter, awaiting my next "score." It was not just me. It was all around me. The system was such that it engulfed everyone. It did not discriminate. . . . The light dawned the day my son said: "You're a policeman, Daddy? I want to be one too." The thought of my son becoming what I had become sickened me.[1]

From what we had been learning in the course of our investigation, Droge's experiences were fairly common throughout the Department. Cops who normally would not have become involved in illegal behavior got caught up in what was "the thing to do." Unless one wanted to be like the two odd-ball officers in the 80th Precinct, they all went along and became "one of the boys." We even heard of instances where police officers bragged about "scores" they had never made.

Since Droge had taken a leave of absence to go to California, he was of little use to us as a potential undercover operative, until he could arrange to return to active duty. Even then, his use as an operative would be problematic since his targets of opportunity were few, and his absence would make him stand out. Nevertheless, we kept our eyes open for a possible circumstance where Droge could be of use as an agent, while debriefing him about his experiences as a "grass eater."

With Droge, we had a third police officer to feature at our projected hearings. Droge would testify about what life was like as a "grass eater" while Phillips would describe his career as a "meat eater," and Waverly Logan would tell about life in a "special unit." Our public hearings agenda was filling up.

---

1. Edward Droge, *The Patrolman: A Cop's Story* (New York: New American Library, 1973), p. 16.

15

PHILLIPS AT WORK

It was clear that Bill Phillips would be the star of our public proceedings. He was, in the classic sense, a "rogue." With a swagger, he had shaken down bar owners, construction foremen, prostitutes, thieves, businessmen, other cops, pimps, gangsters, loan sharks, gamblers, and anyone else whom he could threaten or for whom he could do an illegal favor. He boasted that he never gave up trying to "score" a victim. If his solicitation for a bribe at the time of an arrest was rejected, he would continue to make overtures even up to the point of trial. Expected testimony could always be altered at the last minute, for a price. "It's never too late to do business," he said. Of course, circumstances differed, and there were "good" precincts and "bad" ones. Phillips most feared being assigned to Central Park, which would have tested even his ingenuity. "What are you gonna do there," he mused, "shake down the squirrels?"[1]

In Phillips, we had stumbled upon one of the real "meat eaters" in the Department. Under longtime corruption fighter Chief Sidney Cooper's

---

1. About five years after our work was over, I, with a group of others, was waiting on a corner in Manhattan for a traffic light one dark, rainy night, when a formation of about a half-dozen mounted policemen, who customarily spent much of their time in Central Park, went by on their horses. As the last of them passed, I heard a voice from the gloom above me: "You never got anything on the Mounties."

characterization of corrupt police officers as "meat eaters" or "grass eat-ers," Phillips had all the attributes of the most voracious of meat eaters.

Phillips was also one of the best raconteurs I had ever encountered, and he used this ability to enthrall friends and victims alike. He had a superior intelligence, great physical courage, a thorough knowledge of the law, an en-gaging personality, a remarkable street sense, an attractive physical presence, an understanding of the ways of New York City, nerves of steel—and no conscience at all.

There was one item in Phillips's list of past adventure that perhaps should have given us pause. He had killed a man. Several years before, early one morning on a deserted street in Harlem, Phillips shot a man to death whom he reported as having attacked him with a knife. It was one of those situations where a police officer is either brought up on charges or given a citation. Phillips was decorated. I have never doubted Phillips's version of what happened that night, but there would come a time when others would see it differently.

At the outset, it was necessary to cut some sort of a deal with Phillips, and that could only be done with the cooperation of some law enforcement au-thority. Having surrendered Bob Leuci to the federal authorities, along with a supervisory attorney and two agents, I felt the government owed us one. My problem would be to get the government to see it that way. Prosecutors have notoriously short memories when it means giving up a juicy case.

I carefully prepared the pitch I would make to the U.S. Attorney, Mike Sey-mour. I didn't know Seymour very well and wasn't sure exactly what buttons to push with him. The son of one of the most prestigious lawyers in New York, Seymour, by age forty-five, had made a reputation for himself chiefly as a formidable Wall Street lawyer with connections in the WASP Republican establishment. He was tall and personable, with something of a patrician's demeanor. Although he may not have commanded full respect in rougher, more traditional law enforcement circles, he was self-consciously fair—a real straight arrow. I relied on his feeling indebted to us for turning Leuci over to him. This time, it was our turn.

The less genteel breed of crime-fighter was typified by the wiry little man Seymour inherited as his chief assistant when he took over as U.S. Attorney, Silvio J. Mollo. Normally, Seymour would have made the selection of his chief assistant himself. But Mollo had become a fixture since he came to the office in 1939 with John Cahill (he had been the office manager at Cahill's firm, Cotton & Franklin, later to become Cahill Gordon Reindel & Ohl). Cahill had been appointed special counsel to prosecute Martin Manton, Chief Judge of the

U.S. Court of Appeals for the Second Circuit (covering New York, Connecticut, and Vermont), on a charge of accepting bribes. Manton was convicted. Cahill then became U.S. Attorney for a while and when he returned to his law firm, Mollo stayed behind at the U.S. Attorney's Office. Rising through the ranks, Mollo became Chief of the Criminal Division and, finally, Chief Assistant. U.S. Attorneys came and went, but Mollo went on, seemingly forever— and pretty much ran things in the Criminal Division.

But the office had changed somewhat under Seymour. Sil Mollo and his band of tough professionals had less influence, and things were not always done in quite the usual way. I counted on this change in attitude as I prepared my pitch to keep Bill Phillips for our commission. I had little hope of getting any sympathy from Mollo for any argument that a television spectacular was more important than sending crooked cops to jail. I was hoping Mike Seymour might think differently.

I called Seymour, told him I had something important to discuss, and made an appointment. With some trepidation, I entered Seymour's office and my heart sank as I saw that Mollo was there. I loved and respected Sil, but this was one time I wasn't happy to see him, no matter how warmly we greeted each other. I began hesitantly, describing our investigation of Phillips, Hollander, Schweitzer, and Germaise. Then I told about "turning" Phillips and about his demonstrated potential for productive undercover work. I reminded Seymour of Leuci and, with a quick nervous look to see how Mollo was taking all this, I began to suggest how valuable Phillips would be as a witness in the Commission's public hearings.

Before I had much of a chance to get into my sales pitch, Seymour said, "It's clear to me. This one's for you." I listened, nodding appreciatively, as Seymour ticked off the very arguments I had carefully prepared in order to persuade him to do what he immediately decided to do anyway. As he saw it, Phillips would be most useful working with us to develop evidence for our hearings, rather than spending his time making individual cases. Unlike Leuci, his knowledge was widespread, touching many facets of the Department. The picture he could paint would be tremendously effective in rousing people to do something about corruption. Since he was not involved in narcotics or organized crime, we were not faced with the dilemma of sacrificing the chance to arrest drug dealers or important mobsters in order to put on a public show. Seymour finished by asking, "How can we help you?" I didn't dare look at Sil.

Mollo had sat quietly while considerations of general law enforcement had been placed ahead of the immediate parochial needs of the U.S. Attorney's Office. But he was certainly going to salvage something for "the Office" in making practical arrangements. It was agreed that we would keep Sil apprised of Phillips's progress. Whatever Phillips turned up would be used to make federal cases once our hearings were over. This was fine with me, because I received a promise from Seymour that he would see to it that Phillips got immunity from federal prosecution for his confessed misdeeds if he gathered information resulting in significant prosecutions, of either police officers or serious malefactors, such as members of organized crime. Seymour also promised that if Phillips produced cases of value, Seymour would do his best to prevail upon Manhattan District Attorney Frank Hogan to go along with giving Phillips immunity on the State side.

The deal was struck. Phillips immediately began working hard to win the rewards he had been promised.

Finding a place to meet with Phillips on an ongoing basis, without danger of exposing his undercover work, posed a problem. We couldn't be seen with him in public, and certainly not in the Knapp offices. We needed a private venue with a number of anonymous entrances, so as to avoid observation. I settled on using my law firm, Cahill Gordon Reindel & Ohl, which was located in a large downtown office building with multiple elevators to its many floors.

The only problem was that a number of my partners had indicated that they were not thrilled with forging too close a physical connection with the Commission's activities. Cahill Gordon, with about one hundred twenty-five lawyers, was one of the largest and certainly one of the most politically connected law firms in the city. Cahill, who had passed away in 1966, and his senior partners had never been hesitant about becoming active in various political efforts, but they did not like getting involved in controversial matters that they didn't control. As a very junior partner, I did what I was told in this area. In connection with reassigning Robert Leuci, I had attempted to arrange a discreet meeting among the police commissioner, Whitman Knapp, and the then–Attorney General of the United States, John Mitchell. The firm, fearing involvement in "something controversial," refused my request. If they didn't want the attorney general and the police commissioner visiting the firm after hours, how would they feel about a self-confessed corrupt policeman like Phillips? I was pretty sure I knew what the answer would be. So—remembering the principle "Forgiveness is easier to get than permission"—I didn't ask. We just went ahead, gave Phillips the "stage name" of Barry Sanders, just in case he ran into anyone, and used the firm as our undercover headquarters—without telling anybody at Cahill Gordon.

As Phillips became a part of our operation, Teddy Ratnoff, knowing nothing of the change in Phillips's status, lived in constant fear. We never told

Ratnoff that Phillips had agreed to cooperate with the Commission. Had we done so, he immediately would have sold the information to whatever publication would give him the highest price. So since the day that he had been unmasked in Germaise's office, Teddy had been convinced that Phillips would search him out, and kill him.

Teddy was not too far wrong. Phillips never forgave Ratnoff's betrayal of him. On the ride down from P. J. Clarke's to our office on the day our agents picked him up, Phillips had begged to be given a few minutes with his fingers at Teddy's throat. Over the next months, this request was repeated every once in a while, with such fervor that I could never be entirely sure whether Phillips was serious. I once asked him what he would have done if the electronic device he found on Ratnoff in Germaise's eighth floor office had been a self-contained recorder instead of a transmitter, so that he needn't have feared eavesdropping agents.

"I'd have thrown the recorder out the window," he said—with a slight smile intended to keep me wondering whether he would first have removed it from Ratnoff's body.

We satisfied ourselves that it was not necessary, at this point in time, to worry too much about Phillips actually getting violent with Ratnoff. However enraged he might still be, Phillips would not jeopardize his deal by doing something foolish.

Ratnoff, not knowing that Phillips had made an accommodation with us, saw no reason for comfort. He called us, often several times a day, pleading that we have Phillips arrested. Sometimes he would attempt to lure us out of the office by pretending to have seen Phillips at some location or other. I would be sitting talking to Phillips in the office at Cahill Gordon, while Ratnoff was telling me on the phone that he had just seen him and that I should send some people to come and look for him. Ratnoff apparently reasoned that once some agents were out searching, he could somehow point them in what he thought was Phillips's direction. "Don't worry," I repeatedly told Teddy. "We have Phillips under constant surveillance. We can't pick him up until we chase down some leads we have on Germaise, but don't worry, Teddy, don't worry."

"Don't worry?!! Maybe you don't have to worry," Ratnoff would squeal, "I'm the one he'll snuff!!"

Our attempts to soothe Ratnoff were only partially successful. He finally took off to England, so as to be safely out of Phillips's range.

Phillips slid smoothly into his role as an undercover operative. He needed no instruction as to the techniques involved in getting people to incriminate themselves. He needed only to be pointed in the right direction. What was "the right direction" was, of course, largely up to him. In repeated debriefings, he recounted his corrupt adventures, ongoing and in the past, many of which afforded us springboards for future investigations. He also told us of situations into which he felt he could inject himself that he was confident would be profitable. His task was made easier by the fact that our objective was not to make criminal cases against any individuals, but merely to gather evidence about the patterns of corruptions generally. A description by some cop of a corrupt event in which he had not personally been involved would be inadmissible in court against the subject of the tale, but could be used, with caution, to demonstrate that such things happened.

It wasn't really necessary to make things easy for Phillips. He was a natural and skillful operative. The direction he took in using those skills was, however, something of a problem for us, because it was a problem for him. He had no qualms at all, as he proved to us on the first day after he agreed to help, in gathering information and making cases against hoodlums. He quickly set about picking up the monthly pad from known gamblers in the 25th Precinct, many of whom were listed in departmental records as Mafia members. He collected amounts ranging from five to thirty-five dollars each visit from men with names such as "Muzzi," "Louie Fats," "Joe Fats," "Farby," "Big Sam," and "Joe Tough Guy." Two thirty-dollar payoffs were taken from a policy operator with the unlikely name of Frank Serpico (no relation, of course, to "our" Frank Serpico).

But Phillips was reluctant to turn his attention to the people we were really after—his comrades "on the job." Throughout the period he worked for us, there was a constant tug of war, as we tried to point him toward cops and he did his best to interest us in "civilian" crooks instead. The information we picked up in the course of his dealings with mobsters about the way things operated was useful, so, to some degree, we accommodated him. For example, we didn't ask him to go against any of his partners. There really was no need to push him to such betrayal because we had more than we could handle with other leads he could be persuaded to pursue. Known throughout the Department as a genuine "super thief," Phillips was trusted, immediately and completely, by just about any crooked cop.

The activities of the Department's 450 plainclothesmen, which had been the subject of Frank Serpico's initial revelations, were of particular interest to us. Had Serpico been accurate in describing the organized corruption in the plainclothes unit to which he had been assigned, and did such conditions exist in other plainclothes units? According to Phillips, it was common knowledge that all plainclothesmen were corrupt. The graft was so well-organized, no one could serve in a plainclothes unit without participating.

Phillips told us that when he joined the force, cops didn't fear getting caught taking bribes because sanctions were lax and graft was so common that it was easy to deal with people. The tide seemed to be changing recently. Discipline was getting stricter and sources of money were drying up. He told us of Farby, a known gambler and a key organized crime figure, who approached Phillips with a complaint about a lieutenant in Patrol Borough, Manhattan North. Farby had the fix in with the Department but this lieutenant kept making arrests and Farby assumed that he was trying to jack up the pad. Phillips talked to another patrolman, who also assumed the lieutenant was getting greedy. He assured Phillips that the lieutenant's superior would be very angry if he knew that anyone was tinkering with the pad. When Phillips met with the lieutenant, however, he heard a very different story. Apparently, the lieutenant felt the 25th Precinct had become too "hot"—full of undercover agents and stoolies. The lieutenant said the investigators had movie cameras that could read what you wrote from three blocks away, so unless you parked blocks from a policy operation, and disguised yourself before going in, it was just too dangerous to get involved. His inspector also rode with him as he checked out suspected gambling locations, so he couldn't avoid making arrests. Apparently things were somewhat different from five years before.

Once, while Phillips was wired and waiting in a bar, Farby came in and began to complain to Phillips about the precinct commander. Farby had been paying this captain a hundred dollars each month through a "bagman"—someone authorized by the captain to pick up graft for him—and yet friends of his in the Department had shown Farby five confidential memos the captain had written to headquarters turning in Farby's policy operation. Phillips did not know whether the bagman was keeping the hundred dollars or not.

Shortly after going undercover for us at the 25th Precinct, Phillips was added to a gambling pad that covered a crap game run by a gambler known as Joe Tough Guy. He was told that three sergeants were on this pad, and that the lieutenant wanted to get on. Phillips knew the lieutenant (he had once given him twenty-five dollars to be assigned to an unmarked car), and asked him if he could attend his meeting with Joe Tough Guy. At the meeting, which we recorded, Joe Tough Guy paid the lieutenant ninety dollars: twenty dollars for each of the five lieutenants who wanted to be on the pad, less ten dollars, which would be paid the following month. The next day Phillips saw Louie Fats and picked up the rest of the "nut" for the pad, $220, which he distributed. A month later, Phillips's partner gave him twenty-five dollars for the pad, so he assumed everything was set.

Phillips claimed to know nothing about corruption in narcotics. He assured us that although he had never worked in narcotics enforcement, he was sure that cops who were doing narcotics work were straight. We knew, of course, how wrong Phillips was, because Bob Leuci had described in detail extensive corruption among narcotics cops. But Phillips seemed genuinely unaware of such things. He repeated to us the traditional "dirty" money and "clean" money distinction that we had heard was common among cops of his, and earlier, generations. Money from narcotics and, in the view of some, from prostitution, was "dirty" money and, as such, was taboo.

Phillips drew his own distinctions, for his own reasons. He purported to disdain narcotics for what we understood to be the accepted reasons—it was beneath him, and he hated drug dealers. As for prostitutes, he had no qualms about taking their money, but always felt that he could not trust them enough to take graft from them. One of the few times he relaxed this principle was when he proved his point by unwisely getting involved with Xaviera Hollander.

The only man I ever saw Phillips fear was a PBA delegate in an East Side precinct by the name of Jim Doyle. Brash, self-confident, and streetwise, Doyle was out of central casting for the part of a tough New York cop. He was the PBA official who had set Alfonso Jannotta up with a phony story when we filmed Jannotta taking a bribe from George Burkert, our in-house tow-truck driver. We had reason to believe that Doyle was at the hub of a good deal of the corruption going on on the East Side, and Phillips emphatically confirmed that impression. However, when we suggested setting something up with Doyle, Phillips became very nervous. "The guy's got a sixth sense," Phillips said. His usual bravado seemed to pale a bit at even the mention of Doyle's name.

We pressured Phillips into making a run at Doyle, but he did so with obvious doubts, and without his usual touch. Adopting the approach of claiming that he had some people he wanted to set up in a gambling operation, Phillips said to Doyle that he wanted to get clearance as well as rates from those handling the action in that area. Perhaps it was Phillips's manner. Perhaps Phillips was right and Doyle was clairvoyant. Perhaps, like Phillips's partners, Doyle was a friend, to be protected or privately warned. He might even have been innocent. In any event, the scam was a bust. Doyle was noncommittal. He listened to Phillips's proposal and grunted something about looking into it, but by no means showing enthusiasm, or even familiarity with, the kind of thing Phillips was talking about.

Doyle never actually turned Phillips down, but kept stringing him along until it became obvious to us that he wasn't going to do anything. We wound up with nothing more than some unremarkable tape recordings evidencing the unsurprising fact that a PBA delegate was unlikely to turn in a police officer who comes to him with a corrupt proposal. We never were successful in finding anything to corroborate what was said about Doyle. He went on to become a high-level official in the PBA.

Even as an operative for us, Phillips never really gave up trying to make money. He actually tried to persuade Bruh to skim payoff money he collected in Commission "sting" operations. They would split it, he said. Later, Phillips claimed he was kidding.

One of the most chilling tales of corruption related to us by Phillips involved a patrolman named John Roff. Roff had confided to Phillips about two years earlier that he had taken $5,000 in order to cover up for a high-level mobster who had personally committed a murder. Phillips told us that the cop had bragged about his being an actual eyewitness to a gangland killing of one Desiderio Caban, done by Arnold Squitieri, an underboss in the Gambino family. Roff had confronted Squitieri with his information and accepted the $5,000 that Squitieri offered him to forget about it. Phillips said that he had told Roff at the time that he was crazy to risk taking money in a mob homicide. But, Phillips said, the guy was greedy.

We worked out with Phillips a plan to capitalize on the two-year-old conversation. Phillips telephoned Roff and told him that he had to see him about something very important. Wearing a wire, Phillips pretended to have inside information from the District Attorney's Office indicating that they were opening up the Squitieri investigation and had suspicions about Roff. Phillips said that he might be able to do something to sidetrack the investigation but he needed Roff to tell him the story, in detail, once again. Roff, frightened and grateful, laid it all out, and we got the whole tale on tape.

As it turned out, we never used this tape in our public hearings. As in Leuci's case, we had to concede that a discrete investigation of the matter was too important to be compromised by exposing it on television. So we waited until our hearings were finished and turned the information over to the District Attorney's Office. Armed with the Commission tape, police confronted Roff and got him to cooperate to make the case against Squitieri. The final result, two years after the hearings were over, was a guilty plea from Roff to a corruption charge and a murder conviction of Squitieri.

Phillips's efforts on our behalf were succeeding beyond our expectations. In my view, his testimony, backed up by his undercover work, complete with tapes and films, would be a solid cornerstone for any hearings we might hold. Other testimony would fall into place around a powerful main event. I knew that Phillips would be mesmerizing. But it was difficult to get across to the commissioners just how good a witness he would be. The issue of whether we held public hearings at all was unsettled in the minds of the commissioners. Our original plan, to hold hearings in the spring, had long since gone by the boards. Now the only question was, would we shoot for hearings in the fall, or just wind things up without any hearings and write a report. In considering this decision, the commissioners did not have access to the day-to-day operations that were building in such a promising way. So, I sat Phillips down and taped an interview, roughly approximating some of the things about which he would testify at a hearing. Whit Knapp took the tape home one night. When he called me the next day, any doubt that we would have public hearings in the fall was removed. "My God, the man is a Baron Munchausen," he said.

Tucked away in the mass of information Phillips gave us was an apparently insignificant account of his shakedown of a pimp operating a house of pleasure in an apartment on 57th Street. The incident—and the very fact that Phillips told us about it at all—would prove to be of immense importance not to our investigation, but to Phillips himself.

Chief Counsel Michael Armstrong   *Photo courtesy of Ralph Cipriani*

Knapp Commission chairman Whitman Knapp speaks to press.   *Photo by Evelyn Straus, © Daily News, L.P. (New York); used with permission*

Commissioners (*left to right*): Cyrus Vance, John Sprizzo, Whitman Knapp (chairman), Joseph Monserrat, Franklin Thomas   *Photo by Jim Garrett,* © Daily News, *L.P. (New York); used with permission*

Agent Cipriani testifying   *Photo courtesy of Ralph Cipriani*

Police officer William Phillips
Photo by Gordon Rynders,
© Daily News, *L.P. (New York);*
used with permission

Madam Xaviera
Hollander *Photo*
by Gene Kappock,
© Daily News, *L.P.*
(New York); used with
permission

Mayor John Lindsay
Photo by Jim Garrett,
© Daily News, *L.P.*
(New York); used with
permission

Patrolman Edward Droge   *Photo by Dan Farrell,* © Daily News, *L.P. (New York); used*
with permission

Informant Ted Ratnoff   *Photo by Dennis Caruso*, © Daily News, *L.P.*
(New York); used with permission

Police Commissioner Patrick Murphy
Courtesy of New York City Police Department

Former police
officer Waverly
Logan *Photo by
Paul DeMaria, ©
Daily News, L.P.
(New York); used
with permission.*

Tow truck driver
George Burkert *Photo by
Frank Hurley, © Daily News,
L.P. (New York); used with
permission.*

Agents Brian
Bruh and Ralph
Cipriani *Photo
courtesy of Ralph
Cipriani*

Cop's liquor order to addict-informant to be paid for with narcotics
Photo courtesy of Ralph Cipriani

Members of the Knapp Commission listen intently as William Phillips (l.) is questioned by Chief Counsel Michael Michael Armstrong. Commission members (from left) are: Cyrus Vance, Chairman William Knapp, Franklin Thomas, John Sprizzo, and Joseph Monserrat. *Photo: Dennis Caruso, Daily News, L.P. (New York); used with permission*

Police detective Frank Serpico (*right*), with attorney Ramsey Clark *Photo by Jim Garrett, © Daily News, L.P. (New York); used with permission*

Reporters at commission hearing   *Photo courtesy of Ralph Cipriani*

Detective
David Durk
Photo: Frank Russo,
New York Daily News,
*L.P. (New York); used
with permission.*

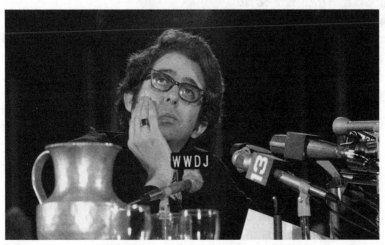

Mayor Lindsay's chief of staff, Jay Kriegel   *Photo by Paul DeMaria,* © Daily News,
L.P. (New York); used with permission

WEATHER
Tonight: Clear
Low around 50.
Tomorrow:
Fair, 65-70.
Fair, Warmer
Thursday
SUNSET: 6/9
SUNRISE TOMORROW: 7/17

New York Post
FOUNDED 1801. THE OLDEST CONTINUOUSLY PUBLISHED DAILY IN THE UNITED STATES.

Vol. 170
No. 294

NEW YORK, TUESDAY, OCTOBER 19, 1971
© 1971 New York Post Corporation

15 Cents

CLOSING
MARKET
P. 60-68

FINAL

7 RACES

THE PAYOFF
Cop Tells the Whole Story

Patrolman William Phillips testifying today.

Post Photo by Richard Cummins

By Andrew Porte
with Carl J. Pelleck, Marvin Smilon and Marc Kalech

A policeman today spelled out for the Knapp Commission the full details of how the cop payoff system worked.

Patrolman William R. Phillips told the commission: "I never knew a plainclothesman for more than two months that wasn't on the pad," an expression meaning that all plainclothes cops accepted payoffs.

"If he's not equipped for the type of work, he's transferred out, and the type of work is taking money."

Phillips said that in six months as a plainclothesman assigned to break up gambling in Harlem, he netted $6000 in payoffs. He said that every other member of the 16-man squad received about the same amount.

Phillips traced his career as a policeman, describing how he could make $40 a month as a beat patrolman, then $80 in a radio car until his assignment to the plainclothes staff.

He said that on his first day on the gambling detail a man called "Eggy" pulled his car to the curb and "was waiting for us to arrive. He knew that new men were coming up and he said to us, 'You get $20 a day, O.K.'?"

Phillips said Eggy explained that it was all right to take the money because all the policemen at the division and borough level had been taken care of.

The two policemen watched the policy operation and were shocked. "This was so obvious" that they

Continued on Page 5

Canada Bars Kahane While Kosy's There

By Dick Belsky and Arthur Greenspan

Rabbi Meir Kahane was ousted by the Canadian government today because he was trying to meet Soviet Premier Kosygin to protest the treatment of Russian Jews.

The Canadians sent Kahane and six other Jewish Defense League members back to the U. S. follow-

ing an unarmed attack in Ottawa on Kosygin by a young Hungarian refugee.

Kahane said today he'll try to return before Kosygin leaves.

"Had I been allowed into Canada," Kahane told The Post today, "nothing would have happened. The Canadians certainly did not cover themselves with any honor," he said.

"But what happened in Canada is the best thing that could have happened to Soviet Jews," he insisted.

Kahane and the other JDL members had flown to Canada to protest the treatment in a Soviet prison camp of Silva Zalmanson, one of nine Soviet Jews convicted in an al-

Continued on Page 5

ON THE INSIDE

WALSH THREATENS to punch Pretel in mouth. Page 5.

SECRET SERVICE hounds out agent who guarded Johnson after JFK assassination. See Jack Anderson. Page 40.

FBI IGNORED pleas from hijacked pilot who died. Page 5.

NIXON adds civil penalties to pay price bill. Page 4.

JUDGE indicted in election case here. Page 2.

CITY COMPLAINS to OEP over $1M hike in oil bill. Page 5.

LOTTERY WINNERS
Page 28

Front page *New York Post*   Photo: New York Post

16

PROBLEMS

At the end of June 1971, the Knapp Commission came to the point where, just as we were hitting full stride, the jury-rigged operation was about to come apart. We were running out of money and on July 1 we would lose most of our personnel. The commitments of our supervisory attorneys were over, and all of them were about to return, or already had returned, to private pursuits.

Our funds, such as they were, were just about exhausted, without any prospect of replenishment from the City. The Federal Law Enforcement Assistance Administration came up with an additional $75,000, but it wasn't enough. Whit again hit all his foundation contacts, but most of them were tapped out. The agents who were on loan to us from the various federal agencies had more than overstayed their leaves of absence. I had finagled extra months, using every argument I could think of. I let each agency think that the other agencies would stay as long as the one I was talking to. But all arguments had run out, and the time had finally come. All three federal agencies set July 1, 1971, as the date their agents must return to them.

It was really too bad. The Phillips undercover operation was getting into high gear. We were finally developing some other very profitable leads, and our surveys of bars, restaurants, hotels, and construction sites were showing promise but were not yet finished. After all those months, lurching from one fruitless effort to another, we were finally in a position to put together meaningful public hearings, in the fall—but we were running out of resources.

Then, a gift from heaven—or, an even more unlikely source, the Internal Revenue Service, which relented, and agreed to allow Brian Bruh to remain with us as long as we needed him. Not only that, the agency forgave our outstanding bill to them for the last several months of salaries for the four agents they had loaned us (two of whom had left us to work with Leuci). Freed of this substantial obligation, we now had enough money to continue to pay Ralph Cipriani, who was an attorney as well as an ex–FBI agent of considerable experience. He could work with Bruh for the two or three months remaining before public hearings, if any, would begin.

The unexpected financial boost provided by the forgiveness of our obligation to the IRS enabled us to take on an attorney who had the ability and willingness to double as an investigator. Julius Impellizzeri was a single practitioner who was an acquaintance of Whit Knapp and was having a slow time professionally, so he could give us a few months. Now in his fifties, Impellizzeri had been an assistant district attorney under Frank Hogan. He was sharp, experienced, knowledgeable in the criminal justice field, and willing to assist in any way possible.

The two young Justice Department lawyers we had obtained in the Leuci deal, John Sweeney and Dave Ritchie, could also stay, and were enthusiastic about doing so. Sweeney's eagerness to help had actually gotten him into a bit of trouble one hot morning in the early summer. He arrived at the office before everyone else, and ran into some workmen making a delivery. It was a window air conditioner. Sweeney signed for the item and had the men put it next to the window for which it was destined. Then, after the workmen had left, it occurred to him that installation would be a relatively simple operation. Unfortunately, he miscalculated the weight of the machine and, while attempting to put it in the window, he dumped it out instead. The air conditioner plummeted ten floors, landing on a first-floor overhang. Fortunately, no one was killed. It was a tribute to the strength of Sweeney's character that he held up quite creditably under the ribbing to which he was subjected, and continued to do first-rate work.

Warren Colodner, a young litigation associate at Cahill Gordon, volunteered to give up his summer vacation to help. I had worked with Warren on several cases. He was an excellent lawyer, upon whom I knew I could rely. He was also a friend, and in years to come, I would prevail upon him to leave Cahill Gordon in order to join me at another firm, Barrett Smith Shapiro & Simon. My partners at Cahill Gordon later agreed to extend a leave of absence to Warren so that he could remain with us when his vacation was over. Cy Vance persuaded his partners to give a similar leave to a young associate named Paul Ford. He was a fledgling corporate lawyer with no experience in litigation, much less investigative work, but he was extremely bright and willing.

Carol Ash, our administrator, left us at about this time, but her assistant, Anne Beane, stayed on.

With this pared-down group, aided by a few part-time volunteers, we could get through the last several months of our investigation. It was to be the final belt-tightening.

We had earlier made an important personnel change that could hardly be categorized as "belt-tightening." Commissioner Arnold Bauman had found it necessary to resign—he soon thereafter became a federal judge—and was replaced by Professor John Sprizzo, from Fordham Law School. Sprizzo had served as chief appellate attorney and assistant chief of the Criminal Division during the time I had been at the U.S. Attorney's Office in Manhattan. As important, from my point of view, he had been an extremely formidable blocking back (at 275 pounds) on the office's touch football team. He was one of my closest friends. Sprizzo was enormously intelligent and learned in the law—he was later to become a federal judge. He also took no nonsense from anyone. We had, in Sprizzo, another commissioner whose integrity would be questioned by no one, even those who disagreed with his strongly held and vigorously expressed views. In a reunion of commissioners some years later, Bauman and Sprizzo, then both on the federal bench, got into a political argument that, characteristically for both of them, became so heated that Whit Knapp was moved to propose a toast to John Lindsay, "For his wisdom in not appointing Arnold and John to the Commission at the same time."

Another thing ending as of July 1, 1971, was the Commission's power to issue subpoenas and administer oaths. The City Council had reluctantly extended these powers for six months at the end of 1970. It was perfectly clear that a further extension would be impossible, at least not without our making full disclosure to the City Council of what we were doing. It was, of course, out of the question for us publicly to reveal to a Council laden with pro-cop legislators the details of our undercover operations, particularly those of Bill Phillips.

With respect to our power to administer an oath, we had a good legal argument that the mayor's executive order, which granted us the right to "hold hearings," necessarily included a grant of the authority to swear witnesses. We could not be sure the argument would prevail if challenged, but witnesses we called to testify would not know of the frailty of our authority. We would go ahead and administer the oath, and witnesses would still feel the impetus to tell the truth that results from the threat of a potential perjury charge.

We had no backup authority for the subpoena power granted by the City Council resolution that was about to die, so we rushed to complete, before July 1, the executive session testimony that was part of our fact-gathering process. The Commission ended up questioning a total of 183 witnesses in executive sessions. We wouldn't need subpoenas at our public hearings, because all of the witnesses would be appearing voluntarily. In a few instances, chiefly involving Department or City officials, like First Deputy Commissioner John Walsh, we obtained agreements to testify in executive session after the cut-off date, without requiring a subpoena.

As the deadline approached, we managed to get testimony, or a promise of voluntary testimony at a future time, from every relevant witness save one: former Police Commissioner Howard Leary. We were aware that Leary's testimony would be a simple denial of any knowledge of Frank Serpico's allegations and, unless one of his underlings contradicted him, it would be difficult to show otherwise. Nevertheless, it was important to get him on the record. We also wanted to explore some of his general views about anti-corruption efforts in the Department while he was in command. But Leary proved to be elusive, and our polite inquiries as to his whereabouts came up with nothing. After a while, it became obvious that he was deliberately ducking us. Whenever we left a message at a location where he was supposed to be, he was either "in conference," "not in," or "gone for the day," or he simply did not answer. It began to be a little embarrassing—a commission charged with investigating the whole New York City Police Department could not find the former police commissioner. Finally, about one week before our deadline, we located him. He ignored several attempts to make contact with him. Then, on June 24, 1971, I left an urgent personal request that he call me. He did so on the morning of June 29, the next-to-last day for our subpoena power. I explained that our subpoena power was running out and asked if he, like John Walsh and others, would agree to testify later, in July. He declined, saying that he saw no purpose in testifying anyway. It was too late for protocol or the amenities that normally would be extended to an ex–police commissioner. I instructed Brian Bruh to serve him with a subpoena.

First thing the next day, Bruh called in to report that Leary was refusing to accept our subpoena. I told Bruh to leave the subpoena with Leary and come on back to the office. We didn't have time to get a court order compelling him to honor the subpoena. If Leary wanted to flout it, we would deal with him in court later. If we ultimately were unsuccessful in taking his testimony, we would include in our final report the fact that he had refused to testify. The readers of the report could draw their own conclusions. One of the advantages of conducting an investigation, the purpose of which is to make things public, is that public figures can be coerced into cooperating merely by threatening to make known any refusal to do so. Apparently, Leary didn't care what we said about him. Bruh dropped the subpoena in his lap and bid him good day.

A small party was scheduled that afternoon at 2:00 P.M. in the Commission offices to say farewell to those who were leaving—which was practically everyone. Only the commissioners, Bruh, Cipriani, Impellizzeri, and a few young volunteers would remain, including those from the Justice Department and our law firms. We gathered to reminisce about the wild ride we had shared and to wish ourselves luck. We had hardly begun our little celebration when we were interrupted by a knock at the front door. It was Howard Leary, announcing that he was ready to honor our subpoena. He would testify. Whit Knapp, Otto Obermaier, and I put down our drinks and ushered Leary to our makeshift hearing room, stopping long enough to send for a court reporter.

Before Otto began questioning Leary, Whit attempted to make sure he understood what he was doing:

KNAPP: Mr. Leary, before we begin the formal questioning, I would like to
    advise you that you have all of the rights and privileges—you are aware
    that you have the right to—
LEARY: I would like to hear them because you are kind of discourteous, so
    I suppose you know—
KNAPP: What?
LEARY: I said you have been discourteous so far, so I would like to know
    my rights as you understand them.
KNAPP: Your rights, as I understand them, is you have the right to refuse to
    answer any question that may be put to you on the ground that it may
    incriminate you. You have a right to an attorney if you want to.
LEARY: Can I postpone it and come back tomorrow?

At that point, Leary engaged Whit in a series of nit-picking exchanges about what had or had not happened during our efforts to get him to testify. The preliminaries finally ended:

KNAPP: Mr. Armstrong was trying to get ahold of you last week and he
    was unsuccessful. You have asked for an adjournment. Do you want an
    adjournment or don't you?
LEARY: No, no, we will do it now.
KNAPP: May I inquire why you asked for one if you don't want one?
LEARY: I just wanted to know whether you would grant it or not.

KNAPP: I'm telling you I would.

LEARY: I'm telling you I don't need it.

Leary's substantive testimony continued in this vein. As Otto attempted to adduce meaningful responses, Leary was obstructive, at every turn. Fortunately he did not have much to say, so we made our record and called it a day. We went back to our party, shaking our heads. How could a man like that have undertaken to run the largest police department in the nation?

Our farewell party was a bittersweet affair. Commissioners, investigators, attorneys, volunteers, and staff assembled in our ramshackle offices and we splurged a few of the dollars we had left on a reasonably sumptuous spread of food and drink. It was a blend of confused emotions. We had struggled together to overcome a series of obstacles and, although things were looking up, we still couldn't say for sure whether we would ultimately succeed. We had assembled a great mass of information and embarked on some very promising paths. Now the few of us who remained would have to pull together and organize what we had collected while pursuing the unfinished investigations that lay ahead.

17

TANK AND SLIM

Among the matters comprising unfinished business was our just-beginning investigation into a particularly bizarre manifestation of police graft—cops ordering stolen merchandise and paying for it in drugs.

Waverly Logan—our PEP Squad witness who had first surfaced on a Channel 5 television show—had been unable, because of his notoriety, to work undercover for us. But he was able to put us in touch with two people who could. He introduced us to two youthful drug addicts who went by the names "Tank" and "Slim." I never knew the real names of the two young men, and it is at least possible that they didn't either. They were registered police informants and had developed a special relationship with the cops they served. In addition to providing the cops with information, the two junkies exchanged stolen merchandise for narcotics.

Raised in the heart of the ghetto, they had little to look forward to in life beyond surviving until the next day. Tank was about nineteen years of age, small, wiry, and constantly jittery. Slim was a little older, tall, laconic, and seemingly half-asleep almost all of the time. Both were very intelligent. Nervous, voluble Tank had a lively and winning personality, and he acted as the spokesman for the pair. Slim almost never said anything.

Logan had stashed away enough evidence of Tank and Slim's criminal behavior to put them behind bars for decades, and had used this leverage to get them to cooperate as informants. When Logan turned them over to us, he did so along with the proof of their misdeeds, the threatened exposure of which—with a few dollars now and then—seemed to motivate them. They agreed to help us gather information about the cops with whom they had been dealing.

What Tank and Slim had to offer was immediate access to an ongoing corrupt arrangement they had developed with the seventy or so officers in a narcotics enforcement outfit called Group 6, stationed at the 23rd Precinct in central Harlem. The two were in constant need of narcotics. The cops in Group 6, like anyone else, had personal needs of various kinds and they often found themselves short of money to pay for what they wanted. But they had lots of what Tank and Slim needed—drugs.

It was not unusual for narcotics agents to skim a little off the top of any drug stash confiscated in the course of an arrest. In this way they accumulated a supply with which to pay informants. Just about the only way to make narcotics cases was by using informants, who had to be paid. Since almost all of them were junkies who would use the money they were given to buy narcotics, there seemed to be little wrong with eliminating the middleman and paying them directly, with junk. With Tank and Slim, the cops took it one step further. They exchanged drugs not merely for information, but for merchandise. A cop would "order" some liquor, a household appliance, a television set, and the like, and Tank and Slim would steal the item for him, or get it from a fence, taking payment from the cop in heroin or cocaine. Sometimes they would use some of the drugs to pay for the merchandise. Tank and Slim were running a thriving business in stolen-to-order merchandise, paid for in drugs—by cops.

We set about plugging ourselves in to this trade. Tank and Slim went on operating as usual, but now they did so wearing a wire and under surveillance. The cops had been dealing with the two young men for so long that they no longer thought it necessary to pat them down, and they talked freely in front of them about the details of transactions that, by this time, had become routine. For us, it was a marvelous opportunity.

Impellizzeri, the only full-time attorney we had left, most often handled the surveillance. Usually a natty dresser, middle-aged Impellizzeri cut quite a figure, in scruffy clothes, slumped on a doorstep or curb, apparently slugging wine out of a bottle encased in a paper bag. He reported that "one lady threw me off a stoop because she didn't like winos around that house." Bruh and Cipriani, our only remaining agents, were pretty busy with Bill Phillips, but they lent a hand now and then.

On one occasion, captured on wire and film, Tank and Slim met with a dozen cops from Group 6 at their headquarters. The boys had brought with them only ten of the thirty cartons of cigarettes ordered by the cops, because their supplier, who was taking payment in narcotics, wanted to move slowly, first doing only a third of the deal. A discussion ensued as to how to measure one-third of the narcotics.

TANK: Hey, the reason why I didn't want to do that thing last night, 'cause they had a carnival in that park.

COP: Get it?

TANK: Them motherfuckers. They had a slight riot in there. Did you read the papers today?

COP: Get the cigarettes?

TANK: Yeah; you got the thing?

COP: Yeah.

TANK: Go down here. I got to go get them they're in the basement.

COP: Oh. They're in the basement?

TANK: Yeah.

* * *

COP: Got thirty cartons?

TANK: I got ten.

COP: Hey man . . .

TANK: You can break it down and give me a little something. They have stamps and everything and I can go back tonight and get the rest of them. But the man just wants to see something. You understand?

COP: How am I going to break that fucking thing down?

TANK: That's not no problem. Put the thing on a piece of paper or any-thing, 'cause the man, he the type of guy who wants to see something, then he'll come up with the rest, don't you understand what I'm say-ing, 'cause this is the first time I'm working with this cat.

COP: Aw, fuck it. I ain't gonna break that thing.

TANK: You never broken a quarter down?

COP: I ain't gonna go breaking quarters up.

TANK: All right. I'll tell you what I'll do . . . 'cause we got some whiskey too, ya dig it?

COP: I want the fucking cigarettes.

TANK: Yeah, but he wants something up front first. You don't understand what I'm saying; he wants something up front first, you dig what I'm saying?

COP: But I got the fucking thing with me now.

TANK: I know you got it. He says take ten and see what the man says 'cause he figure you weren't gonna show or something . . .

COP: How the fuck am I gonna break this thing up? Where am I gonna break this thing up?

TANK: You can drive around the block and break it up. It's easy man; get a piece of paper . . .

COP: I'll give you one-third of the fucking thing and I'll give you the other two-thirds when you bring the rest.

TANK: That's what I'm talking about.

COP: I don't want to keep fucking around breaking this thing up.

The police officer was quite particular about getting just the brands of cigarettes he wanted.

TANK: Hah? Yeah, my Marlboro and Salem. Hey, dig it, but he got Pall Mall too now.

COP: I don't want Pall Mall. Either Parliament, you know . . .

TANK: What about Winston?

COP: No, I don't know anybody that smokes Winston.

TANK: Parliament, Salem, Marlboro.

COP: Marlboro, couple of cartons of Tarrytons.

TANK: Right.

COP: O.K.

The cop also wanted delivery of a mini-bike he had ordered:

COP: Get the fucking bike tonight. If you come, I'll give you another one for the bike.

TANK: You said, like, a motorcycle you wanted, right?

COP: Yeh, a mini-bike and . . . cigarettes, and I'll give you another one. I'll give you a full quarter.

TANK: Can you take forty more packs, uh, cartons?

COP: How many more?

TANK: Thirty more. That's all you can handle with a quarter. I see that. But the guy got as many as you want.

COP: Well, when do you want the stuff? I want the mini-bike tonight.

TANK: Tonight. Well, that's all I'm gonna do then.

COP: I'll tell you what. You want to bring up fifty more cartons?

TANK: If you can handle it, I'll bring it up. I can give you fifty more. But you're going to have to take the mini-bike the next day.

COP: Tomorrow—I explained that.

TANK: Yeah, I did it. That's the best . . .

COP: All right, wait—come here. I want that fucking mini-bike tonight.

TANK: Right; as soon as I come back with this here, I'll start working on it.

On another occasion, a police officer had placed an order for liquor and an eight-track car stereo, but he did not show up to collect and pay off. Without much difficulty, Tank and Slim disposed of the material to another cop.

Another transaction involved a power saw and some liquor of a particular type:

TANK: How ya doing, Harry?

COP: All right.

TANK: Say, do you own a home?

COP: Mm. [*assent*]

TANK: Take a look at that. [*displays power saw*] Let's go in the park.

COP: Sherry Herring.

TANK: Not Sherry Herring.

COP: Cherry Heering, Cherry Heering.

TANK: Heh, heh.

COP: If you're going to be a dealer in liquors you have to know your stuff.

TANK: You said Sherry Herring. We got two Harvey Bristol Cream and three Cherry Heering. Now you got it all. I'll give you two for nothing. . . . I mean one for nothing. I already owe you one.

TANK: What do you think that this is worth, Harry? [*referring to circular power saw*]

COP: A quarter?

TANK: Should be, I know that for a fact. The price tag ain't on it. I know it at least costs that much.

COP: I know. To be honest with you I don't know offhand.

COP: I got a half.

TANK: For the bottles?

COP: For that. [*referring to the circular saw*]

TANK: Can you go two . . .

COP: I only have one. I got some coke if you want some coke.

TANK: Good.

COP: All right?

TANK: Good. This is all right though? The coke?

COP: Yeah, the coke is fine.

TANK: You want to look in the box first?

COP: No, I know where to find you if there's something wrong.

TANK: You can open up the . . . oh Harry, listen, that's why I want you to open it up now so we don't get in no trouble.

COP: If I'd thought that then I would have opened it up first, right?

TANK: Yeah, that's true.

Tank and Slim apparently were not the only ones who were involved in these types of exchanges. Nor were their transactions limited to the narcotics group with which they were registered. They seemed to have easy, trusting relationships with a number of cops from the area. If an officer from outside Group 6 placed an order and then didn't show, Tank and Slim would just go back to Group 6 and see who they could get to take the merchandise off their hands.

One officer placed an order with Tank and Slim for thirteen bottles of liquor for his daughter's wedding shower, giving a list of exactly what brands he wanted. Another specified that liquor should be delivered to his home, after going with Tank and Slim to Group 6 headquarters in order to get the heroin that constituted payment. The same cop, four days later, ordered more liquor, again for home-delivery. After being delayed because he had to go to an anticorruption meeting, the cop turned over the heroin, wrapped in a dollar bill.

COP: Got a dollar bill?
TANK: Yeah . . . Let me use the knife . . . This is the same thing right? It's the best. That was nice. Watch it now.
COP: Is that good enough?
TANK: Yeah, this dollar's too big.
COP: I'd better crimp the corners.
TANK: Put a little more in there. How are you wrapping that. Don't wrap it up. That's how coke comes, wrapped up, and I can't open it good.
COP: You ain't opening it 'til you get home.
TANK: We might get off in the train station. I'm sick now.
COP: Don't fuck around in a train station.
TANK: Yeah, not up where you live.

Another operation involved an officer from outside Group 6, a uniformed cop assigned to a regular precinct. The officer ordered six bottles of liquor, met with Tank and Slim about two doors away from the precinct house, and made the exchange. Because he had quite a bit of heroin he arranged to see them again, that night, for another exchange. He arrived in uniform, took the liquor (eight more bottles) into the precinct house and returned a few minutes later with the drugs.

TANK: Hey, John—John.
COP: You're kidding?
TANK: Johnny Walker Red. Yeah, it's all right.
COP: Yeah, I know. Alright, listen, I have to pay you in about fifteen minutes.

TANK: Mm.

COP: All right, wait back up in there about fifteen minutes. I'll be right back.

TANK: Grab it now. Hold it by the bottom. Don't drop it.

COP: I'll, uh.

TANK: Bring enough this time.

COP: I will. Now, just wait here.

TANK: All right, I'll be out here.

COP: 'Cause I don't want these dudes to start connecting us.

[*Pause*]

TANK: [*Under his breath, to our agents in surveillance car*] He's coming up now . . . He's coming up now . . .

COP: What is that thing, coke?

TANK: Some of it's speed, I've been using heroin or coke.

COP: I know that.

TANK: I got some, uh, tomorrow night . . . like, uh, the same thing.

COP: Yeah.

It was clear that the cops in Group 6 did not see themselves as being in danger of exposure by their comrades. Tank and Slim had one meeting—in which they haggled extensively over the amount and quality of the heroin they were to receive—just two doors down from the precinct house. The openness of these transactions was startling. Our agents saw and overheard a uniformed patrolman walk into the precinct house with an armload of liquor that, he announced to everyone present, he had just "bought" from Tank and Slim.

Our targets were not completely oblivious. Tank and Slim told us about another junkie who apparently suspected that Tank and Slim were acting as "double agents," for money, and said he wanted in on the deal. First, he wanted to meet Tank and Slim's "boss." Bruh and I met with the junkie on a secluded corner near the FDR Drive in Harlem in order to size him up. He was very nervous, and things just didn't feel right, so we broke off discussions before letting him know who we were or what we were up to. It was a good decision. We learned much later that the junkie had been set up by the cops in Group 6, to check on Tank and Slim.

One of the hazards of an enterprise that rests on the efforts of young drug addicts is the fact that you are dealing with young drug addicts—not the most reliable of individuals. In fact, it was necessary for us to support the drug needs of the two boys in order for them to be able to function. We paid them for their services and had no doubt in our minds as to what they did with most of the money. We didn't stop too long to worry about the irony of our deliberately supporting the drug trade.

Every once in a while, we were forced to face directly the fact that we were paying money to buy narcotics. Late one night, when I was comfortably asleep at my suburban home, I got a call from Julius Impellizzeri. He had met with Tank and Slim, who were scheduled to transact business with some police officers, only to find the two young men completely strung out. They needed a fix so badly that they could not operate coherently. Julius, dressed for undercover surveillance, had no money on him. I was too far away. There were of course no ATMs as yet. A former colleague of mine at Cahill Gordon lived in a fashionable apartment on 82nd Street and Fifth Avenue, so I called him up. We were good friends and, without asking any questions, he got dressed and went to a designated corner to give twenty dollars to two extremely disreputable-looking young men. Tank and Slim used the money to obtain the means of straightening themselves out. I paid my friend back the next day. A few months later, I told him what it had all been about.

As valuable as the information gathered by Tank and Slim was, we thought we saw an opportunity for more. With proper backup, they might be able to expand into other areas of the Department, using their contacts in Group 6 as springboards. However, as the time for our hearings approached, the Commission's investigative resources were extremely limited. Our only remaining agents, Bruh and Cipriani, were feverishly winding up the various operations centering on the undercover efforts of Bill Phillips. They had little time for a new venture. Only Julius Impellizzeri was available. He had already been working with Tank and Slim and, as someone they knew and trusted, would be necessary to any effort involving them. We decided to turn to the Feds. Our public hearings were imminent and there probably wouldn't be time for us to be upstaged. In any event, I knew that I could trust completely the person to whom I turned, Bill Tendy, chief of the Narcotics Unit in the U.S. Attorney's Office in Manhattan.

Bill, in his fifties, was a fixture. Rugged, bald, and assertive, he had been putting narcotics violators in jail for about twenty years, after growing up in a tough neighborhood in what was then Irish/Italian East Harlem. Among the scalps on his belt was "Godfather" Carmine Galante, who—with "Big John" Ormento, "Colly" DiPietro, and several other top hoods—had been convicted in a prosecution led by Tendy that went through two five-month trials. The first ended in a mistrial. The alternate jurors had been used up for various reasons—one juror, for example, had received a bottle of wine with ground glass in it, prompting him to seek to be excused. On the eve of summations, the foreman of the jury was found at the bottom of a staircase in a deserted warehouse with a broken back. When he recovered, he somehow could not remember any of the evidence that he had heard during the previous five months of trial, so the judge was obliged, under the rules as they then existed, to declare a mistrial. In the months before the case could be retried, two government witnesses were murdered. Nevertheless, Tendy, after another five-month effort, obtained convictions of all of the defendants. He was formidable, and he was a close friend. I could trust him. He would use Tank and Slim to make cases, but would wait until we used them first in our hearings.

The operation didn't turn out the way we had hoped. Impellizzeri and Tendy didn't get along that well, each of them being accustomed to calling the shots. In addition, Tendy was a traditionalist and was accustomed to making cases in the usual way, going through the usual procedures. He was not thrilled with unorthodox schemes, or Impellizzeri.

A federal taskforce of a half-dozen agents was devoted to the effort, but it yielded little that we were able to use. A meeting was held in a bugged hotel room in Harlem, and a disguised truck was employed on several surveillance operations, but in the time before our hearings we were unable to progress much beyond the level of drug violators, to the point of getting information about the police who obviously protected them.

Even though this last venture with Tank and Slim did not go as planned, the overall effort with the two was a significant success. We had retrieved something of what we had given up when we surrendered Bob Leuci to the Feds, namely, firsthand information about police-narcotics corruption. Tapes and films of considerable impact had been generated, and they would be quite suitable for showing in a public hearing.

18

PHILLIPS, IN HIGH GEAR

Meanwhile, the Bill Phillips operation was proceeding full blast. Under the direction of Brian Bruh and Ralph Cipriani, Phillips went from one corrupt situation to another, generating films and tapes.

In an operation that lasted for most of the three months of Phillips's undercover work for us, he targeted two plainclothes units to the east and south of Central Park. The Third Division covered lower Midtown Manhattan, stretching from Central Park South to 14th Street. The Fourth Division stretched east and south of the park. Approaching two Third Division cops he knew, Fanelli and Laviano, Phillips inquired about getting protection for what he said was a big floating crap game that a supposed friend of his, a gambler by the name of "Little Artie," proposed to establish in locations throughout both the Third and the Fourth Divisions. "Little Artie" was the name of an actual gambler, with a record, who was currently out of town and, as Phillips knew, had no intention of returning in the near future. Phillips presented himself as "Little Artie's" agent for the purpose of seeing to it that he was put on the pad.

The overture was met with routine interest. This was nothing new to the plainclothesmen of either division. Phillips went on to discuss with Fanelli and several others—the ones in charge of setting things up—the establishment of "Little Artie's" business. Everything was, of course, to be done in a future that was never to be. We had neither the resources nor the inclination to follow through by setting up an actual "sting" operation. All we needed for our purpose were tape recordings of police officers talking freely about the way it would work. After enough preliminary conversations had been taped to show what the plans were, Phillips would procrastinate in their implementation, and hope that "Little Artie" didn't decide to come back to town.

The details of the arrangements were set up in conversations—taped, of course—between Phillips and the "inner circle" of the Third and Fourth Division plainclothesmen. These were the "heavy hitters," whose skill in the business of taking bribes merited their leadership positions. It was the only measuring stick for success that made sense, because the division cops did little else. Arrangements were made with care: the "nut" was set at $2,000 per division, a total of $4,000 per month; "kites" (complaints by customers) were to be taken care of by a lieutenant; suitable locations were selected, and a method of identification was agreed upon—using matching photographs of a particular dollar bill. Precinct cops would be given their share and would not bother anyone. All of this was recorded on tape.

It became apparent that, as Phillips had predicted, every plainclothesman in the Third and Fourth Divisions was involved, each doing his share of picking up money and taking his established percentage of the overall monthly "nut." Phillips claimed that his experience in thirteen years on the job left him in no doubt that all of the seventeen plainclothes divisions in the city operated precisely as in the Third Division. This was what we had consistently heard since Frank Serpico first described conditions in the Seventh Division in the Bronx. Now we had tape recordings to back it up.

The cops also discussed setting up a pad in the Public Morals and Administration Division (PMAD), run out of headquarters. Fanelli and Laviano would take a piece of that pad as well. Fanelli bragged about making many scores in the area, saying that he would regularly "flake" a group of individuals, then make them pay to avoid being charged for possession of the planted drugs. He would force one or two of the group to plead guilty anyway so his record would look good. Fanelli also told—on tape—of making an arrest that he later learned was fixed with the trial judge. Since he hadn't been paid himself, he testified truthfully and the defendant was convicted, which, said Fanelli, did not please the judge.

In another tape, Fanelli discussed checking out six possible locations for the "Little Artie" gambling operation in order to make sure the locations had not been known gambling spots and were the "right types" of places. Fanelli was recorded being given two hundred dollars of Commission money for his services.

Phillips was careful to indicate that the game probably couldn't start until after Labor Day, and managed to resist the plainclothesmen's attempts actually to get in touch with "Little Artie." In the course of their taped conversations, the plainclothesmen casually exchanged stories about graft: one new lieutenant unsuccessfully tried to get a double share of the pad and bypass his two-month waiting period; another lieutenant tried to increase the pad for the Borough Office, even after the plainclothesmen assigned there had been transferred out and the office no longer dealt with gambling. One plainclothesman told of an arrest he made with his lieutenant. They caught four prostitutes, let two off, and had the other two plead guilty, collecting money from them later.

Negotiations for the "Little Artie" "contract" were coming down to the wire, when Phillips met with Fanelli and a cop named Luzzi from the Fourth Division. Phillips had just been transferred to the First Division, and we decided to use this opportunity to end the operation. The Commission didn't have the necessary $4,000 to actually get the pad started, so Phillips told Fanelli and Luzzi that "Little Artie" wanted Phillips to take the game to the First Division with him. Phillips claimed that Artie had helped put through this transfer and that he wanted to do anything Artie wanted. Naturally, Fanelli and Luzzi weren't pleased about the move because this left them out in the cold. Phillips said he didn't want to close any doors, so he gave them each "a hat" (fifty dollars), in order to keep things open. Luzzi pointed out that there was a borough command in the First Division that would have to be included in the new pad, and they all joked about the possibility of drawing in the borough corruption team as well. Luzzi then said that if Phillips wanted to extend the game back into the Third and Fourth Divisions, the price would be $4,000 per division, not $2,000 as Fanelli had said.

This was the last meeting with Fanelli and his cohorts in the Third Division. Perhaps they got suspicious when Phillips indicated he wasn't going to follow through. The operation had lasted for more than two months and, with the Commission hearings approaching, Phillips just withdrew quietly.

Things did not always go smoothly, and even Teddy Ratnoff's equipment occasionally went awry. On one such occasion, Phillips was in a bar, pumping a corrupt cop for information. The bar was one frequented by cops, and a number of them, along with other customers, were drinking and watching television at the far end of the room. Phillips's attention to his conversation was distracted by sudden loud complaining from down the bar that the television set was malfunctioning. Turning to see what was going on, Phillips was horrified when he realized that the signal from his transmitter was somehow being picked up by the television set. His conversation with the cop was being broadcast, in somewhat garbled tones, to the entire bar. It would only be a matter of minutes before some cop at the bar figured out what was going on. Mumbling something about a better bar around the corner, Phillips hastily paid his tab and ushered his companion out of range of the meddlesome television set.

On another occasion, Phillips's attempt to set up a loan shark met with a frustrating lack of cooperation from the hoodlum. The plan was for Phillips to introduce an agent to the shark, from whom the agent would borrow money and not pay it back. Loan sharks have ways of making people repay. We reasoned that when the inevitable threat was made, the agent would disappear, with the crime recorded on tape. Phillips would explain that his acquaintance had double-crossed both of them and skipped town. We would later confront the shark and put pressure on him to cooperate with us against cops with whom he was dealing.

The only problem was that the loan shark refused to get nasty. Probably because the borrower was supposedly a friend of Phillips, the shark merely repeated his requests for payment in terms no more ominous than those customarily used by one's local banker. Finally, he even modified the terms of the loan so as to make it more easy to be repaid. With nothing but a possible charge of usury, we had to abandon our hopes of pressuring the shark for information.

Phillips also introduced us to one of the "hot spots" of gambling activity in the city—the "office" of "Louie Fats." It was a telephone booth on the corner of Pleasant Avenue and 118th Street in Harlem, where Louie hung out, with his confederates, "Muzzi," "The Fish," and others. The area, carved out of the expanding black and Hispanic neighborhoods around it, was home base for the Italian American mobsters who ran the numbers racket and other gambling enterprises in the minority communities.

Phillips arranged a taped meeting with a lieutenant, for the ostensible purpose of making sure the various payments made by "Louie Fats" would go smoothly. They were to meet "Joe Tough Guy," one of Louie's sidekicks:

PHILLIPS: Hi, Chief. What do you say? You busy?
LIEUTENANT: Yeah, come here.
PHILLIPS: I spoke to your number-one boy yesterday and I saw Louie, and he says that, uh, Joe is going to be here at one.
LIEUTENANT: Yeah.
PHILLIPS: He's supposed to meet you at one about the dice game?
LIEUTENANT: Yesterday?
PHILLIPS: No, today.
LIEUTENANT: Albert [another cop] told me yesterday he was supposed to meet him yesterday.

PHILLIPS: No, it's today at one. That's what Louie told me to tell you. Look, I couldn't get a hold of "the Fish." "The Fish" is fucked up, you know.

LIEUTENANT: Yeah.

* * *

PHILLIPS: Right, so could I meet the other guy with you or see what he wants to throw us?

LIEUTENANT: Where's he gonna meet us?

PHILLIPS: In the bar.

LIEUTENANT: Next door?

PHILLIPS: Yeah.

LIEUTENANT: Okay.

PHILLIPS: I'll go have a beer.

Phillips and the lieutenant moved to the bar, where Joe Tough Guy was waiting:

LIEUTENANT: I wanna get out of here as quick as possible. How ya doing Joe?

JOE: All right.

LIEUTENANT: [*indistinct*] I'm the other guy.

PHILLIPS: Oh, good.

LIEUTENANT: What do you want to do, Joe?

JOE: What do you want to do?

LIEUTENANT: All right, listen. There's four lieutenants on the desk and myself; that's five guys. There's two fly captains.

JOE: Forget the captains.

LIEUTENANT: OK, five lieutenants.

JOE: Five lieutenants . . . you get fifteen apiece, all right?

LIEUTENANT: Forget about it. Division gets a hundred.

JOE: All right. We'll go for twenty apiece.

PHILLIPS: Do I hear twenty-five?

JOE: You guys have been pushed for ten dollars apiece.

LIEUTENANT: Ten dollars is nothing.

JOE: Let me see if I got it with me. One-hundred-dollar "nut," here's ninety dollars and, uh, there's five of you, right?

LIEUTENANT: Right.

JOE: I owe you ten dollars.

LIEUTENANT: Okay.

JOE: The end of the month.

PHILLIPS: Want me to loan him ten? [*laughs*]

JOE: Louie Fats will have the money every month.

LIEUTENANT: Okay.

JOE: All right?

LIEUTENANT: Good.

JOE: This way I won't have to see you again.

LIEUTENANT: That's right.

PHILLIPS: Whose going to take care of the dough, uh, the thing? The whole thing? You going to take care of it yourself, do you want me to pick it up when I'm over there, or what?

LIEUTENANT: You pick it up.

PHILLIPS: For everybody, for everybody, all right?

LIEUTENANT: Why don't you give it to Louie Fats, and Al will pick it up on Sunday. Al was going to see Louie anyway.

JOE: What do you mean by everybody?

PHILLIPS: I could pick the whole, one shot, pick the whole fucking thing up for the cars.

JOE: All right, that's all right with me, but I mean, uh, the sergeants come and pick up their own.

PHILLIPS: The sergeants pick up their own okay, but I figured I'd get it all in one "nut," the sergeants, lieutenants, the cops all in one shot.

JOE: Vinnie, uh, Vinnie will take care of the, the, uh, radio cars.

PHILLIPS: All right. This way, this way, you see, you eliminate all the traffic. It's like a one-shot thing.

JOE: He, he, he, uh, anyway, he takes care of it.

PHILLIPS: You do it your way, all right. Okay, see you later.

JOE: Uh, when Vinnie gets it this month there'll be an extra twenty, I'll tell him to give it to you. You ask him for it.

PHILLIPS: Okay, thanks.

JOE: Tell him I, uh, promised you that.

PHILLIPS: Okay, thanks.

JOE: All right.

Louie Fats operated quite openly from his telephone booth and a nearby storefront. Everyone in the neighborhood knew that the booth was for Louie's use only and it stood pretty much empty when he wasn't using it. Phillips told us that cops in the area, detectives, plainclothesmen, patrol car cops, and foot patrolmen, would literally line up on the first and fifteenth of every month to collect what was owed them by Louie Fats and his people. All we had to do was find a way to hide a camera within range of the phone booth and we would be able to chronicle this parade.

We set about making the arrangements. I contacted a rising young investigative reporter whom I knew at NBC News, Ira Silverman. He was later to become a nationally known TV investigative reporter and producer, but at this time he was just beginning his career. Pursuant to our usual agreement with NBC, Silverman would follow our directions in taking his film, and then turn it over to us, pending our hearings. Our instructions were precise. Silverman and one African American cameraman, equipped with a small portable television camera, were to station themselves at the window of a second-floor apartment in a decrepit rooming house just opposite Louie Fats's "office." The apartment had been made available to us through the efforts of a local priest, who was sympathetic with our endeavors and who had influence with the building's landlord. A side door was to be left open so that Silverman and his cameraman could slip into the apartment undetected. He was thoroughly briefed on the need for secrecy in the operation, where to park, what to wear, and, generally, how to blend into the local scene.

Halfway through the morning on the day of the operation, I got a hysterical phone call at home from Silverman. He was desperate. The operation was blown, and he was in immediate personal danger. What should he do?

What had happened was that the cameraman assigned to Silverman had not shown up. In seeking to replace him, Silverman encountered the paralyzing bureaucracy of the labor union to which the cameraman belonged. Not being free to explain what his special needs were all about, Silverman had been obliged by the union to take a full crew, complete with full-sized cameras and lots of equipment. He decided to go ahead. Soon he found himself leading his gang of a half-dozen—mostly white—cameramen and technical assistants, laden down with clearly marked NBC equipment, through the streets of Harlem.

They somehow managed to reach the apartment relatively unnoticed, and set about putting their equipment in place. Things seemed to be functioning smoothly, and they began to shoot pictures through cracks in the window's musty drapes. All might have gone well if, during a break in the filming, an assistant cameraman had not leaned out the window to take a reading with his light meter. Just at that moment, one of Louie Fats's lieutenants looked up, directly into the face of a fat white guy leaning out a window pointing a black object in his direction. The alarm was sounded, and Louie's people headed for the apartment. Everyone fled, in hysterical confusion. They had only gotten a few shots, and weren't even sure they were of policemen.

Now Silverman was distraught. His equipment was inscribed with large NBC logos. Louie apparently made a couple of quick phone calls, and soon cops were inquiring at NBC, stating that they needed to identify a film crew, operating on the corner of 118th Street and Pleasant Avenue. When the question was put to the union leader, he identified Silverman. That's when Silverman called me in a panic. He was certain that he had become an instant target to be rubbed out, if not by cops, certainly by mobsters. We told Ira to stay with his mother for a few days until things blew over. Nothing ever happened to him.

Silverman's crew had gotten some film of individuals dropping in at Louie Fats's establishment and, after a few minutes, moving on. None were in police uniform, and we had no idea who they might be. We arranged for Phillips to come to NBC for a secret viewing of the film, but he said he couldn't identify anyone. Maybe some of them were Phillips's friends, but we had no way of knowing.

The fiasco apparently had wider implications. Shortly thereafter, Phillips had a taped conversation with a nervous cop:

COP: I've been going out of my fucking way to stay away from that fucking East Side.

PHILLIPS: Yeah.

* * *

COP: The whole fucking East Side is bad. Very bad. I don't talk to nobody over there.

PHILLIPS: Yeah.

COP: Especially in uniform, radio car.

PHILLIPS: I don't do nothing over there no more.

COP: If you want to go you gotta park your fucking car three blocks away, disguise yourself—they're taking movies.

PHILLIPS: Yeah.

COP: They got these fucking cameras that from three blocks away they could see what you're writing.

PHILLIPS: That powerful?

COP: That's how good they are. And then they got the shotgun mikes— they can hear what you're talking about, too.

PHILLIPS: Yeah.

COP: They put one on you, one on the guy you're talking to.

PHILLIPS: I know, matter of fact they had something over there the other day. Somebody was taking movies over there and they, that was blown. They had an apartment and somebody gave somebody up and they found out about it.

* * *

COP: And you talk to somebody, uh, they get apartments in the neighborhood, they move in, they live there, for months, and they start to trust 'em and they fucking work. They're actually taking numbers.

PHILLIPS: On the payroll for the Commission.

COP: So you may be talking to Farby and the fucking guy next to him may be working for the Department of Investigation. You don't know who you're talking to. That's what I say. I wouldn't talk to nobody. Fuck these guys.

PHILLIPS: Yeah.

COP: I say, if you're in civilian clothes, by yourself, away from where they work . . .

PHILLIPS: Right.

COP: They want to give you a fucking hat, fine. Otherwise, stay away.

Later Phillips had a talk with "Muzzi," in the course of which he collected a casual ten dollars and got further confirmation that Louie and his people were laying low:

MUZZI: How are you, how do you feel?

PHILLIPS: How ya doin', Muzzi? What happened with the Fish?

MUZZI: If you don't want to go to jail, you better listen to a friend of yours. You gotta stay away from here. The FBI . . .

PHILLIPS: That's why I come in civilian clothes.

MUZZI: Well, that's what I'm trying to tell you.

PHILLIPS: We ain't seen you since January.

MUZZI: Here, we haven't been doin' much.

PHILLIPS: Yeah.

MUZZI: Well, that's all I got.

PHILLIPS: I'll take a ten. It's that hot, huh?

MUZZI: Either way . . .

PHILLIPS: That's why I go in civilian clothes.

MUZZI: What's your name?

PHILLIPS: Bill, Bill Phillips.

MUZZI: That's what I'm tryin' to tell ya. The best you can do is [indistinct] . . . The FBI, now they come after cops too.

PHILLIPS: Yeah, right.

MUZZI: It ain't that they don't come after us, that's uh, that's what they're looking to do.

PHILLIPS: So he's out of action, the Fish?

MUZZI: Sure he's out of action, there's nobody there.

PHILLIPS: I seen it, a fucking federal rap, uh? That five-year thing you're going to do?

MUZZI: For what?

PHILLIPS: Yeah.

MUZZI: We haven't been doing nothing.

PHILLIPS: Yeah.

MUZZI: So make yourself scarce.

PHILLIPS: OK, Muzzi, I will. Bye.

Preparing Phillips for an operation one night, it occurred to us that he would fit in more easily in the setting we had targeted if he had an escort. Lisa Barrett had already left us, as had most of the female staffers, like Carol Ash. We tried locating one young associate at Cahill Gordon who would have been perfect. She was bright and attractive, with enough spirit of adventure to find it intriguing to pose as Phillips's romantic interest, but she didn't happen to be working in the office that evening, and could not be located at home. So Phillips went to his meeting unescorted. His would-be date was most disappointed when she learned what she had missed.

Among the creature comforts that Phillips had accumulated during his profitable years as a New York City policeman were two airplanes. We never did find out authoritatively to what extent Phillips used these planes for reasons other than weekend recreation. Later there were rumors spread that the planes were involved in drug smuggling. We found no indication that any such thing was happening, and for a variety of reasons I thought it highly unlikely that Phillips would have engaged in the drug trade. For one thing, I found credible his protestations that dealing in drugs was different than the normal corrupt activities in which he engaged. His reservations were not necessarily based strictly on moral grounds. It just was too risky.

The availability of the airplanes, however, was an opportunity for us. Although he had no entrée into the supply of drugs themselves, he had heard another cop talk about making money by importing quinine, to be used in "cutting" heroine. Phillips followed up this lead, with the view to making his planes available for shipment of quinine from Canada. Things were just getting underway when one of the key contacts, with whom Phillips was beginning to deal, was murdered. The drug trade was indeed risky, even at its peripheries. The killing chilled Phillips's interest in setting up the quinine deal, and we didn't push him. We were satisfied to trim our sails a bit.

A plainclothesman in the Bronx once told Phillips about his partner's personal wiretapping racket. He would put a wire and a recorder on a phone in a bar for a day or so and return to see if there was any "useful" information on it. Recently the cop had learned, from the wire, about a bookmaking operation in another division. Phillips offered to buy the information, and the recording, but the plainclothesman apparently had become suspicious of Phillips. There was no deal.

In another sting operation in Queens, Phillips came up with more than he expected. He had inveigled a plainclothesman stationed in the Sixteenth Division in Queens to discuss with him setting up an illegal card game. In doing so, the plainclothesman described in detail the arrangements that would have to be made and who would get paid off. The "nut" would be about $1,500 per month. Phillips gave the cop fifty dollars to check out some locations and they began to discuss, in detail, how money was made in the Sixteenth Division.

Then the plainclothesman began to get confidential with Phillips about something more serious. It seems he had participated not merely in gambling corruption. He had made an $80,000 narcotics score as well. Probably out of pride in his accomplishment, the cop described the whole thing. He had made an arrest involving two or three kilos of heroin and $217,000. He and his two partners turned in only $137,000. The other $80,000 was carried out of the station house in a shopping bag and split among the three. Despite a loud jukebox in the bar in which they were talking, Ratnoff's equipment worked perfectly, and the plainclothesman's prideful self-congratulations, about both gambling and narcotics, were recorded clearly.

One day, fairly late in the investigation, Phillips came to us with news that he thought was significant. He had been wrong about narcotics cops being straight. He told us of spending a day riding in a patrol car with an ex-detective recently transferred out of the Narcotics Division. Apparently, because of Phillips's reputation, the detective had spoken freely in front of him. Phillips took it all in and then repeated to us a description of corruption in narcotics enforcement that meshed pretty closely with what we had learned from Bob Leuci and our surveillances of Tank and Slim. Phillips seemed truly surprised by what he had heard and purported to be disdainful of cops who would mess around with narcotics. He continued to insist that he had never participated in or even known about narcotics corruption.

We found, in the course of our investigation, a number of other indications that a line was drawn on narcotics by cops of Phillips's generation, even by the "meat eaters." To people of Phillips's age, raised in the Depression and World War II, drugs were genuinely to be feared and despised. To younger officers, growing up in a society where drugs were increasingly common, taking money from a drug peddler did not have much more impact than taking payoffs from a gambler or a loan shark. It appeared that the "clean money–dirty money" distinction had been seriously eroded, particularly among the younger officers. Evidence of this trend could be seen in the growing number of narcotics-related corruption tales we were told by Bob Leuci and others.

On the other hand, it was possible, of course, that Phillips was conning us. We had heard the rumor that Phillips himself was involved in the narcotics trade, and that he actually transported "junk" in his light airplane. We didn't believe the rumor, but with Phillips, anything was possible.

With only Bruh and Cipriani available to devote full time to Phillips's undercover operation, things sometimes got a little tight. On a few occasions, even I was called upon to fill in, taking the unfamiliar role of street agent. Once I was relaxing at home one evening, when the phone rang. It was Brian Bruh, and he needed help. Impellizzeri and Cipriani were tied up. Bruh had set up a meeting that night with a gambler to whom he had been introduced by Phillips. He needed backup, to surveil and record the meeting. I was his only available candidate. So I climbed in my car and drove into the city. We somehow managed, even though I was relatively hopeless when it came to technological things. I could sit in the car and listen, while Bruh went about his business. But operating the recording equipment was a different matter. With a little intense instruction, I got enough of the hang of it. The tape actually came out in fairly understandable form.

Another time, when Bruh and Cipriani were shorthanded, I got the opportunity to see Phillips in action, up close. I was called upon again to act as Bruh's assistant, minding the electronic equipment while Phillips met with people under Bruh's visual surveillance. Bruh and I met Phillips, for the purpose of rigging him up with his transmitting equipment, on an out-of-the-way street on the Upper East Side, near Gracie Mansion. Bruh and Phillips were in the back seat of the car, taping the equipment on Phillips's body, when a patrol car came around a nearby corner and pulled up alongside. There was Phillips, half-naked, and Bruh with a pile of electronic equipment in his lap. I sat, transfixed, in the front seat. Phillips immediately took over. Slipping his shirt back on, he jumped out of the car, whipped out his badge and flashed it quickly at the officers. "This is an IAD undercover operation," he barked authoritatively, "get out of here right away!" The cops hesitated for a moment and moved on. Phillips coolly returned to the car and Bruh finished wiring him up. We proceeded to make several stops, Phillips engaging in conversations that I dutifully made sure were recorded correctly. It was illuminating for me to have a chance to see Phillips in action.

On one or two other occasions, I was forced, because there was no one else available, to take a turn as an agent, in one form or another. The experiences necessarily involved the normal drudgery, excitement, anxiety, and quick decision-making that characterized the routine day-to-day work of an agent. I was able to get a slight idea of the difference between ordering agents around and actually doing the work.

We had always done the best we could to keep Phillips's undercover activities secret, but we knew that it would only be a matter of time before someone connected with law enforcement would get wind of what was going on. It finally happened. Apparently, Jerry McKenna, counsel for the State Joint Legislative Committee on Crime, from whom we had gotten the $1,500 whose tardy delivery had caused me to borrow from my law office's safe, made some inquiries about getting immunity for Phillips, with an eye toward calling him as a witness in his own hearing. One thing led to another, and I received a telephone call from an assistant district attorney in Manhattan named Joe Phillips—no relation to Bill—requesting that I come to his office to discuss with him reports he had gotten about our using an undercover cop. I dutifully complied.

Joe Phillips, assigned to the Rackets Bureau in Frank Hogan's office, greeted me from behind a huge desk in a huge office. Seated next to him, on a couch, was a detective from the so-called "bat cave," an elite group of anti-corruption police officers working directly with the first deputy commissioner. Just about the only effective anti-corruption outfit in the Department, they had recently developed an important corruption case reaching all the way up into the police commissioner's office, only to have the case thrown out after a ruling by the Supreme Court of the United States rendered the wire taps they had used no longer legal. The detective said practically nothing during the meeting. He just sat on the couch, smoking his pipe.

Joe Phillips, on the other hand, did not hold back in expressing himself. A large, thickset man, with a typically Irish face, he was not given to communicating in subtleties. "We understand that you have a police officer working undercover for you on corruption cases and we want you to turn him over to us," he said. When I answered, ambiguously, Phillips got more direct. If we were uncovering crimes that had occurred in Manhattan County, it was the D.A.'s job to pursue those crimes and anyone interfering with those efforts would be guilty of obstruction of justice. He wanted me to turn over our informant, together with all tapes, films, documents, and other information related to our investigation.

As politely as I could, I told him that I would not comply with his request. He responded by saying that he would issue a subpoena for the information. I replied that I would not honor the subpoena. He retorted that he would have me held in contempt. I said I didn't think so. Our Commission had been appointed by the mayor to investigate, among other things, whether the district attorneys had been ineffective—perhaps deliberately so—in dealing with police corruption. Did he really think that it was wise to seek a contempt citation against the counsel of a commission that might be looking into his office?

I was not being courageous. It was clear that Phillips was bluffing and had no intention of seeking to hold anyone in contempt. He blustered a bit and lapsed into a demeaning commentary on the value of our Commission's work. Remarking on our as-yet unexpressed conclusions, he speculated with a sneer that we probably would purport to find corruption everywhere in the Department, and invoked the old saw about not drawing conclusions from a "few rotten apples in the barrel." To support his point, Phillips turned to the detective sitting silently on his nearby couch. "You're the real expert here," he said, "by way of example, just how many Captain's bagmen [people picking up graft for precinct commanders] are there in the seventy-eight precincts in New York City?"

The detective calmly took the pipe out of his mouth and said, dryly, "Seventy-eight."

Phillips exploded. "Don't say that in front of him," he sputtered.

The detective shrugged. His name was Richard Condon and he would, in later years, become police commissioner—and my very close friend. As often was the case with Condon, his cryptic reply to Phillips's question said more than appeared on its face. Condon was not saying that every precinct commander in the city was corrupt, but only that the economic opportunity afforded by the public perception that precinct commanders are susceptible to bribes was too good an opportunity to be turned down. Whether the precinct commander was on the take or not, there was always someone ready to collect, saying it was for him.

While my conversation with Joe Phillips ended with a polite but flat refusal on my part to turn over information to him, I arranged to keep in contact with Condon. The relationship with Condon grew quickly. He was sharp, knowledgeable, sympathetic with our goals, and most importantly, he became a friend. I could trust him. Before long, we were coordinating our investigative operations with him. Down to two investigators, with hearings looming in the near future, there wasn't much time left. I grew to rely on Condon for his ability to get things done in the Department, including technological help—he could legally tap a phone, while we could not. Most of all, I grew to know that I could turn to him for sound advice.

Overall, Bill Phillips's efforts were a resounding success. We had a wealth of material to show the facts about corruption in a broad representative section of the Department. We weren't after criminal cases, but the extent of Phillips's work could partly be measured by the fact that during a three-month period, in the sixty-nine wired operations in which he was engaged, he accumulated evidence that ultimately resulted in the indictments of more than thirty policemen. And he wasn't even trying.

19

THE DYNAMIC DUO—AGAIN

Ed Droge had given us a good deal of valuable information about his past activities and had also worked on a few relatively routine projects. It was difficult to develop much of a plan to use him as an undercover operative because he had little to offer in the way of targets. He didn't know any "meat eaters" and, even if we had the personnel to amass proof against a proliferation of "grass eaters," we really didn't need more individual examples. In any event, we didn't have manpower or time enough to spread a net for little fish.

Then, in filling us in on what he had done and whom he had met, Droge mentioned two cops he had run across while taking a course in the Department prior to his leaving for California. The word was that they were heavy hitters. Their names were Robert Hantz and David Greenberg—our old friends, Batman and Robin. Tales of the activities of these two were fresh in our minds, particularly since we shared Brooklyn District Attorney Eugene Gold's frustration at being unable to prove conclusively the murders Hantz and Greenberg were suspected of committing. So we leaped at the chance to capitalize on Droge's acquaintanceship to get proof against the two.

We decided to use the same approach that Phillips had used so successfully in flushing out evidence of gambling pads in Manhattan. Droge would telephone Hantz or Greenberg, reintroduce himself, and seek information about how to obtain protection for a supposed gambler friend who wanted to operate in the area where they were assigned.

It was risky. Droge was no Phillips. He did not carry Phillips's automatic stamp of trustworthiness among corrupt cops. Moreover, Droge's acquaintance with Hantz and Greenberg was slight, and they had no personal reason to trust him. Nevertheless, the hearings were almost upon us, and our investigations would be ending in any event. Besides, Droge had pretty much completed his work for us, and we didn't stand to lose that much if he was blown, or the operation turned out not to be successful. The possibility of getting Batman and Robin was too tempting to turn down. We decided to take a chance.

Droge called Greenberg. At first wary, Greenberg became friendly enough and did not immediately balk at the hint that he might give Droge some help in arranging protection for a gambler. In several telephone conversations over the next day or so, Greenberg seemed receptive, but guarded. One call gave us pause—Greenberg phoned Droge from Greenberg's precinct house. Was he really that casual? We wondered. Finally, at about four o'clock on an afternoon late in September, Greenberg agreed to a meeting. He set a price of six hundred dollars to pave the way for Droge's gambler. The money would be paid that evening at the Green Tea Room, a coffeehouse in the Red Hook section of Brooklyn.

It sounded too easy. Perhaps it was a setup of some sort. But we decided that we had nothing to lose. I called Brooklyn District Attorney Eugene Gold and told him that we had an operation going that night which might come up with something on his two "friends."

"Not *those* friends?" he said.

"Those are the guys," I responded.

Gold was ecstatic. He offered to give us any help he could, saying that he was off to a function that evening but I was free to interrupt him at any time. I said that I did not see any need for immediate help, but I took the telephone number where he could be reached.

Carrying a concealed wire and an envelope with six hundred dollars in cash, Droge went to the Green Tea Room at the appointed time. He walked inside and sat down at a table. He was shortly joined by Hantz and Greenberg. Our agents, Brian Bruh and Ralph Cipriani, listening in a car parked a little down the street, recorded the conversation.

Then Bruh saw someone, parked a few cars down, whom he thought he knew. The man was a detective from the Internal Affairs Division (IAD) of the police department, with whom Bruh had worked a number of times during the last few weeks on investigations involving Bill Phillips. Bruh walked over to the cop, while Cipriani continued to monitor the conversation in the Tea Room.

"Hi," said Bruh. "What's up?"

"I'm covering a meet," said the officer.

"It's not going down in the Green Tea Room, is it?"

"Yeah, how did you know?"

"Involves Batman and Robin?"

The officer was incredulous. "How the hell do you know about it?"

Bruh laughed resignedly. "We've got the other side."

Hantz and Greenberg had taken the opportunity of Droge's approach to them to win a few brownie points by turning Droge in to the District Attorney's Office. They had reported that a corrupt cop was trying to make a deal with them and, prompted by an assistant D.A., who swung into action on the case, agreed to meet with the cop, wearing a wire.

Bruh explained that Droge was also wired, and acting as a Knapp agent. The officer called in his comrades working on the surveillance. IAD had done a thorough job. A dozen or so officers appeared from various vantage points and congregated on the street outside the Green Team Room. Joe Hynes, chief assistant D.A. in Gold's office, later to become district attorney himself, was there, too. Obviously he had not had an opportunity to speak to Gold.

"Well, you may as well call in your men," Bruh was told.

Bruh turned to Cipriani. "Hey, Ralph, come on in."

Meanwhile, Droge, Hantz, and Greenberg continued their conversation, transmitters going on both sides of the table.

Once it was perfectly clear what the situation was, there was little more to do than to tell the three in the Tea Room what was happening, so everybody could go home. One officer showed the ingrained nature of his training by suggesting that they wait until the money changed hands before interrupting the meeting. Everyone looked at him, oddly.

Droge, Hantz, and Greenberg were immersed in their discussion when Bruh, Cipriani, and a couple of IAD cops came in to inform them that they were working at cross-purposes. It took a moment for the facts to sink in. Then the three quietly nodded to each other and went their separate ways.

In their book, Hantz and Greenberg described this incident in somewhat more lurid terms. According to this version, Hantz knocked Droge off his seat, snarling, "Pay the checks, motherfucker! You just bought dinner." The account continued:

As they walked out, every customer in the restaurant got up and followed, leaving unfinished meals on the counters and tables. All went to pay their checks. All were Knapp Commission plants—not only the customers, but the man pushing the broom, the counter man, the grill man, and the waitress. . . . The crowd [of Knapp agents] included representatives of the

Knapp Commission . . . the F.B.I., the Police Commissioner's Confidential Investigating unit . . . and even the Internal Revenue Service.[1]

In fact, the tapes—on both sides, of course—show that everything went quite amicably, and of course there were only two Knapp agents. It was not until the "meet" was over that Batman and Robin saw an opportunity to cause mischief.

Back in my office, I was waiting to hear the results of the surveillance. The phone rang; it was Ralph. "Well, we were right to be suspicious. It was a setup." He gave me the details of the fiasco.

"Nothing to do but go home, I guess," I responded. "Tell everybody good-bye, and I'll see you tomorrow."

A few minutes later the phone rang again, and Cipriani told me that Batman and Robin were making a fuss over the incident and everybody was going back to IAD headquarters at Division Headquarters, in the 84th Precinct station house, in Brooklyn, just south of the Brooklyn Bridge. I told him that I would hang out in the office and that he should call me if he needed me.

About a half-hour later, the phone rang again. It was not Cipriani this time, but Chief Sidney Cooper.

"Hi, cousin," he said sweetly, "you and your girlfriends caused a dilly this time." Sidney never beat around the bush.

"What's the matter?" I asked. "We were after them. They were after us. The cops are going to have a healthy laugh because we looked silly. But why should anyone lose any sleep over it?"

"Cousin, I've got half the brass in the police department heading down here. I've got PBA delegates threatening to call a strike. I've got people saying they want to sue the police commissioner, Whitman Knapp, and you. I've got an assistant district attorney who is talking about locking everybody up. I'm afraid the press has gotten hold of the whole thing. And I still really don't know what the hell went on. Got any suggestions?"

"I think I hear you telling me that you'd appreciate it if I came down to see you."

"Be so kind as to get your ass down here right now, cousin."

By the time I got to the 84th Precinct, the place was really buzzing. People were scurrying around everywhere. Various groups were huddled together, talking excitedly. Hantz and Greenberg were angrily stalking up and down,

---

1. L. H. Whittemore, *The Super Cops: The True Story of the Cops Called Batman and Robin* (New York: Stein and Day, 1973), pp. 346–347.

gesticulating to a group of agitated PBA officials and cops. Our people were trying to be inconspicuous.

I was ushered into Cooper's office, where about a dozen high-ranking police officers and prosecutors sat in a crowded circle of chairs. Cooper was at his desk. As I took a seat and looked around the room, I saw that Dick Condon was there too.

"What are you doing here?" I whispered.

Condon took his pipe out of his mouth. "Just came down to laugh," he said quietly. Actually, he had heard about the incident over the police radio and had hustled down as fast as he could, thinking it might involve Phillips. Once there, he decided to stay.

Cooper had now been filled in on the facts by various people, and he undertook to lay out for the assemblage what apparently had happened.

"As I understand it, you Knapp birds used a cop named Droge to approach these two heroes, Hantz and Greenberg, to set up a meeting where Droge was to give them six hundred dollars in exchange for protection for a phony gambler. You guys had the whole thing wired. Unfortunately for you, Hantz and Greenberg squealed to the Brooklyn District Attorney's Office. Our friend Joe Hynes, Gene Gold's trusted right arm, came along with a bunch of D.A. squad officers to pick up this corrupt cop. Hynes didn't know you guys had filled Gene Gold in on the whole thing because Gold had left the office without telling Hynes about your call. So everybody gathered at the Green Tea Room with both sides wired, until you found out that each other was there. Have I got it about right?"

Condon took his pipe out of his mouth again. "I've seen this on *Get Smart* a number of times," he said, in a voice everyone could hear, "but it was never this funny." The reference, to a contemporary TV series about bumbling spies, made even Sid Cooper smile.

Hantz and Greenberg didn't see anything funny about it. They ranted and raved, making threats to bring charges against everyone. The PBA delegates, seeing a golden opportunity to embarrass the Commission, egged Hantz and Greenberg on, threatening to sue, to strike, and to arouse a furor in the press.

Finally, Cooper calmed everyone down. Hantz and Greenberg may have been energetic, but they weren't too bright, and Cooper succeeded in convincing them that they were part of a broader anti-corruption picture, and that everyone was on the same team, and that we should all pull together, and that everyone makes mistakes, and so on and so on.

With Hantz and Greenberg mollified by Cooper's romancing, even the PBA delegates realized there was nothing of substance to make a fuss over. Two organizations authorized to conduct electronic surveillance had done so on each other. However foolish they may have looked, there was nothing to do now but go home, which we finally all did.

Almost as amusing as the event was the account of it later given by Hantz and Greenberg in their book. Although I had never even spoken to them during the course of the entire evening, they claimed to have arrested me and charged me with "entrapment," only agreeing to free me when Joe Hynes promised I would be indicted. The charge was repeated a number of times as the two hawked their book on various TV and radio talk shows. I didn't have anything to worry about. First of all, "entrapment" is grounds for defending a charge, not bringing one. Secondly, my version of what happened was backed up by the surveillance tapes from both sides, Joe Hynes, and a dozen cops as witnesses. I toyed with the idea of suing the "dynamic duo," donating any recovery to the Patrolmen's Benevolent Association. I never got around to it.

We never did manage to find enough evidence formally to charge Batman and Robin. Neither did IAD nor any of the district attorneys. In fact, the Dynamic Duo worked their way through the byzantine political maze of the police department with such skill that the police commissioner promoted them to the grade of detective.

In his book, *Target Blue*, Robert Daley, who took a year off from being a reporter to serve under Commissioner Murphy as deputy police commissioner in charge of press relations, said that Murphy saw the promotion of Batman and Robin as an opportunity to take headlines away from us. The commissioner got his publicity. Without ever checking with us or, apparently, any other knowledgeable source, Murphy decided not only to promote Hantz and Greenberg but to do so personally in a public ceremony. The two showed their lack of respect for the commissioner and the Department by appearing at the affair resplendent in Batman and Robin costumes. Murphy went ahead with the presentation and awarded the new detectives their gold shields. The film of the event was just right for the opening of *Super Cops*, the movie.

Greenberg, at least, did not go forever unpunished. He quit the job in 1975 and was elected to one term in the State Assembly on the strength of the heroic deeds described in his book and movie. He managed to serve for a year and a half before being indicted and convicted in an $86,000 fraud scheme, for which he was sentenced to two years in federal prison. Later he became involved in an alleged $350,000 insurance scheme in which his business partner was murdered on the eve of his scheduled interview with investigators. Hantz remained on the job, suffering no mishaps other than an arrest on a marijuana charge. He was acquitted on the charge, but "flopped" to patrolman, and retired in 1988.

20

THE EVE OF THE HEARINGS

As the time for the hearings approached—they were set to begin on October 18, 1971—things became increasingly frantic. With only weeks to go, we still had operations going on, but at the same time we were preparing witnesses, collecting documents, and editing tapes.

One fundamental decision we had to make concerned the scope of the hearings. How much of the mass of material we had collected should be presented in the public session, and how much should be left to be treated in our final report.

Phillips would be our lead-off witness. Interspersed with undercover tapes and films, his testimony would dramatically present the life and times of a true "meat eater." He would be supplemented by the testimony of a typical "grass eater," Ed Droge. Then we would lay out the various aspects of what we had found that leant themselves to public presentation: the operations concerning Tank and Slim; George Burkert and the tow-truck payoffs; Waverly Logan; gamblers, hotel operators, and some others. We had more than enough to get and keep public attention. The rest would be detailed in our report.

But what about Frank Serpico, and the charges that led to the creation of the Commission in the first place? Without Serpico, there never would have been a Knapp Commission. It seemed to us that events had overtaken Serpico and his story. Our investigation had succeeded in uncovering a picture of what was currently going on. It was a serious picture of generalized corruption throughout the Department, the existence of which had been generally ignored.

We had the opportunity, by staging a set of hearings that would perhaps be a bit theatrical in spots, to apply some shock therapy that would awaken the public, confront the police brass, and force politicians to stop talking about a "few rotten apples in the barrel." Maybe something could then be done to lift the fog of corruption that enveloped the Department.

However, it might distract from this focus on current conditions if we shifted public attention to the issue of whether Serpico's charges had been promptly addressed four years before. The commissioners debated the issue and, somewhat tentatively, decided to leave Serpico for the final report. For now we had to concentrate on the hearings we were about to present and, specifically, our first witness—Bill Phillips.

The preparation of Phillips was a formidable job. Assisted by Warren Colodner, the young lawyer provided by my law firm, Cahill Gordon, I met with Phillips late into the night—night after night. We went over his proposed testimony, selecting the portions of the tapes we wished to use, preparing transcripts, and sorting through various documents. All the while, Phillips continued to work undercover with Bruh and Cipriani.

Phillips's success in exposing conditions in the Third and Fourth Plainclothes Divisions prompted us to explore last-minute ways of broadening his activities. We discussed with him the possibility of moving him back into plainclothes and of arranging a transfer for him to the First Division in downtown Manhattan. We had a plan, but it needed the cooperation of Commissioner Murphy.

In the waning days of our investigation prior to our hearings, it was no longer a matter of vital necessity that the police commissioner be kept in the dark about what we were doing. We had somewhat compromised the security of our undercover operation anyway, because we found it so useful to work with Dick Condon. Condon, utterly trustworthy himself, had occasionally found it necessary to call on other police officers for help. We were no longer operating in a pristine vacuum of security. So we went to Murphy, explained the Phillips undercover operation to him, and said that we needed his assistance in getting Phillips transferred into plainclothes.

Murphy and Smith were completely willing to help us, and concocted a scheme to do so. They would announce the formation of a group of senior patrolmen to be transferred from uniform into plainclothes, for the ostensible reason of bringing maturity and stability to the plainclothes division. Hopefully, older police officers, closer to retirement, would be less willing to risk their pensions by becoming involved in corruption. It was an idea that Murphy had been thinking about anyway, and implementing it at this point would facilitate getting Phillips into plainclothes, because he could be selected as one of the senior police officers for the program.

While Murphy and the police brass were mulling over the means of putting the new senior plainclothesmen program in place, Phillips took things in his own hands and got himself transferred. He apparently had connections with a borough commander who, incidentally, was one of those about whom rumors of shady behavior had been widespread. Phillips used this connection, and all of a sudden he had been transferred to the First Plainclothes Division in lower Manhattan. Without looking too hard into how he had managed to accomplish this feat, we tried to take advantage of it.

Phillips approached several of the plainclothesmen with the suggestion that a pad be set up for a fictitious gambler, as we had done with "Little Artie." There was an initial meeting of a number of Phillips's new comrades at a restaurant directly across the street from Manhattan District Attorney Frank Hogan's office. The meeting was taped, and it looked as if we had launched another successful operation. There wasn't much time. Our public hearings were to begin shortly. But we might as well continue collecting information, right up to the end.

Phillips's undercover efforts on our behalf had to be squeezed into his normal duties as a police officer. One night, Bruh and Cipriani had gone home while Phillips, with a partner, did a late tour of regular duty. It was morning when the tour was up, and they would have to be on duty early enough to make going home not practicable. Phillips was tired. He didn't feel like spending the night on the lumpy cot that would be provided for him at the precinct. "Tell ya what," he said to his partner, "let's just find a good hotel and sack out. A nice bed, a little room service, and it won't cost us a thing." His partner got very nervous. "We can't do that," he murmured darkly, "the Knapp Commission is watching *all* of the hotels." Phillips decided not to make a fuss and went with his partner back to the precinct, mumbling to himself, "You jerk, the Knapp Commission is two guys—they're friends of mine—and they're home in bed."

Then, at almost the last moment, in the midst of all the pre-hearing frenzy, we were faced with a situation that demanded our attention. It involved, of all things, a cop taking a free meal. But not just an ordinary cop.

From the outset, we had resolved to steer clear of the issue of policemen eating free, even though it was perhaps the most obvious and prevalent manifestation of police corruption in the city. We considered it beneath us to focus on individual police officers dining on the arm, and we said so, publicly.

As a matter of fact, the practice was a symptom—if a minor one—of the pervasive attitude in the Department we hoped to help change. If cops proudly thought of themselves as public servants instead of freeloaders, they would consider themselves above taking petty graft and would be much less likely to be susceptible to the temptations of more serious corruption opportunities. But the notion of a dozen investigators snooping around to canvas the eating habits of 32,000 policemen was, if nothing else, a practical impossibility. And any such efforts would trivialize what we were trying to do.

Of course, when it happened right under our office window, as with the unfortunate patrolmen who pulled their cars up to the back of Gassner's restaurant each day, there wasn't much we could do to avoid taking note. Similarly, included in the encyclopedia of wrongdoing revealed to us by Bill Phillips was what he called his "electric chair meal." He had certain favorite restaurants—only the best—where he would regularly polish off the most sumptuous repast, literally from soup to nuts, liberally lubricated by cocktails, wine, and brandy. Phillips described himself as finishing off such a feast and settling back in his chair, unable to move. "Go ahead, and pull the switch," was the way he described his near-helpless state, "I can't move, anyway." He always left a generous tip. Phillips would be permitted to testify at our public hearings to a toned-down version of this account.

From a broad point of view, when considered in the aggregate, rather than targeting individuals, the issue seemed to be a proper one for our investigation. So, we went through the tedious task of examining hotel and restaurant records to see how widespread and costly it was to let cops eat for nothing. However, if our broad canvass of hotel and restaurant records unearthed a prominent figure, we would have to do something about it, to avoid the accusation that we were covering up for someone influential.

It was in the course of this general examination of records that, just before our hearings were to begin, we came upon a dinner check at an upscale restaurant in the New York Hilton Hotel, for four people in the amount of $84.30. In those days, when a dime was worth roughly what a dollar is today, this was a fairly significant bill. The police officer who hosted the party signed his own name, Albert Seedman, the Department's Chief of Detectives.

Seedman was one of the most powerful individuals in the Department. He headed the elite detective bureau, whose three thousand members worked in squads assigned to each precinct and were charged with solving crimes rather than performing uniformed patrol duty. The detective's gold shield was much coveted. Seedman's personality matched the power of his position. A rugged, assertive man, his rise through the ranks was marked by spectacular and always highly publicized exploits. As a captain, he had once been reprimanded for staging a second "perp walk" (publicly escorting a handcuffed defendant to his court appearance) when news photographers had missed the first one. A cigar-chomping Seedman was photographed pushing up the defendant's face to allow newsmen to get a better view.

The rough-and-tumble image he vigorously courted did not include a reputation for being overly fastidious when it came to cops taking a buck or two. We checked the signature on the bill. It appeared to be his.

We would have to mention the incident in our final report, but we did not want to distract attention from our more serious revelations by raising it in our public hearings. Knowing Pat Murphy's defensiveness—if not paranoia—where we were concerned, and realizing that our inquiries of hotel personnel regarding Seedman's identity might well get back to the commissioner, I thought it best to assure both of them that we were not going to raise Seedman's peccadillo in our hearings. So, Impellizzeri went to tell Seedman, personally, what we had found, make sure that it was his signature on the bill, and assure him that when our hearings began, a few days hence, he need not worry that the meal would be mentioned. I called Murphy to say the same thing.

I did not count on the depth of Murphy's fear and distrust of the Commission. Apparently he did not believe me. According to a lengthy discussion of the incident in then–Deputy Commissioner Robert Daley's book *Target Blue*, our revelation to Murphy triggered a firestorm of speculations, meetings, late-night telephone calls, arguments, decisions, counter-decisions, and general confusion, all premised on the fear that the Commission might have something nefarious in mind, like blindsiding Murphy during the hearings with as-yet unrevealed charges against Seedman. They all frantically wondered what we were going to do.[1] Had anyone asked us, we would have assured them that we had absolutely no interest in bringing out the incident. I suppose they wouldn't have believed us.

Faced with the perceived threat of his chief of detectives being exposed in a public hearing, Murphy decided to move first. Seedman was suspended, and Murphy issued a press release to announce the action. The media, gearing up for our hearings, jumped on the story. "Seedman Relieved of His Command" said the front-page headline of the *Daily News*. Seedman's sin, together with his picture, was emblazoned on the front page of every paper in town. The fact that he was reinstated five days later did little to dampen the initial public impression.

The publicity was not welcome. It was nice that our hearings were being advertised, but we did not need the implication that we would be centering our attention on free meals. Our opponents sneered that this was what they

---

1. See *Target Blue: An Insider's View of the NYPD* (New York: Delacorte, 1973), pp. 275ff.

had been saying all along—our commission had spent a year and a half chasing cops around for accepting freebies.

When Gabe Pressman, who had become something of a friend, interviewed me, on the air, about the Seedman incident, I had an opportunity to even the scales a bit for his accusing me of "McCarthyism" during my maiden appearance on TV. Since we were attempting to minimize the Seedman meal payment, Pressman naturally took the other side. What right, he charged, did we have to play down an act of dishonesty. Corruption was corruption! "Tell me, Gabe," I asked, innocently, "did you tip your mailman last Christmas?" He acknowledged doing so. "That was a federal crime," I said. "It's against the law to give a gratuity to a federal employee for doing his job." Gabe got the point. As a matter of practical fact, some corrupt acts are worse than others, and some are too trivial to spend much time on.

A side result of our uncovering Chief Seedman's dinner party was to provide grist for the humor mill that always was one of the Department's chief characteristics. The word spread throughout the Department that they now had a standard—it was permissible accept free meals—up to $84.30.

Then—just as the hearings were about to start—Phillips's cover was blown. I was at home late one night when I got a call from Dick Condon. It was urgent. He would prefer not to talk to me on my home telephone. I took his number and went out to a street telephone booth to call him back.

Condon's detectives had been maintaining a wiretap on one of the First Division plainclothesmen with whom Phillips was becoming involved. By law, we couldn't tap phones, but Condon could. He had a tape of a wiretapped phone conversation in which one of the plainclothesmen, who had undertaken to do some checks on Phillips, reported back to another cop. Phillips's switch into the First Division had been unusual enough to cause notice. It was hard to understand how someone with Phillips's reputation could have swung the transfer. Moreover, Jimmy Doyle, the East Side PBA delegate whose "sixth sense" Phillips both feared and respected, had a brother in the First Division. Jimmy may have warned him about Phillips. For whatever reason, the First Division plainclothesmen had decided to check Phillips out. Condon's wiretap had picked up what the check revealed. He played the tape for me:

"Hello, Charlie? This is Tony."

"Hi, Tony. What's up?"

"Remember that guy that I was checking on?"

"Yeah, what about him?"

"Think the worst."

There was a long pause. "Shit!" said Charlie, softly.

"I'll tell you more when I see you," said Tony.

"Are you talking from a good phone?" Charlie was dying.

"I don't really know. How about yours?"

"Oh, mine's okay."

"But you can never be sure. I'd better wait until I see you."

"Just one thing, Tony, how long have you—"

"Charlie, I don't think we should talk about this on the phone."

"Yeah, yeah, I know, but I just want to know—"

"Charlie!"

"I know, but . . . "

"CHARLIE!!"

"O.K., O.K. I'll talk to you later."

"Goodnight Charlie."

It was clear that Phillips had been exposed. For the few days remaining before the hearings, he would no longer be safe, much less useful. It was not that he had any real fear of physical retaliation from fellow officers, but he had engaged in undercover work against a score of mob figures. It would not take long for the word to filter back to these gangsters that Phillips had become a Knapp agent, had made cases on them as well as on cops, and was about to testify on television. The people on Pleasant Avenue had ways of dealing with problems like that.

Phillips was not the least bit fazed. He insisted upon continuing his usual routine. In particular, he intended to spend the night before the opening day of the hearing at home. We urged him to find some other place. It would not have been difficult, since he had a girlfriend in town with whom he customarily spent a good deal of time. Phillips was adamant. He wanted to go home so that he could tell his wife what was coming. She knew nothing, he said, about his corrupt activities, much less his work with the Commission. He did not want her to learn about both, for the first time, on television.

We did not have anyone to send with Phillips for protection, and besides, our agents were not armed. But Phillips was. "If anyone comes after me," he said, "I'll take a couple of the pricks with me." He really seemed to find it a complete answer to the prospect of his being in danger that, if he were killed, he would exact simultaneous revenge. He went home for the night.

As it turned out, word about Phillips did not get out that fast. Apparently, the cops who discovered him kept the information to themselves, spreading the word only to their close friends. When Phillips's activities as a Knapp agent were revealed at the hearing, the news came as a bombshell.

Another loose end was Teddy Ratnoff. He had fled to England to avoid Bill Phillips, and returned from self-imposed exile to assist us with the electronics we would need during the hearing. We required a sound system to be heard throughout the hall, and our radio tapes and films had to be edited and prepared for presentation. Teddy undertook to rent the necessary equipment for us, set it up, and handle all the necessary editing. It seemed like a good deal because, uncharacteristically, Teddy did not charge us very much. Teddy's generosity should have been a tip-off that something was fishy. But I missed it.

Later we were to find out that Ratnoff's largesse undoubtedly sprang from something more than friendship. He used the authorization we gave him to act on our behalf to rent equipment for us. Then, when the hearing was over, he apparently stalled the company he had dealt with long enough to steal the rented equipment, pocket the proceeds, and skip town.

With the hearing about to begin, it was now time to tell Ratnoff that Bill Phillips had been cooperating with the Commission. Teddy would be doing the final editing of Phillips's tapes, so he had to know.

Ever since the confrontation in Germaise's office, Ratnoff had lived in terror, thinking that Phillips was coming to kill him. When Teddy showed up at the hearing room, the day before the public hearing was to begin, he came resplendent in a wig, for disguise, and armed with a tire iron, for defense.

As for Phillips, he enjoyed thinking about things he might do to Ratnoff. "Before you tell him that I'm working with you guys, give me just one last chance," he pleaded. "Honest, I've given up the idea of killing him—I just want to make one threatening phone call." Phillips leered. "I want to call him up and say 'Hey, you baldy headed little fuck—do you know who this is?'"

We did not think it would be productive to terrorize our technical expert on the eve of the hearing. Phillips's request was rejected and we took Teddy aside to tell him what was going on. Teddy's amazement equaled his relief.

When the day for the hearing was finally upon us, it became apparent that the press was actually interested in what we were doing. Based on the attention given by the media to other seemingly similar hearings, I had expected only limited coverage. Because the *New York Times* had broken the Serpico story, which led to the creation of the Commission, we could expect from them a discrete, front-page item on the first day of the hearing. After that, I assumed the stories would quickly become smaller and move further back in the paper. I guessed that the other papers would carry us perfunctorily on the inside pages of the paper for a little while, and then drop us entirely. If we were lucky, one or two local TV stations would cover us for the first day or so.

I was wrong. In the days before the hearings opened, we received more and more inquiries from reporters. It became apparent that we would receive quite heavy TV and radio coverage. Then, on the eve of our first day, Channel 13, the local public television station, decided to cover the hearing, live, gavel to gavel.

Live coverage on public television gave us a tremendous publicity boost, but it caused a problem we had not anticipated. In 1971 people still had the quaint notion that obscene language should not be presented in mass media entertainment, particularly to a daytime audience that undoubtedly would include small children. In those days, TV and radio network censors watched closely to see that words presumably offensive to the viewers, and therefore to the sponsors, were not permitted on the air.

The people whose voices were heard in the tape-recorded conversations we intended to play on TV included street cops, junkies, drug dealers, prostitutes, and others whose normal means of expression comprised, from time to time, an off-color phrase or two—to say the least. Our hearing sessions were now to be broadcast live in a time slot normally occupied by, among other things, children's' shows, like the tremendously popular *Sesame Street*.

Since I shared the perhaps old-fashioned view that children should not be exposed to the language of the street, I wrestled with the problem of editing our tapes. It was impossible. The tapes were hard enough to understand, even without cropping them. We had prepared written transcripts to be shown on a screen in the hearing room, and on a TV "crawl" simultaneously with the playing of the tapes. Without them the tapes would have been impossible to understand. We simply did not have the time to redo all the tapes and transcripts. In any event, the offensive expletives were so prevalent—often every other word or even every other syllable—that to remove them would be to make the tapes unintelligible. So we worked it out with the television people that they would warn the viewing public prior to the showing of the tapes that they would be hearing language unfit for children.

We had fully expected, in many of the Commission's activities, to break new ground. But I don't think any of us anticipated that one of our breakthroughs would be the introduction of "dirty" language to daytime television.

21

THE PUBLIC HEARINGS: PHILLIPS'S TESTIMONY

Our public hearings began on October 18, 1971, in the Grand Hall of the Association of the Bar of the City of New York, in Midtown Manhattan. Whit Knapp, as an officer of the association, had gotten permission to use the room. Contrary to the association's established policy, we were permitted to admit the press, including radio and television. It was a magnificent setting. A lofty ceiling, paneled walls decorated with huge imposing paintings of former presidents of the association, and, overall, the ambiance of one of the most prestigious bar associations in the country.

Along one wall of the room was a long, carved wood dais, behind which the commissioners sat, each behind a set of microphones. In the well in front of the dais, small tables faced each other, about thirty feet apart. One of them was for the witness and one for me and whoever was helping me with the questioning, usually Warren Colodner. Seats for spectators were arranged facing the commissioners' platform and circling around on each side of the ends of the room. There was space for several hundred spectators.

When I got to the hall on that first day, I realized how much I had misjudged the interest of the press and the public. The room was overflowing with spectators and swarming with reporters. A long platform had been erected against the wall opposite the commissioners, in order to accommodate television cameras, but it became so crowded that it had to be extended. Channel 13 had set up live cameras, not only on the media platform but on each side of the witness area, facing both the witness and counsel tables. Photographers and cameramen with portable equipment were everywhere.

I thought that we must have hit a "slow news day." Whatever the reason, we were about to get a lot of attention.

Whitman Knapp started the proceedings on a dignified, low-key note by giving a short opening talk on the purposes of the Commission. He concluded:

> In brief, then, it is the purpose of these hearings to inform the public about—and to focus attention upon—the corruption-related problems faced by the Department and its individual officers.

I followed by delivering a specific outline of what we intended to show and the kinds of witnesses we intended to call. As a teaser, I promised that "we will call corrupt police officers" to describe both their own illegal activities and their work as undercover operatives for the Commission. This was the first indication that we claimed to have broken the famed *omertà* among cops. The hint caused a noticeable stir in the room. Momentum began to build.

Then, as the feature event—the only substantive presentation of the day—I laid out the story of the Xaviera Hollander–Teddy Ratnoff–Bill Phillips investigation. I told in detail, with frequent interruptions for audio tapes and films, the story of how Ratnoff had acted as an intermediary between Xaviera Hollander and Phillips and how our agents had carefully taped and sometimes photographed what was happening. When a tape was played, a transcript of what was being said was projected on a large screen, accessible to both the audience and the TV cameras.

Only Xaviera was identified by name. She had no interest in anonymity. In the films of Phillips, one of which showed him actually taking an envelope of money, we had camouflaged his identify by superimposing a black spot on the film to cover his face. He was identified only as "Patrolman P."

I also kept Ratnoff's name out. Ratnoff had insisted that his ability to earn a living, if not his life, would be seriously jeopardized if his identity were revealed in the hearing and, although I suspected that his reservations had more to do with his creditors than his safety, I had promised not to mention his name. So, Ratnoff got a black spot too, and became "Mister T."

It was pretty spectacular stuff. Here was a faceless police officer caught on tape and film actually taking payments from the mysterious, also faceless, emissary of a flamboyant lady of the night, for the purpose, among others, of bribing a judge. The presentation culminated in playing the tape of the dramatic confrontation in Irwin Germaise's office, when "Patrolman P" discovered "Mister T's" secret transmitter. "Patrolman P's" growing rage, as he realized what was happening, and "Mister T's" terrified and desperate attempts to stall long enough for help to arrive came across loud and clear in the hushed hearing room. Then the tape ended with Brian Bruh and Gordon White bursting into Germaise's office. "We want him out of here," Bruh is heard to shout, "I'm from the Knapp Commission." I turned to Whitman Knapp. "That's all for today, Mr. Chairman," I said, quietly. "We will begin hearing testimony from live witnesses tomorrow."

The reaction of the media was tumultuous. The story was a fascinating one and, perhaps because of Phillips's personality as it came across in the taped conversations, the tapes were riveting. We actually had color films of money changing hands. The whole thing was high drama, and the reporters ate it up. The story was the highlight of every local television and radio news show that night and was featured in national news programs as well. Video clips showed the illegal meetings between Ratnoff and Phillips, both of whose faces were obscured by black blobs. The next day, the front page of every newspaper in New York City was dominated by our opening salvo. The headline for every story focused on the suddenly-famous "Patrolman P." The papers carried, prominently, his faceless picture, taking bribes. Who was "Patrolman P"? The press clamored to know. I muttered something about protecting witnesses— an obviously irrelevant point—and refused to give any information.

David Burnham, the *New York Times* reporter who had started the whole thing with his article on Frank Serpico, was particularly persistent. David had been very helpful in the course of our investigation and knew more about what was going on than any other reporter, by a long shot. He started asking some questions that indicated that he had fairly good sources of information. I took him aside and said to him that I would tell him who Patrolman P was—if he promised not to use the information immediately. If he wanted to use it in tomorrow's paper, I told him, he had to find it out himself. Burnham decided to keep hunting.

The next day, testimony began before a packed press corps and a standing-room-only gallery that had swollen in numbers since the first day. Whit Knapp called the hearing to order and directed, "Mr. Armstrong, please call your first witness."

"Mr. Chairman, I call William R. Phillips."

Phillips took the witness chair, looking cool and well-groomed in a gray sports jacket and light orange shirt with a patterned tie. Everyone strained to see him, all but a very few wondering who he was.

"Will you please state your name and occupation," I began.

"William Phillips. I am an officer in the New York City Police Department."

"Yesterday in these hearings we heard about a certain "Patrolman P." Are you that man?"

"Yes, I am."

My little blockbuster was a total success. Spectators gasped, and began loudly to buzz, until Chairman Knapp called for order. Reporters, including David Burnham, looked genuinely stunned. The hook was firmly set. The Knapp Commission had gotten everyone's attention.

As good as he had been as an undercover operative, Phillips was an even better witness. A consummate showman, he knew exactly how he should come across, and played his role perfectly. I had never met anyone who could outdo Phillips as a raconteur. From a bar stool, his wit, energy, and enthusiasm, coupled with a knack for detail and a marvelous way of expressing himself, had made even the most unlikely story seem credible. His steely toughness was somehow melded with a wide-eyed little boy quality that choked off the skepticism of listeners, who found themselves both afraid to question him and hesitant to do so lest they hurt his feelings. As mesmerizing as he was over drinks as an undercover agent at a bar, he was more so on the witness stand. Toning down his normal act by a notch or two, he spoke in quiet, respectful tones. His infectious energy, although subdued, was still very much evident. He spoke with a monotonous ring of authority underlined by an obvious command of facts. There could be no question that he knew exactly what he was talking about. He was utterly believable.

Phillips's credibility rested on another fact—he was telling the truth. He was well aware that we had done our best to check everything he had to say and, more importantly, he was aware that his future depended upon the assumption that nothing he said would ever later turn out to be untrue.

The testimony began with the episode that had been the subject of the first day's hearing, Phillips's dealings with Teddy Ratnoff and Xaviera Hollander. The public had heard the day before about these events from the investigators' prospective; now they heard it from the viewpoint of "Patrolman P." He told about meeting Hollander and putting her on the pad, collecting five hundred dollars a month in order to allow her to operate undisturbed by police. He described the arrangements with Ratnoff whereby the payments were supposedly to protect Xaviera against headquarters' cops as well as division plainclothesmen and precinct patrolmen. He admitted that he put all the money in his own pocket and took his chances that other units would not find out about Xaviera and arrest her.

Phillips next testified about fixing Xaviera's court case, describing how he got Patrolman John Ryder to take $3,500 for "softening" an affidavit to the point where it could not be the basis of a prosecution. Then Phillips told about Xaviera's boyfriend, Larry Dreyfus, who was arrested on a charge of passing on a phony $250,000 check, and on whose behalf Phillips was attempting to arrange to bribe Judge Schweitzer. Phillips described in detail his efforts and those of Irwin Germaise. His testimony was laced with references to events that had been recorded by Teddy Ratnoff.

Phillips testified with great specificity about events, times, and places, but, following our general policy, we had carefully instructed him not to identify anyone by name. Our job was to set forth patterns of corruption, not to nail any particular individual. Since we couldn't, as a practical matter, give people who might be named the right to defend themselves, we did our best to keep names out of the hearing. There were some unavoidable exceptions. Where an individual was inextricably involved in a fact pattern or on a surveillance tape, we could not keep his or her name out. In some cases, as with Xaviera Hollander, who was writing a book about her exploits, the individual could hardly object.

We had explained to Phillips the particular importance of keeping Teddy Ratnoff's name secret. Ratnoff had insisted vehemently that his business would be ruined and he would be in personal danger if he were identified as the go-between in the Hollander–Phillips transactions. Whether for these reasons or some other less savory ones, it was a matter of tremendous importance to Ratnoff, and it was in our interest to keep him happy. I had emphasized the restriction to Phillips. He had solemnly given his agreement.

Then the time came in the narrative for Phillips to describe Teddy for the first time. He said, deliberately, "The go-between was a short, bald, fat man who said he knew Xaviera Hollander." Phillips paused. Looking me squarely in the eye, betraying what I thought was the flicker of a smile, he said evenly, "That man's name was Teddy Ratnoff." He came down hard and clear on the last name.

Phillips had said to me, the night before, when I told him he couldn't make a threatening phone call to Teddy, that he had an ace up his sleeve. This was it. He had given up on the idea of killing Teddy, but he still wanted revenge. I suppose he figured that one mischievous transgression would not be sufficiently serious to jeopardize his deal with us or with the prosecutors.

For a moment, I stared blankly back at Phillips, and then went on with my interrogation. A question or two later, just to nail it down, Phillips again identified Ratnoff by name in a clear, loud, distinct voice. He had taken a small step toward getting even.

Phillips then turned from the events that had ended his life as a corrupt cop to a description of what that life had been like. His father was a cop, and Phillips gravitated to the job at age twenty-seven after a "dead end" position as a tool and die man. In his fourteen years as a policeman, he had worked in most of the precincts in Manhattan in one capacity or another—patrolman, plainclothesman, detective, youth squad member, and cruiser car operator.

Phillips told of being assigned, upon graduation from the Police Academy, to the 108th Precinct, in Queens. Like 90 percent of his young rookie comrades, he was enthusiastic, idealistic, and eager to do well by making good arrests. Gradually, he learned that taking graft—petty at first—was part of the job. He was soon assigned to the 19th Precinct in the Upper East Side of Manhattan. The area was largely one of fashionable apartment buildings and a growing number of bars and restaurants.[1] Phillips told of being treated to his first free meal by a restaurant owner eager to make friends and ensure himself sympathetic treatment in the future. The foot patrolmen customarily got five or ten dollars per night from bars and restaurants. Construction sites yielded about the same.

Phillips explained that there was no way, in this crowded, high-rent area, for construction of a new building to be accomplished legally. There were simply too many regulations to be complied with, involving such things as sidewalk clearance, congestion of materials, trucks blocking traffic, and the like. Police officers got paid for allowing construction to go forward. Phillips said that he didn't even have to ask. All a cop had to do was walk on a construction site and ostentatiously brush imaginary dust from his sleeve. The timekeeper in charge got the message—there was an ordinance against creating the kind of dust that is inevitable on a job site. It would cost a few bucks to avoid a summons.

After a time, Phillips said, he was transferred to a sector car, where payoffs became more regular. Cruising the bars, cabarets, dance halls, and construction sites in his sector, he collected about seventy-five to a hundred dollars per month. The money was shared with his supervising sergeant, and sometimes the precinct captain.

In addition to routine graft, Phillips told of individual payoffs. Phillips said that when a fight occurred in a bar or restaurant, the owner faced a fine, or at least an investigation by the State Liquor Authority. In exchange for anywhere from two to four hundred dollars, the police report of the incident would list it as having taken place on the sidewalk outside the establishment. Phillips told of a particular fight, when he collected two or three hundred dollars for not reporting the fight at all. On another occasion, he took three hundred dollars to drop charges against an inebriated patron who

---

1. It was here that we conducted our "midnight raid," by picking up memo books from cops visiting bars. See chapter 4.

took a punch at him. His testimony ranged over a variety of other forms of graft, including regular Christmas payoffs from business establishments; payments from tow-truck operators for favorable treatment; traffic payoffs; money from diplomats to make their lives even easier than normal; payments from city marshals to allow them to function unimpeded at foreclosures; and payments made by the cops themselves to their clerical men and desk officers in order to get choice assignments. Construction payments were regularized for sector cars, each site paying forty to eighty dollars per month, per site, for each car. Phillips also learned how to check out a fellow officer's reputation for being "on the take" by making a discreet phone call or two.

None of this extracurricular activity prevented Phillips from doing a pretty good job. During his time in the 19th Precinct he made six felony arrests and got five citations.

Perhaps as a reward for good work, Phillips was assigned to a special plainclothes unit in the detective bureau in 1961. He was to undergo six months of training, preparing him to be a detective. Assigned to the Sixth Division, covering three precincts on the Upper East Side of Manhattan and in Harlem, Phillips was now to focus on gambling and vice. This was fertile territory to make money.

The chief sources of revenue were the policy spots sprinkled throughout the area where people played the illegal "numbers" game. Phillips said that a typical spot in Harlem paid $3,500 a month to patrolmen, plainclothesmen, sergeants, and lieutenants, all of whom had their pieces of the pie. It was the plainclothes force that had primary responsibility for enforcing the gambling laws, and they were the ones who made the most money. During his six-month stint as a plainclothesman–in training, Phillips made approximately $6,000. Each member of his sixteen-man group made the same. Phillips's group was accustomed to picking up twenty to fifty dollars per day from each of the policy spots in their area. They were so diligent that they aroused the ire of one gambler, who complained to an inspector at division level that the group was picking up graft every day, when payoffs were supposed to be made only weekly.

The policy people were a colorful group and Phillips named a group of them, all operating around a particular location, which he also identified. "Eggy," "Spanish Dave," the "Bell brothers," "Gimp," "Gout," "Tampa Charlie," and "Crappy" were identified as openly conducting business at specific known locations, each of which Phillips identified. This testimony prompted Commissioner Monserrat to ask, somewhat incredulously, "Can we go and see them operating right now?" Phillips smiled and answered, "Not right now. Fifteen minutes ago, maybe, but not right now."

In addition to regular payoffs, Phillips testified about individual "scores" and identified "Johnny Cigar," "Joe Cuba," "West Indian Dave," and "Spanish Raymon" as having had occasion to pay him as much as five hundred dollars on a particular occasion when, in apparent violation of the overall agreement, Phillips had picked up their "work" and refused to give it back until he was paid.

Phillips closed his first day of testimony by opining that he believed that the situation with respect to gambling enforcement was pretty much the same throughout plainclothes divisions in the city. I ended the questioning for the session by thanking Phillips for his testimony and announcing that he would resume on the following day.

At the conclusion of the testimony, Knapp, acting on impulse, chose to deliver an impromptu, on-the-record summary of what had gone on during the day. The commissioners did not take kindly to what he had done and they called for an immediate, private meeting, right there in a room adjacent to the hearing room, to let Whit know in no uncertain terms that any reactions the commissioners, including him, might have, were to be reserved until the hearings were over. As was his wont, Knapp immediately recognized that he had made a mistake and vowed it would not happen again.

The reaction in the media to Phillips's testimony was even greater than on opening day. Again the story filled the TV news shows and covered the front pages of all of the New York newspapers. A large photograph of a scantily-clad Xaviera Hollander adorned a *Daily News* centerfold comprised entirely of pictures of her, the grouped commissioners, Ratnoff, Phillips, and me. The *Times* ran a front-page story and three full pages on the inside of the paper, giving long excerpts from the testimony and reproductions of the pictures that had been shown. The giant headline covering the front page of the *Post* said it all: "THE PAYOFF—Cop Tells the Whole Story."

As captivating as the testimony was to the general public, there was a special audience for whom it had a particularly intense significance—the cops. I doubt if there was a single precinct house in the city that did not have a television set tuned in to Bill Phillips's testimony. All over town cops watched, with varying degrees of interest. Those who did not know him were amazed that any police officer would publicly testify about such matters. For the many who knew and worked with Phillips, or had done so over the years, the sight of his taking the stand was not only astounding, but—in many cases—personally threatening. Years later, a police officer who had had more than a little involvement with Phillips told me that he had been settling down to watch the hearings with a morning pick-me-up at a bar. When he saw it was Phillips taking the stand, he literally fell off his bar stool, onto the floor.

Many other police officers, glued to their TV sets, had a particular reason to be interested in what Phillips had to say. Would he say anything about them? Had he told the Commission about things that didn't make it on television but for which they would have to answer? One problem for Phillips's nervous former comrades was the fact that we were careful not to indicate the date of the confrontation between Phillips and Ratnoff in Germaise's office, so that no one could tell, within a month or two, when Phillips started working for us. We felt that this ambiguity would help the prosecutors who would follow up on our information. People who had had dealings with Phillips in the months prior to his starting to work for us could never be sure that their conversations were not taped.

In one instance, this deliberate imprecision had tragic consequences. Phillips had told us about a sergeant with whom he had had dealings shortly before he began working with us. In the course of our investigation, we tried to reawaken the relationship. Phillips met with the sergeant, equipped with the usual transmitter. For some reason, the sergeant was wary, and we obtained nothing from the recorded meeting that was incriminating. But the sergeant had no way of knowing, when he saw Phillips testify on television, that the illegal deals he had had with him occurred before Phillips began cooperating. For all he knew, his early guilty conversations were on tape, in the possession of prosecutors. As many police officers have a tendency to do, he assumed the worst. He became more and more morose in the weeks following the hearing. When the IAD investigators approached him in a routine follow-up of Phillips's allegations, he closed the door of the office in which he worked at the 23rd Precinct, took out his service revolver, and killed himself.

Of course, people had a perfect right to resent and disapprove of the hearings if they wanted to, but some people took it too far. The first day of Phillips's testimony was interrupted, about halfway through, by the police security unit, which reported to us that a threat had been received claiming that a bomb was planted somewhere in the hearing room. The hearing was suspended, while we conferred with the security cops to decide what to do. It was simply impracticable to evacuate everyone. Besides, if we did so, we could be certain that the threat would be repeated, continuously. So we waited while the cops made as thorough a search of the room as was possible. When they found nothing, we resumed the testimony and managed to finish that day's hearing safely. During the rest of the hearings, we got only one more bomb threat, a few days later. In a less unnerving expression of disapproval, an enraged spectator charged the dais one day, screaming at Knapp, "You're a liar! You should be indicted for perjury." He was escorted from the room.

In his first day of testimony, Phillips had exploded the myth of the "blue wall of silence." Here was a cop—a thoroughly corrupt one—describing exactly what was going on, and backing it up with tape recordings.

As he took the witness chair for a second day, the air of suspense that had surrounded him was replaced by one of expectancy. Phillips had opened the door to his world and invited the public in for a firsthand look at what police corruption was, and how it worked. His second day's testimony was to be more of the same. He began by describing his experiences with pads in plainclothes units throughout the city. What he said echoed Serpico's description of his experience in 1967 in the Seventh Division in the Bronx. Monthly cash pickups, in regular fixed amounts, were made from gambling locations. Sometimes the pickup duties were delegated to a civilian "service," for 10 percent of the gross take. The money was divided up in equal shares and the value of a "share" differed from division to division, depending on how lucrative the area was. The more open and numerous the gambling establishments, the more opportunity for making money. A new transferee to the division would not get his "nut" until two months had passed, so that he could be checked out. After he left the division, he received two-months' "severance pay."

Phillips went through ten different divisions, giving his view as to what the "nut" was in each. Payments ranged from four hundred to fifteen hundred dollars, and Phillips carefully indicated which figures were based on his firsthand knowledge, and which were based on secondhand information. In one case, he gave an estimate and said he was "not sure." After the hearings, a friend of Whit Knapp's told him that he had been in a hospital bed watching the hearings on television. He shared the room with a cop. Every time Phillips would begin to indicate the amount of the "nut" in a division, the cop would quickly state the figure, as he knew it. Phillips's number was the same every time.

Phillips testified that large gambling operations paid pads of $3,000–3,500 but could get a discount if they ran more than one spot. Smaller operations, who couldn't afford full protection, paid a few officers on separate contracts. If an unprotected gambler got arrested, the arresting officer could write the arrest affidavit in such a way that, if he were offered some money, he could tailor his testimony to get the case thrown out.

Some plainclothesmen, at one point, were assigned to borough commands and had their own pads, often totaling $1,000 per month, per cop. At the time of the hearings, plainclothesmen were no longer assigned at the borough level, but some supervisors still collected payments for themselves. At the precinct level, not all precinct captains were crooked, but all precincts had "bagmen," who were, supposedly or actually, collecting for the captain.

Phillips described the program of which he had recently been a part, in which thirty-five men with ten–fifteen years' experience were assigned to plainclothes, on the theory that concern for their pensions would drive them to withstand temptation, and their doing so would set an example. This was the program that Commissioner Murphy had made available to Phillips, at our request, in order to facilitate his transfer, only to discover that Phillips had already wangled the transfer without help. According to Phillips, the program didn't work out as planned. Of the thirty-five veteran cops, five or six didn't want the transfer because they thought plainclothes duty, and the corruption it entailed, was too risky; four or five were reluctant, but went along; and more than twenty were "elated" at the prospect of making extra money.

Phillips told in blow-by-blow detail of the "sting" he had run for us, involving plainclothesmen in the Third and Fourth Divisions, when he pretended to set up a pad for "Little Artie." He explained that gamblers in such a game could win or lose $15,000 in one night, and it was worthwhile for the operator of such a game to make sure he wouldn't be disturbed. Since the game that "Little Artie" was supposedly considering would operate in both the Third and Fourth Divisions, he arranged for payments of $2,000 or $2,500 each month to each division. Tape recordings of the various conversations captured discussions between Phillips and officers Fanelli and Laviano, the two representatives of the "inner circle" in each of the Third and Fourth Divisions. TV viewers and the hearing audience heard the cops say that there were thirty men in each division and everyone was on the pad. Twenty out of the thirty were described as "dunces" because they were content to sit back and receive their money without coming up with new contacts, but every man took his share. The figures finally quoted, in supposedly setting up the new dice game, were $2,000 for each division each month.

Phillips next told of being transferred to the youth squad in November 1961. With jurisdiction over bowling alleys, pool rooms, dance halls, bars, and other places where teenagers congregated, the opportunities for graft were considerable. Phillips testified that he was assigned to the Manhattan South Youth Squad, with about twenty men, assigned to four different zones. Everyone shared in the pad. Phillips was assigned to a slow zone and got only forty dollars a month. The zone, which included Times Square, had a pad of between one hundred and one hundred fifty dollars a month. Only the lieutenant who commanded the outfit was straight. He threatened to arrest anyone who was caught taking bribes, so they didn't tell him. Even his two sergeants were on the pad. Phillips's friends throughout the Department informed him that conditions in other youth squads were the same as in his own.

Phillips testified that after leaving the youth squad he was transferred to the detective squad in the 17th Precinct, in mid-Manhattan on the East Side. At first he was assigned to a unit operating outside the 17th Precinct itself, covering a broad area on the East Side. Phillips took no graft while assigned to this detail. It was spread too thin to be safe and, besides, he was intent on becoming a full-fledged detective. He made twenty-four felony arrests in the first month and eventually received his gold shield, elevating him from probationary status to being a full-fledged detective. Then, at Christmas time, the clerical man in the 17th Precinct gave him an envelope with three hundred dollars in it. Six months later he was assigned to the 17th Precinct Detective Squad itself. With a touch of pride in his voice he testified about making forty to fifty arrests a year, including one involving an individual who planted a bomb in St. Patrick's Cathedral, and another individual who tried to rob Cardinal Spellman's residence.

Graft in a detective squad, said Phillips, took a different form than in plainclothes. Although the squad had a small pad, twenty or thirty dollars per month, detectives mostly made their money not from individuals making regular payments or in organized pickups from locations, but from individual "scores" in individual cases. Of the twenty-eight men in the squad, ten or twelve were actively corrupt and about 80 percent took something now and then.

Phillips's second day of testimony ended, as had the first, with a promise of more to come.

In Phillips's testimony about payments made to plainclothesmen, we ran into our first example of how our story could get seriously distorted in the press's reporting. The *Times* and the front page of the *New York Post* each carried a map of the City of New York showing the boundaries of the seventeen divisions into which the police department was divided. On the map, next to each division, was the amount of the "nut" that Phillips had ascribed to that division—what each plainclothesman got each month as his share of the graft. The papers hardly mentioned, if at all, the fact that the entire plainclothes contingent for the whole city consisted of only about 450 men out of some 32,000, or that Phillips had not pretended to have firsthand information about each division. It was easy to look at the map and come to the erroneous conclusion that every police officer within the geographical boundaries of each division received a monthly payoff in the amount indicated.

Police organizations sent up a howl. Originally stunned into relative silence by Phillips's revelations, the Commission's opposition began to regroup. Some of the criticisms apparently got to Commissioner Murphy. In the early morning, before the third and final day of Phillips's testimony, Murphy went on the police radio. Speaking to every patrol car and precinct in the City, Murphy mocked Phillips's testimony. "Why should the best police department in the world," he said, "feel it necessary to be defensive over the self-serving statements of a rogue cop?" He urged the listening cops not to be discouraged "because one or another traitor to the uniform that you wear so proudly seeks to justify his own dishonesty by pretending none of you is honest." Murphy was, as usual, careful. Everything he said was literally, if narrowly, true. Phillips was indeed a rogue. That's what his testimony was all about. The clear implication of Murphy's words, however, was that Phillips was not to be believed, and that the conditions he described did not exist. Murphy knew better, but faced with a tirade of resentment and anger by cops who focused only on their feelings that they were being attacked and betrayed, he chose to go with the flow.

The cry of protest from pro-cop quarters was not limited to head-on denials of Phillips's testimony and attacks upon his credibility. We had already heard stories that now became fodder for those who took the seemingly inconsistent positions that "cops aren't corrupt" and "others are corrupt too." One police officer had told us of an alleged incident where a shakedown by an FBI agent had been covered up, to preserve then–FBI Director J. Edgar Hoover's oft-repeated boast that there never had been a corrupt FBI agent. Another cop said to us that the best anti-corruption device would be to "issue the firemen skin-tight boots."

In answer to such comments, we chose to defer, saying that we had no jurisdiction to do anything but look at police, and that was quite enough.

The second day of Phillips's testimony brought another hostile reaction of a more ominous kind. In order to avoid reporters, Knapp and I were accustomed to exiting the hearing room, at the end of the day, by means of a back route, emerging on the street behind the Bar Association building. The police informed us that a threat had been telephoned to them, indicating that the caller had a familiarity with our route and an intention to shoot Whit.

The Department unit assigned to security at the hearings was concerned. "If anything happened to you," said the commander of the unit, "we would be really embarrassed." Whit assured them that he had no desire to cause them embarrassment. For the rest of the hearings, and some time thereafter, Whit was given 'round-the-clock protection, in the form of two detectives who went with him everywhere.

I too was the target of a few threats. One evening, when my wife Joan picked up the phone at home, the caller was menacing and specific. "You tell that Jew-bastard that we're going to shoot him when he gets off the train tonight," he snarled. Joan's defining sense of humor remained unquenched, even under such frightening circumstances. She reported to me that she wasn't really worried, because, as she told me, "You're not Jewish and you took your car to work."

It may have been that the caller knew more than we did. Four years later, my seventy-five-year-old father revealed to me—for the first time—that his name was not really Armstrong . . . but Aronstein. Born in Brooklyn in 1900, he had moved to Manhattan as a young man and changed his name in order to get a job as a copy-boy in his chosen field, advertising, then virtually all Christian. Over the years, he and my Irish-Catholic mother had visited his Brooklyn relatives often, telling my sisters and me that they were going for a drive in the country. Once the ice that had been formed in another age— when survival sometimes depended on such decisions—was broken, we eventually had warm reunions of the Armstrong-Aronstein clans. No one ever shot anybody.

Taking the witness chair for the third day, Phillips continued telling, in greater detail, his account of his experiences as a detective. Although the monthly pad was insignificant, collections got well organized at Christmas time in the form of a list of givers that was ten or fifteen legal-sized pages long. Each detective got about four hundred dollars, and could supplement that, individually, by up to about two hundred dollars, by contacting people for whom he had done personal favors. The major source for illegal money was from "scores" extracted in individual circumstances, as they arose. Phillips told of his first score, occurring on his first day at the 17th Precinct squad. Acting on a complaint about a bookmaker, Phillips and two partners found policy records in the subject's car. The bookie suggested that he might buy his way out, and they asked for $1,000 each. The two other experienced cops told Phillips that the lieutenant had to be cut in. The lieutenant gave each detective one hundred dollars and kept the rest for himself. He had a rule: "If you make a score, you can cut me short, but don't cut me out." After that, Phillips said, he always cut the lieutenant in, but took his share first.

On another occasion, Phillips falsely told a hood, accused of a serious assault, that he had been identified in a lineup. In fact, witnesses had been too frightened to say anything, and the man went free. Phillips collected $3,000 for supposedly fixing the case. He told the lieutenant that he had collected $1,000, giving him his share—$300. Another time, Phillips collected five hundred dollars from an alleged assailant of a woman. This time, he happened to tell the lieutenant the truth about how much he had collected. It was a good thing, because the incident was actually a test of Phillips's loyalty. The assailant had borrowed three hundred of the five hundred dollars from the lieutenant himself.

Phillips testified to a number of other "scores" made by others as well as himself, some of which were significant. In one investigation of three subjects who ran a newsstand and got suspended sentences on charges of possession of untaxed cigarettes, two detectives and the bosses told Phillips that they split a $10,000 score.

Phillips testified that, in addition to money he had collected, he had enjoyed a comfortable lifestyle. He stayed, gratis, in premier hotels whenever he wished. At least once or twice a week he would be treated, at one of the expensive restaurants in his East Side precinct—one of his "electric chair meals."

In his testimony, Phillips touched upon another source of illegal money for cops—other cops. Clerical men, of course, got money for handing out lucrative assignments. Money also went to the fingerprint bureau, the bridgeman in court, who called cases sooner for those who gave him money, the borough commander, the district commander, and, supposedly, the chief of detectives.

Among the ways that the detective squad was different from the plainclothes division, or normal patrolman, was their relative silence about what they were doing. Since payments were not part of a systemic organized collection effort, but rather arose on an individual basis, detectives did not freely discuss them. You discussed scores you had made with those you could trust. As to others, it was none of their business. They would probably want a share.

Phillips told how in August 1965 he was unexpectedly demoted from the detective squad. He was working night duty when he went into a bar and grill with his partner and ordered a couple of soft drinks. The bartender was a friend of Phillips. Phillips's partner recognized two men in civilian clothes at the end of the bar as cops, and Phillips warned the bartender. Phillips and his partner left, and one of the two cops followed. The bartender then went to the other one and told him that his pal was a policeman, not realizing that the man he was warning was also a cop. Phillips and his partner were dropped from the Detective Division the next day, and he was assigned to the 25th Precinct.

Having been "flopped" to the status of patrolman, Phillips deliberately shied away from illegal activities in the 25th Precinct for about a year. He kept his eyes open, however. The 25th Precinct was a high-crime precinct with a lot of gambling activity. Phillips got to know the various gamblers, and he spiced his testimony simply by mentioning their nicknames, some of which had come up before: "Dickie," "Chico," "the Fat Man," "Farby," "the Fish," "Muzzi," and "Louie Fats."

Slipping the roll call man ten dollars to "take care" of him, Phillips was otherwise content to watch the illegal activities from the sidelines for a change. Patrolmen who were interested in making money would pay (five dollars per assignment on average) to have themselves assigned to key gambling areas around the first of the month when the payments were made. You could earn about a hundred fifty a month that way. Bodegas—small, usually Hispanic grocery stores—would pay two to three dollars each Sunday in order to stay open in violation of the blue laws, and that was another source of cash. Apparently there was no trouble getting cops in the 25th Precinct to work on Sundays. (If there were no foot patrolmen around, the man in the sector car would collect the bribes, often spending much of his day picking up from as many as forty-five different bodegas in a sector.)

After about a year, Phillips decided he wanted to get back into the illegal operations and let it be known that he wanted an assignment to a sector car. It was understood that, upon his assignment, he would pay the roll call man thirty dollars. Once assigned to a car, Phillips began scoring gamblers he knew, putting them on his own private pad. He and his partner together eventually made over four hundred dollars every month, including about one hundred to one hundred fifty dollars from gamblers, thirty or forty dollars from construction sites, and the rest from bodegas, crap games, card games, and social clubs. One establishment paid ten dollars each night of each weekend to the sector car to be allowed to operate as a cabaret without a license, and an additional fifteen dollars went to the sergeant. There was a "gambling car" at that time, and it was the responsibility of the three patrolmen and one lieutenant assigned to that car to lock up gamblers who were operating in the precinct. The gambling car pad amounted to six hundred dollars per month for each patrolman and nine hundred dollars for the lieutenant. Phillips said that, at the time he left the 25th Precinct a month before, all the sector cars in his sector were taking money, and all the men regularly assigned to the cars were involved.

Phillips testified that, in the last year or so, he had noticed a change in the Department. Corruption was not as widespread as he had known in the past. He said that there were some cops who actually did not participate in illegal activities. As for himself, some things were different, too. If he rode with a young cop, he wouldn't take bribes, in order not to expose the rookie to things that might get him into trouble. Phillips had a talk with his own partner, advising him not to get involved in graft because pressure from federal and police sources was getting too great.

Change was coming slowly, however. Out of four lieutenants in the 25th Precinct, Phillips only knew of one who definitely never took money (he was known to be honest, and "a clear sign of that was that he brought his own lunch to work"). Phillips had evidence on one of the lieutenants and information regarding the other two that suggested that they, too, were on the take. Three out of the twelve or fifteen sergeants would take money, but just a few years before it would have been only three who *wouldn't*. Both captains were straight, even though there were rumors that a captain's "bagman" still collected from gamblers, saying the payoffs were for the captain.

Phillips ended his testimony midway through the Commission's fourth session, by testifying about a number of miscellaneous incidents of corruption, including one involving a PBA delegate and the use of illegal wiretaps to uncover potential sources of shakedowns.

He was followed by Commission agent Ralph Cipriani, telling about various Commission surveillances involving gambling locations. Then came the testimony of a seventy-eight-year-old small-time policy "collector" in the numbers business. A self-described "small operator," Everett Cooper had been plying his trade for forty years. He told of regular payoffs, claiming to have occasionally needed to pay them off with his Social Security checks. He described one time when he had been "flaked" by two cops who needed an "accommodation" arrest. He had no policy slips on him, so the cops supplied him with some and then arrested him. Under the supervision of our agents, Cooper had made one payoff, of twenty-five dollars, as a wired-up operative.

As for Phillips, when he finished his testimony, he moved smoothly into the task of transforming his work for the Commission into evidence for criminal cases, the successful prosecution of which would be the basis of whatever deal he could make with the government. He fit right in with the group, headed by Assistant U.S. Attorney Mike Shaw, which was focusing on police corruption and had already been working on the cases being generated by Bob Leuci.

As always, Phillips knew what he had to do. When Shaw later commented on a particularly valuable contribution Phillips had made by saying, "That will be a real feather in your cap," Phillips responded, "I don't need a feather, I need a whole fucking sombrero."

22

THE PUBLIC HEARINGS: DROGE, LOGAN, TANK AND SLIM, BURKERT, ETC.

When Phillips finished testifying, the reaction among members of the New York City Police Department who were watching was one of profound relief. They had been taking hard blows for three days, from a renegade who had broken the sacred code of silence. Now, hopefully, it was over.

But it was not. The Commission's next major witness, the following day, was another cop, telling about the corruption of which he had been a part—Edward Droge.

Droge offered a dramatic contrast to the lead-off witness. Phillips's story, reflecting his career, had been a parade of spectaculars, portraying corruption at its worst. A mild, unprepossessing man, Droge had been for the most part a good, even outstanding, cop. Indeed, he had received medals for bravery. The *Daily News* headline the next morning captured the irony perfectly: "Hero Cop: Graft Is Just a Way of Life."

The corruption about which Droge testified was the garden variety, everyday sort of graft that was participated in by almost everyone having a street job in the Department. Not nearly as spectacular as Phillips's testimony, Droge's story was perhaps even more relevant. Here was a "grass eater," one of the 80 percent of the Department whom Frank Serpico had said "wished they were honest." Our hope was that Serpico was right and that ways could be found to let cops like Ed Droge live and serve honestly, as they wanted to. For now, in the hearings, he was another crack in the "blue wall of silence," another corrupt cop—talking.

I led Droge methodically through his carefully prepared testimony. He was firm, precise, and credible, telling about various incidents contributing to the pervasive atmosphere of graft that had led him to recoil at the notion that his own son might want to become a cop.

Of course, even the most carefully prepared testimony always has a surprise or two. At one point Droge was testifying about the gambler in the 80th Precinct who would make his payment to the sector car by throwing a bunch of folded-up bills into the car window and how, on one occasion, the bills went in one open window and out the other. Concentrating on the irregular nature of the payment, with no awareness of what must have seemed a dreadful attempt at humor, I asked if this method of payment was done on a "catch-as-catch-can" basis. The audience in the hearing room groaned.

According to plan, I saved for last the details of the events that led Droge to be testifying—his acceptance of a bribe, and our confronting him with what he had done. He described the arrest, and his agreeing to accept three hundred dollars for not appearing at a court session that would, he knew, occur after he had already gone to California. He then testified about what happened next:

Q: Was the money actually paid?

A: Two hundred dollars of the three hundred dollars was paid.

Q: And then you, following that, you carried out your plan to go out to California and started school?

A: Yes, I did. I went to California. And I enrolled in college out there that I had been accepted to. And—

Q: And your family was here?

A: Yes, that's correct.

Q: And you planned to go out there and start on your college education and join them when you could?

A: That's correct.

Q: And then on September 15 you were contacted by telephone by us and someone played you a tape recording; is that correct?

A: That's correct.

Q: And what was that tape recording?

A: That tape was one of the conversations I had with the defendant in that narcotics misdemeanor case in which I agreed to accept the money.

Q: And I spoke to you on the telephone?

A: That's right.

Q: And you agreed to come back?

A: Yes, that's right.

According to the prepared script, this was to be the last question and answer. On the spur of the moment, I added two questions that we had not rehearsed:

Q: Officer Droge, do you realize now what you stand to lose for taking the two hundred dollars?
A: Yes, I do, sir.

I paused, looking into his eyes for a moment or two.

Q: Do you think it was worth it?

Tears welled up in his eyes, and his voice broke slightly.

A: No way in the world.

"I have no further questions," I said.

I was later informed that the tape of this snippet of testimony was played for years in the Police Academy, to drive home to recruits the need to remain straight.

Droge testified for one whole session, on a Friday. We spent the weekend preparing for the next week's testimony and dealing with the growing firestorm of press reaction. Reporters came from all over. We even had TV crews from England, France, and Italy. Channel 13, which had been showing the hearings live and repeating the full tape each night, re-ran the whole week of hearings on Saturday and Sunday. They had tried to suspend coverage after Phillips's testimony, on grounds of cost, but it created such a public furor that, with the aid of some specially contributed funds, they quickly resumed full coverage. Newspapers and magazines ran reviews of the testimony, and we were approached by all sorts of people wanting to do specials of one kind or another. *Newsweek* had sent a fledgling reporter named Barbara Davidson to cover what her editors anticipated would be a one- or two-day story. Now Davidson came to us and asked if we could make special arrangements for *Newsweek*'s photographers early in the second week because *Newsweek* wanted to do a cover story—with my picture on the cover. As it turned out, I was not to enjoy that particular distinction. Pictures were taken of me and my family and the story prepared, but then it happened that after twenty-two years of Communist China being kept out of the United Nations, it was admitted during "my" week. I ended up being bumped from the *Newsweek* cover by Mao Tse-tung.

As the hearing became increasingly more of a media event, criticism was heating up from expected quarters. The PBA issued statement after statement attacking what it described as "McCarthyism" and a "circus" atmosphere. PBA President Ed Kiernan said, on a local TV show: "How do you, in good conscience, believe a liar [Phillips] who's admitted that he's lied about everything he's done in his whole time in the police department, and now, because he's on the hook, is lying some more? . . . This isn't an investigation or an interrogation. This is a show boat thing . . . a charade."

Councilman Theodore Silverman, speaking for nine members of the City Council, whose approval had been necessary to our creation, called for a council investigation of the Commission. "These hearings should have been held with dignity," he proclaimed. " . . . An entire police department is being sunk by the infamous testimony of a handful of unsavory characters. . . . Lindsay plays the tune, Whitman Knapp sings the lyrics, and the taxpayers of this city pay for this Roman holiday." The New York Civil Liberties Union, usually ready to string up a cop on any pretext, joined in, calling the hearings a "civil liberties disaster." Some news commentators said much of the same.

Such criticism was inevitable. We were necessarily painting with a broad brush, and we were not as precise in our charges as would have been required in a judicial proceeding. We knew the press would not pick up on fine distinctions, but would report the testimony more spectacularly than we intended. As for the rowdy boisterousness of the press, we would have preferred a more organized and dignified atmosphere, but we really could not complain. Our whole purpose was to attract media coverage about conditions in the Department. We could not very well deliberately titillate and stir up reporters and then complain too much if they went somewhat overboard in responding.

Our next witness, after Droge, was yet another police officer, Waverly Logan. He, of course, had no undercover tapes to present, having first come to our attention when he appeared on local television. He had only his story to tell.

We had spent a lot of time preparing Logan. As a result, he came across not in the somewhat confused, unimpressive way he had in his television appearance. The TV people had not had time to help him organize what he had to say. Now he told the story of his experiences in a resolute and convincing manner. He recounted, in particular, the shame of the PEP Squad, an elite unit formed to fight the narcotics trade in minority communities, which turned instead to profiting from the illegal business they were supposed to help extinguish.

Logan was the third corrupt police officer to testify at our hearings—an effective rebuttal of the supposed irrefutable truth that cops don't talk.

Following Logan, the exploits of Tank and Slim, our two young drug addict–operatives, were presented through the testimony of Ralph Cipriani, who, with Brian Bruh, had been one of the two agents able to stay with us until the very end of our investigation. An ex–FBI agent and attorney, Cipriani was handsomely turned out in a dark suit and tie. He spoke with the authoritative self-assurance of a real professional.

Cipriani's testimony was not subject to attack on the grounds of questionable credibility. He told of the actual observations of agents, backed up by tape recordings and films, of an entire group of police officers busily engaged in the routine business of commissioning the thefts of goods, from cigarettes to mini-bikes, to be paid for with narcotics. The brazen nature of the operation was manifest, as cops talked openly about their "purchases" and shuttled contraband in and out of the precinct house without apparent concern. Cipriani revealed that while most of the merchandise exchanged for narcotics was liquor or cigarettes, more substantial items were "ordered," and in one instance the transaction involved a gun. The revelations also had their lighter side. Cipriani described the cigarette transaction when Tank asked the cop, "What about Winstons?" and the cop answered, "No, I don't know anybody that smokes Winstons." On another occasion, Tank and a cop got mixed about whether they were dealing with "sherry herring" or "Cherry Heering." "If you're going to be a dealer in liquors," said the cop, "you have to know your stuff." One cop was reported delivering Tank and Slim a handwritten list specifying the brands he wanted stolen for his daughter's wedding shower— "two cases of beer, two Jack Daniels, two Harvey's Bristol Cream."

Cipriani told of a time when he was transporting Tank and Slim in a pickup truck, and pulled up flush behind the police car of the cop with whom the boys were to deal: "There we were, two white guys driving, and our black informant hops out of the truck, makes his trade, and hops back in with us. All the cop had to do was look in the rearview mirror to see something was wrong. But we just drove off."

Of particular amusement to the attendees at the hearing was the tape where Tank was emphatically—and falsely—assured that the narcotics he was receiving were genuine. The cop paused for breath, and in the momentary lull that followed, the car radio was heard in the background, winding up a singing advertisement for Coca-Cola with musical assurance, "It's the real thing."

Cipriani finished his testimony by summarizing the results of the three weeks' investigation. Tank and Slim had ten different meetings with police officers, gathering information that made it clear that everyone in the Sixth Group was involved, to some degree or another, in the drugs-for-goods operation. Specific surveillances were made of about twenty-five of the more than seventy officers in the group. Eight of them were caught on tape.

Our next witness was the tow-truck operator, George Burkert. In the course of preparing Burkert for his testimony, we had developed strong reservations that almost led us not to call him at all. He exhibited the same lack of confidence that had caused us so much difficulty at first in using him as an undercover operative. Like the proverbial "deer in the headlights," he froze as he was being coached. His voice kept dropping in volume, his eyes shifted nervously from side to side, he lost his train of thought, and appeared baffled by questions that we had already been over a dozen times. Perhaps, we speculated, he should testify only for the extremely limited purpose of identifying the various tape recordings we had made with him. It did not seem wise to trust him with presenting a general narrative about his experiences. For better or worse, we decided to cross our fingers and go with letting him tell, as best he could, his whole story.

I didn't see Burkert on the day of his testimony until I called his name and he walked—no, rather strode—into the hearing room and up to the witness chair. Resplendent in a lavender sports shirt, he was clear-eyed, erect, and oozed a kind of comfortable self-confidence. I had always thought his Van Dyke beard and small moustache to be a bit scruffy. Now they were trimmed and jaunty. A little bit taken aback, I started to question him. He immediately made it apparent that his transformation had not been one merely of dress and bearing. In a firm, clear voice he crisply identified himself and began to tell his story. Needing from me only a perfunctory cue now and then, he spun his tale of automobile wrecks, greedy cops, and payoffs. Not only was he effective, but he was funny. Telling of a station-house conversation after he and a passenger in his vehicle had been arrested on one occasion, Burkert said: "The officer had reached in his pocket and pulled out something that looked like a cigarette. He said to us: 'Listen. I found this in the back seat of the police car. Which one of you does it belong to?' The cop said it was marijuana. Well, I looked at my friend and he smiled at me and both of us smiled and started laughing. I said to him [the cop], 'Officer, if you found it in your car you better tell your partner to stop smoking.'"

When he got to the story that had led him to us in the first place, the shakedown by officers who gave him thirteen tickets in a twenty-block span, Burkert really got going, mocking the absurdity of a supposed wild chase through the crowded streets of East Side Manhattan, stopping every block or two to issue a ticket. Showing a genuine comic flair, Burkert described the events of the evening to an appreciative hearing room audience, which got more responsive as he warmed to his work. Spectators had become accustomed to hearing depressing acts of corruption recounted by long-faced witnesses. Burkert provided a new element: humor. He made a joke of his misfortunes, and the spectators ate it up.

When his testimony was over, Burkert strode from the hearing room as confidently as he had entered. He was an instant hero. The media, perhaps a little surfeited with grim tales of police crime, leapt to embrace the notion that graft could have its lighter side. Burkert's testimony was emblazoned over TV, radio, and the newspapers. The *New York Times*'s headline read "Underdog Cheered at Knapp Inquiry." Our shy, reluctant witness had become a swashbuckling media attraction.

As it turned out, we perhaps should have been more cautious. Burkert's derisive tale of the improbability of policemen careening down the street after him turned out to be somewhat questionable. The testimony conflicted with the observations of several eyewitnesses who, hearing it on television, came forward to tell a different story. A doorman, an elevator operator, and two businessmen said they actually saw the chase. Since by that time Burkert had repeated the testimony before a federal grand jury, he was indicted for perjury and ultimately sentenced to six months in jail.

Although the hearings hardly needed more livening up, we were all treated to a moment of slapstick comedy one morning, when the chair under 275-lb. Commission member John Sprizzo gave way. It crashed to the ground and Sprizzo disappeared behind the commissioners' table. Fortunately unhurt, he struggled to his feet, got another chair, and signaled us to resume where we had left off.

With George Burkert's testimony, I felt that we had pretty well covered all of the necessary aspects of a hearing. It had been spectacular and compelling enough to get the public's attention. We had suspense, drama, surprise, and now, with Burkert, comic relief. The final two days of the hearing were spent in fairly routine, but important, testimony from our agents and some businessmen, mostly regarding graft in the hotel and construction businesses in New York City.

Our agents and several industry representatives testified about regular organized accommodations given to police officers by hotels in the form of free meals and free rooms. Our compilation of these figures was possible because hotels actually kept lists of police officers who used their facilities, requiring cops to sign bills they were not obliged to pay. This practice led to the scandal, just before the hearings began, that overtook Chief of Detectives Albert Seedman.

The records of one large hotel showed $4,662.77 in free meals to cops in a five-month period. Another hotel provided 168 free rooms to 142 different officers during the same period. None of these "freebees" was reported by the cops as a legitimate expense. Of course no effort was made to check the accuracy of claimed identities, so signatures of "Mickey Mouse," "Whitman Knapp," "Michael Armstrong," and the like abounded.

Commission agent Colonel Mark Hanson, dapper, trim, prematurely white-haired, retired from Army Intelligence, testified that his review of selected records of seven hotels over a five-month period indicated the total payoffs to cops to be more than $60,000.

A somewhat monotonous recitation of compilations made by various hotels and restaurants—the very existence of which demonstrated how routine this sort of minor graft had become—was broken by one last moment of drama created by some unexpected testimony. As part of the mound of exhibits introduced to show hotel and restaurant graft, we offered the 1970 Christmas gratuity list prepared by the Statler Hilton Hotel. It listed amounts for specific police officers "eligible" for twenty-five-dollar Christmas gifts—a total of $335. Hanson testified that lists like this represented proposed, not actual, gifts and stated that we had no idea whether actual payments were made. Further, we had blacked out any actual names on the lists before displaying blow-ups on the large screen provided for viewing on TV and by the spectators at the hearing. We failed to realize that with the back-lighting equipment we used to throw the image on the screen, some of the names that had been blacked out would shine through and could be read clearly. One of these was Aaron Mazen, then a lieutenant of detectives in the 14th Precinct.

Mazen had a reputation for being obsessively honest, and he did not at all appreciate seeing his name on pictures of the blown-up list that appeared on television and again in the newspapers. Enraged, he presented himself the next morning at the hearing room in the Association of the Bar. Confronting me during a break, he aggressively introduced himself, and pointed out that we had no evidence that he ever took a penny. Indeed, we had not. When I embarrassedly protested that, however ineffectively, we had made an attempt to black out his name, he retorted that in any event the supposedly blacked-out name was identified as a lieutenant in the 14th Precinct Detective Squad, and Mazen was the only lieutenant in his outfit.

I apologized and asked him what he wanted us to do. Whit Knapp had publicly offered anyone who felt aggrieved by our proceedings the opportunity of testifying, but no one had come forward, and we didn't really expect anyone to do so. When Mazen said that he wanted to testify publicly in rebuttal, he was astounded when I quickly agreed, and the commissioners backed me up. Spurred on by many of his colleagues, Mazen apparently didn't think we would honor Whit's promise. He was preparing himself to launch in the media a double-barreled public attack on the Commission for defaming him and for refusing to let him tell his side. Instead, he told his story on TV, complete with a public apology from me. The incident came to a close with Mazen concluding his statement by thanking the Commission for treating him "in this fair manner."

Another of our agents, Al Alessi, testified about our investigation into police graft in the construction industry. Alessi was the one ex–police officer among our agents. He had served on the Detective Squad of Manhattan District Attorney Frank Hogan. Tall, angular, with graying hair and an impressively steely demeanor, Alessi summarized interviews and testimony given in executive session by contractors, job superintendents, foremen, and others in the construction business, none of whom was willing to testify publicly.

Alessi told of pervasive and regularized payoffs to avoid harassment for inevitable violations of the tangle of regulations governing building in New York City.

H. Earl Fullilove, Chairman of the Board of Governors of the Building Trades Employers Association also testified, explaining why actual builders declined to do so: "Our members feel that . . . it's a tremendous burden on a member to become a hero for a day and then suffer the consequential individual harassment."

Fullilove zeroed in on the laws that made graft so tempting to cops entrusted with enforcing them: "It is virtually impossible for a builder to erect a building within the City of New York and comply with every statute and ordinance in connection with the work. In short, many of the statutes and rules and regulations are not only unrealistic but lead to the temptation for corruption."

A few more "clean-up" witnesses were called, laying out other aspects of what we had found in our investigations. We were satisfied that we had managed to amass convincing and dramatic evidence showing conditions of corruption in the Department. How far we had come was demonstrated by the fact that we wound up not having time to present the story of our very first success—the "meat robbery" in the West Village. Agent Jim Donovan was prepped to testify about the incident, but scheduling constraints forced us to scrub his appearance at the last minute. Time was tight, and the public had had enough.

The hearing ended with testimony from Captain Dan McGowan. He had been the first to help us, by directing us to the files buried in the Intelligence Division, and had cooperated with us throughout. His testimony was a call to the Department to straighten itself out:

[I would like to] contribute in some small measure to rooting out the weaknesses in the system that permit fine young men with high ideals to come into the Department and within a few years be involved in corruptive practices.

I've spent over half of my life in the police department, I'm the son of a man who spent thirty-nine years in the police department. I want both of us to look back on that service with honor.

And, last, I'm a resident and a citizen of this city. I have a vested interest that the quality of life in this city should become somewhat better, and that my wife and my children and my grandchild, together with all citizens, can point to the police department and truly say, 'It's the finest.'

On that note, the hearings came to an end.

There was to be one more display of fireworks. Whit Knapp had scheduled one of our Yale Club breakfast meetings with Commissioner Murphy and First Deputy Commissioner Bill Smith for the week following the hearings. We needed to discuss with them our cooperation with the Department in pulling together the material we had collected. The breakfast was to be on a Thursday, and Whit called Murphy on Monday morning to confirm. The two had a short chat and Whit went about his business.

Murphy did not bother to tell Knapp what was even then appearing in headlines in the first editions of the afternoon papers. "Murphy Suspends Knapp Cops" was the substance of the headline in each tabloid. Murphy had held a press conference, announcing that Phillips and Droge had been suspended, without pay.

Both officers, in the week or so since they testified, had been assigned to the Department's Internal Affairs Division. Phillips was working night and day with both federal and local prosecutors, collecting and organizing the evidence they were planning to use in scores of indictments arising out of his testimony. Droge, having less to offer in the way of testimony about criminal behavior, was cooling his heels, looking through files in the Intelligence Section. Now both officers were suddenly deprived not only of their guns and badges but, most importantly, their paychecks.

In his book, *Target Blue*, Deputy Police Commissioner John Daley later ascribed Murphy's action to a desire to assert his authority and show the rank and file that he was tough. Whatever the reason, Knapp took it as a personal affront. After all, he had been talking to Murphy that very morning, and the police commissioner had not seen fit to do him the courtesy of informing him what was about to happen.

Furious, Knapp called up Murphy and demanded an explanation. Murphy had little to say in justification of his action and nothing at all about failing to inform Whit that morning. Whit hung up on him.

While Knapp was talking to Murphy, I put in calls to Droge and Phillips. Droge, as usual, was philosophical and resigned. His life had been thoroughly shattered when Joe Foley played him the tape that brought his hopes and ambitions to an end. He had not been able to begin picking up the pieces, and could not yet bring himself to hope for much of anything. To him, Murphy's taking away his pay was just another disaster to be endured.

Phillips, on the other hand, was not going down without a fight. "How do they expect me to eat?" he bellowed. "I'm working my ass off for these bastards, around the clock! What do they want me to do—get a night job, driving a bus? I can't—I'm working for them at night!" Phillips ranted that this was just another example of something he had said all along: Murphy and the City law enforcement establishment were out to get him, and to send a message to anyone who might be tempted to testify against cops. The only way for Phillips to retaliate was to stop cooperating. "No pay, no work," he declared. "What do those sons of bitches think I am? From now on, I'm not lifting a goddamn finger for the locals, I'll only work with the Feds."

I assured Phillips that the Commission was not going to take Murphy's action lying down. He was skeptical.

To deal with the matter, Knapp called a special meeting of the Commission for the following morning at eight o'clock in Cy Vance's office. Whit invited the police commissioner and anyone he wished to bring with him. Murphy said that he would be there, with First Deputy Commissioner Bill Smith and Internal Affairs Division Chief Sidney Cooper.

Cy Vance's office was a wonderful place to meet someone you wanted to impress. On a lofty floor in One Battery Park Plaza, overlooking New York Harbor, it was a huge corner office, beautifully appointed, with a magnificent view of Battery Park, the Statue of Liberty, the Verrazano Bridge, and the entire harbor for background. All of the commissioners showed up for the meeting except Frank Thomas, who was out of the country. We arranged ourselves so as to leave one couch available, on which our three visitors could sit, facing us—and the view.

Murphy, Smith, and Cooper came in and sat down. With hardly a hello, Knapp began in a voice that was almost a shout, "Let's get one thing straight! Bill Phillips and Ed Droge told the truth, and you know it—and you know it—and you know it!" His voice rose in volume as he stabbed his finger toward each of the three in turn. Focusing his attention on Murphy, Knapp lowered his voice only slightly. "Pat," he said, "the fault in this whole thing is mine!" He paused for a heavy moment or two. "Because I trusted you!"

Knapp went on excitedly in the same vein, charging Murphy with betraying the police department as well as the Commission. Murphy was not really serious about fighting corruption. He must have meant to send out a warning to police officers not to cooperate in anticorruption efforts that Murphy only pretended to support.

Each of the commissioners weighed in, making his own contribution in his own way. Vance soothingly tried to point out that Whit had good cause for his anger and that, regardless of Murphy's intentions, an impression had been created that would seriously undermine efforts to fight corruption. Sprizzo confronted Murphy bluntly, saying that what had happened could only be called a "double-cross." Monserrat tried to lay out some of the political repercussions. I told Murphy of the difficulty he was creating with respect to getting cooperation from two cops working on corruption cases, who needed to support themselves.

We made it clear that the only thing that really bothered us was that Phillips and Droge had been deprived of making a living. We recognized the difficulties in allowing two confessedly corrupt cops to walk around with guns and badges. But we pointed out that, at least in Droge's case, it was hypocritical to think that he was any more corrupt than a great majority of active patrolmen. The thing that made Droge and Phillips really different from other cops was the fact that they had testified publicly about their corruption. Perhaps that was why they were now being punished. That's certainly what many in the Department, as well as in the public, would conclude. As a practical matter, if Phillips and Droge had to "moonlight" to support themselves, they would not be available to work with the prosecutors to make cases against cops. Maybe, people would say, that's what Murphy had in mind. For these reasons, we argued, the two officers could be suspended, but with pay. Our arguments were turned down flat. Murphy refused to modify the position he had already publicly taken.

Knapp told Murphy, coldly, what the Commission proposed to do. "Mike has drafted a press release," he said, "which we will release this afternoon unless you reverse your order to the extent of restoring Droge and Phillips to the payroll. The release says that, in our view, you are not sincere in your supposed fight against police corruption, and that suspending Phillips and Droge is a deliberate attempt by you to throttle the resolve of other cops who might be thinking of cooperating in uncovering police corruption." Murphy, intent upon cultivating a public image of liberal enlightenment, would presumably be very upset by such an attack.

The police commissioner did not seem as bothered as I would have expected. Throughout our harangue, he had made little attempt to defend himself or explain his position. It seemed that he felt that he had a trump card, and was simply waiting to play it. I began to think, watching him, that he looked almost smug. Faced with Knapp's threat of a press release, Murphy played his card. "I think you should know," he said. "I have spoken to the Mayor, and he backs me 100 percent in this."

Murphy did not get the reaction he had counted on. The room almost exploded, as everyone started shouting at once. So the mayor thought we would be intimidated, did he? Even Vance showed his excitement. Knapp summed it up for all of us, "Is that what John Lindsay says?" he roared. Turning to me, he commanded, without lowering his voice, "Mike—add the mayor's name to the press release! He obviously doesn't give a damn about fighting police corruption either!"

Murphy appeared thunderstruck. Obviously he had not dreamed that he would get anything like this response. He seemed not to know how to handle it.

Mumbling something inconsequential, Murphy took his leave. Smith, who had said virtually nothing, and Cooper, who looked embarrassed throughout the whole thing, left with him.

We thought we knew where Murphy was going. It was only a few minutes by car to City Hall. Quickly, Joe Monserrat put in a call to Dick Aurellio, the mayor's top aide. Monserrat, the only non-lawyer on the Commission, knew politics, and he knew human nature. While we listened, he briefly sketched out for Aurellio what had just happened and told him that he was sure that Pat Murphy was on his way to see the mayor. "I've got a bunch of really furious commissioners on my hands," warned Monserrat. "I'd hate to see anything crazy happen, but if the mayor allows Murphy to stick to his position, we're going to have the spectacle of the mayor's own Commission publicly charging that both the mayor and the police commissioner are soft on police corruption. The release is already drafted." Monserrat was practical and to the point. The Commission would not relent on this one. Lindsay should realize the political consequences.

I went back to my office to put the finishing touches on the press release. I was told that Knapp would be in touch with Murphy and, if he didn't change his position, I was to send the release—complete with the accusation against Lindsay—to the City Hall press corps.

Later in the afternoon, the police commissioner released a statement reversing himself. Phillips and Droge were to remain suspended, but with pay. The headlines in next morning's newspapers told the story: "MURPHY BACKS DOWN."

23

SERPICO

As originally planned, Captain Dan McGowan was to be the Commission's final public hearing witness. Everything else would be dealt with in our final report—including our conclusions regarding the charges made by Frank Serpico. Serpico claimed that top-level people in the Department and in City Hall, perhaps including the mayor, had, in 1966–67, deliberately or negligently failed to take proper action to look into the corruption Serpico had reported to exist in the Bronx Plainclothes Division in which he then served.

It was important to fix blame, if it existed. But it seemed to us that it was far more important to publicize what we had exposed—the disease of which Serpico's accusations were symptoms.

We were satisfied that we had uncovered what was going on in the Department *currently*. We had found systemic patterns of corruption and had identified an enveloping fog of dishonesty that had crept into all aspects of the Department. The only way to begin to deal effectively with the disease was to expose it—publicly and dramatically. That's what we did. Our public hearings had served well the purpose of focusing the attention of a lethargic public on widespread patterns of police corruption, the existence and extent of which no one had been willing to admit.

This focus might be diverted if we shifted to public questioning of what individuals had done what four or five years earlier, in 1966–67. Frank Serpico's story would be told, all right, but not by calling witnesses at a public hearing. The facts had already been well explored in the press, particularly in David Burnham's seminal article in the *New York Times*. Serpico himself was in the process of preparing for publication his version of what happened, in what was to become a best-selling book. Written by author Peter Maas, the book ultimately would be made into a hugely popular motion picture, for which Al Pacino, as Serpico, received an Academy Award for Best Actor.[1] It appeared to us that what was required of our Commission, with respect to Serpico's charges, was analysis, not any further public exposure of the evidence. We had taken extensive testimony in private session from all of the principals. When, and if, we came to a conclusion as to what happened, and who, if anyone, was to blame in handling Serpico's accusations, we would announce those conclusions in a public report. It did not seem that this analysis would be advanced by presenting, in public, witnesses who by and large had already said what they had to say in very public ways.

So, as our hearings drew to a close, Whit Knapp announced that the Serpico events would be dealt with in our final report, not in continued public hearings. There was a sharp and immediate reaction from a number of sources. The media in general was disappointed. It had been treated to a good show, and Serpico might be an even better one. A curious public didn't want to wait for a report most would never read. Watching TV was much easier. Some groups with anti-cop agendas wanted to keep the pot boiling. Politicians with various objectives saw those objectives advanced by a public examination of the Lindsay administration and its police department.

And then there was David Durk. Serpico himself could not have cared less, but his partner quite clearly did not want to give up what he saw as his day in the sun. Apparently Durk went to a local politician, Queens County Democratic leader Matthew Troy, and persuaded him to object. Troy was a gadfly, and a major political operator in the city. He was later to be convicted for misappropriating funds from a client's account, but at this time he was a formidable and influential figure.

---

1. Almost from the start, Serpico had been working with Maas on a book about his exploits. He used to joke with us about which movie stars we wanted taking our roles. We should have realized that such speculation was fruitless, because Frank's story naturally ended where ours began. There was no real overlap, and therefore no parts for us in his movie. When Bill Phillips appeared in our hearings with his spectacular testimony, Serpico's mentor, Sidney Cooper, commented wryly, "François, you are going to be like the first soldier that fell at Antietam. They are going to be giving copies of your book away free with the one that this guy will write." Cooper was, of course, wrong. Maas's excellent book and the classic movie that followed are properly remembered. Phillips's book, On the Pad, whatever its merits, died with its author, Leonard Schecter, who passed away shortly after the book was completed, but before it could be promoted.

Troy held a press conference and accused the Commission of selling out. We were covering up for Lindsay and his cronies, he bellowed. The media lapped it up.

The commissioners met hastily. We had chosen to avoid public hearings on the Serpico charges because they might shift attention from the hearings we were just finishing on current conditions in the Department. As a result of the stir caused by Troy's well-publicized accusations, it now seemed that not holding hearings on the Serpico charges might distract attention from our real work more than holding them would. To preserve our credibility we had to show that we were not covering anything up. So, on the day before the hearings ended, Knapp announced that they would be resumed in December, for the purpose of exploring the Serpico charges.

Having committed ourselves to holding a set of public hearings, it behooved us to prepare for them. Our first set had been an orchestrated presentation of a picture of police corruption in the city, as we had found it in the course of our investigation. Now we would be focusing on an often-told tale, very little of which had anything to do with facts that we had uncovered in our investigation. There was no question that Serpico had brought his allegations of corruption to the attention of both superiors in the Department and highly ranked City officials. No one had done anything for months. The undecided or disputed issues involved: first, who was responsible for the delay; second, when the Mayor's Office had found out that nothing was being done.

Serpico was to be our first witness and would later be followed by Durk's corroborative testimony. I concentrated on preparing Serpico for his testimony, while my young associate at Cahill Gordon, Warren Colodner, undertook the task of doing the same with Durk. The job that proved to be trickier than we might have thought. Durk was facile, intelligent, and with his own agenda—to get as much publicity as possible for himself and his theories of policing. He appeared for his preparation sessions with his lawyer, prominent attorney Peter Zimroth, who had been an assistant U.S. attorney and was destined in later years to be New York City Commissioner of Investigations.

Colodner bore down on Durk, focusing on Durk's observations of Serpico, and the attempts to get someone to listen to his story. It was important to bring out Durk's background. He must be presented as a real cop, with real experiences, not an Amherst intellectual with nothing to offer but theories. To that end, we wanted him to relate an experience about which he had told us, that occurred early in his career. It involved corrupt police officers in a precinct to which he had been assigned. We didn't ask him to give names and dates, just relate the incident. Durk refused. "I told you guys that story in confidence," he said. "I can't testify publicly about it because I'm working on a number of projects involving cops and I can't have them thinking of me as a stool pigeon." He was adamant on the point and said if he were forced to tell about the incident in question he would refuse to testify at all. "You're just like everyone else," I railed at him. "You'll talk as long as it doesn't affect you." After considerable back and forth, I gave in. I promised Durk that I would not ask him about the incident.

However, I deliberately refrained from informing the commissioners about the deal I had struck. Even though I would not ask Durk about the experience to which he was sensitive, the commissioners, knowing nothing of the commitment, would be free to do so. Indeed, Commissioner John Sprizzo, who could be a ferocious questioner when he wanted to be, picked up on the issue during Durk's testimony and, in a highly confrontational exchange, dragged the story out of him.

Serpico's preparation went comparatively without incident—at first. One potential issue was his physical appearance. Frank was a vision. Unkempt and dirty-looking, his bushy long hair framed his face—also dirty-looking—which was otherwise encased in a large, shaggy beard. He dressed in a grubby pair of torn jeans and an equally disreputable-looking T-shirt. He customarily slipped off his cowboy boots, leaving him barefoot. Tucked into his belt, at front and back, were, respectively, a huge automatic pistol and a snub-nosed .38 caliber. As this apparition left the conference room late one evening, to wander through the near-deserted halls of the Cahill Gordon offices on his way to the restroom, I mused about what the reaction would be should he be seen by any of my partners who had objected to the office being visited by the attorney general of the United States and the police commissioner. Oh well, those partners rarely worked at night. They shouldn't complain.

Frank was relaxed and confident as he prepared to testify. After all, he was just telling the truth. However, as the date for the testimony loomed, he became more hesitant and less cooperative. Finally, one week before the publicly announced hearings at which he was to be the opening—and chief— witness, Serpico informed us that he was no longer willing to testify.

We later found out that Peter Maas, the author of the book *Serpico*, which was then in preparation, had convinced Frank that he was being somehow "set up." We would offer him as our first witness, said Maas, and then we would bury him with contradictory testimony. It didn't make any sense. The Commission did not dispute Serpico's version of what had happened, and the purpose of its hearings was simply to allow those with knowledge of the events to testify about them. Some witnesses would differ from Frank, and some would face sharp cross-examination, but certainly not Frank. We had talked to him to the point of exhaustion—and we believed that he was telling the truth—as he sincerely remembered it.

To present his point of view about why he didn't want to testify, Frank retained former U.S. Attorney General Ramsey Clark, now a partner at a prestigious New York law firm. My efforts to convince Clark that there was no plot against Serpico consumed a number of long telephone conversations during the week prior to the scheduled hearings. These talks culminated in a face-to-face meeting at Clark's office on Saturday morning, prior to the Tuesday opening of the hearings, when Serpico was to appear. That was the only time Clark could make it, and I was forced to compromise an urgent appointment of my own, the "championship" game in an informal lawyers' touch football league, scheduled for Saturday morning in Central Park. I quarterbacked my firm team, mostly comprising lawyers formerly from the U.S. Attorney's Office, including Paul Rooney, Otto Obermaier, and Commissioner John Sprizzo. We were to face a team from Frank Hogan's Manhattan District Attorney's Office. Our Commission had inferentially criticized Hogan's office for not being vigilant enough about police corruption, and the media had made something of a grudge match of the game. It was to be filmed, for airing on NBC News.

I showed up in Clark's office in jeans and sneakers. During the hurried meeting that followed, Clark finally agreed that Serpico would testify. I raced for Central Park. We lost.

As we worked over the final weekend, getting ready for the first day of the Serpico hearings on the following Tuesday, there was one loose end that bothered me. The commissioners had decided that, in the light of what we had learned in private executive session testimony, it would be counterproductive to call John Lindsay as a witness. We knew what he would say—that Kriegel had not told him about any cover-up of Serpico's charges in time to do anything about it—and we had nothing that would contradict him. Of course, there would be value in getting the mayor's statement on the record and there would be a certain symmetry in ending our investigation where it had begun—with the mayor. But the countervailing consideration that prevailed with the commissioners was the desire to prevent all the good work we had done from being lost in political sensationalism. John Lindsay was a rising political star. He had indicated his intention to run for the presidency of the United States. Anything he did was news, and if he testified, that testimony would become the legacy of the Knapp Commission, regardless of its significance, or lack thereof.

The commissioners felt strongly that the revelations we had already made about corruption in the Department should not be obscured—hence, the original decision not to hold any public hearings at all with respect to the Serpico allegations. We had reversed that decision, running the risk of allowing the public to lose sight of the Department's current plight in the glare of personal accusations involving events of four years ago. To put the mayor on the stand would have been to throw in the towel. Later, when the hearings were over, Knapp explained to the press: "If John Lindsay had been put on the stand, no one would give a hoot about anything, except how they could get questions out of him which would either advance or retard his present political activities. I'm not going to have my commission play a part in such a performance." Knapp said that he did not give "a tinker's damn" about the career of Mr. Lindsay but that he could not put the mayor on the witness stand without turning the hearings into a political circus and thus diverting attention from fighting police corruption. Knapp summed up his feelings by saying "If he [John Lindsay] wants national television time, he can arrange it himself."

I fully concurred with his reasoning but as I worked over the weekend to pull the upcoming hearings together, I became increasingly bothered by a nagging thought. It seemed clear that we should not require the mayor's public testimony, but we hadn't even talked to him privately. We were pretty sure we knew what he had to say, but how could we come to any conclusion without hearing it from his own lips?

The more I thought about it, the more troubled I became. So, on the Sunday night before the Tuesday opening of the hearings, I called Whit and explained to him what was bothering me. We really couldn't end this thing without talking to the mayor. The readiness with which Whit agreed with me made me feel that he had been thinking along similar lines.

The next day, Whit arranged a private meeting with the mayor. He and I met with Lindsay, Corporation Counsel Norman Redlich, and Jay Kriegel. We questioned him for more than an hour, learning nothing surprising, but satisfying ourselves that we had done what had to be done.

The hearings began on December 14, 1971, at the building of the New York Chamber of Commerce, on Vesey Street in downtown Manhattan. Only slightly less impressive than the hearing room at the Association of the Bar, where our first set of hearings had been held, the room was cavernous, and it too had huge portraits of important-looking people on the walls. The setup, for spectators and press, was similar to what it had been during the previous hearings, except that now accommodations were made for the fact that there would be even more attention paid by the media.

Knapp began the hearings with a short statement explaining what we hoped to accomplish. He explained that the first set of hearings had been public, in order to share our findings as to current conditions in the Department. He explained how we had originally intended, with respect to the Serpico charges, "to confine to private hearings our inquiries as to the past events, and to deal in our final report with the meaning of such events and their significance to the future." However, he said, it became clear that failing to hold public hearings would itself divert attention "to the futile business of wondering about the past." So: "In these hearings we shall simply endeavor to let each participant in the events under discussion lay before the public in an organized fashion, his recollections and understanding of the events as they occurred." Our own conclusions, Knapp said, would be set forth in our final report.

I called our first witness, Frank Serpico. Apparently, the prospect of being on television had gotten to him. Gone was most of the hippie image. Serpico had trimmed his sloppy beard, gotten a stylish haircut, and put on a dark suit with a buttoned-down, gently striped shirt and a trendy foulard tie. As he approached the witness chair, I kidded him about selling out. He did not smile.

With his attorney, Ramsey Clark, sitting next to him, Serpico testified that he joined the Department in the fall of 1959 and spent the next five and a half years as a patrolman and in a fingerprinting unit as a Spanish interpreter. In 1966 he enrolled in a course given in the department, where he met Officer David Durk. Later that year he was assigned as a plainclothesman to the 90th Precinct and, after six months, he became a plainclothesman in the Seventh Division in the Bronx. In August of that year a black policeman, whom he did not know, gave him an envelope containing three hundred dollars in cash, explaining that it was from "Jewish Max." With Durk, Serpico reported the incident to a captain in the Department of Investigation, Phillip Foran, who told him, not as a threat but as a piece of advice, that if he pressed the incident, he would "end up face down in the East River," and that he'd better forget about it. At Foran's suggestion, he gave the money to the sergeant who was his superior officer. The sergeant put the envelope in his pocket.

Serpico testified in some detail about the organized corruption that he found to exist after he had been transferred to the Seventh Division. He described the systematized collection of pad payments from gamblers, in which everyone in the plainclothes division participated.

Then Serpico related his attempts to expose what was going on. He told of personally informing Commissioner of Investigations Arnold Fraiman, in early 1967, of the "Jewish Max" incident and of later telling him about conditions in the Seventh Division. Nothing was done. The word was that Fraiman, in explaining his inaction, said that he considered Serpico to be a "psycho."

Serpico went on to tell of informing Inspector Cornelius "Neal" Behan in January 1967 about corruption in the Seventh Division. He said that Behan, known for his probity, brought the information to First Deputy Commissioner John Walsh, and that he did so again in February and again in April. Nothing happened.

Serpico claimed that in April he and David Durk told mayoral aide Jay Kriegel of the corruption he had experienced and of Walsh's inaction. When still no action was taken, he again met with Kriegel in the early fall to repeat his charges.

Finally, in October 1967, an investigation was begun into Serpico's allegations. Faced with Walsh's inaction, Behan brought Serpico to Inspector Phillip Sheridan, who was Behan's neighbor and happened to hold an administrative position covering the Seventh Division plainclothes unit. Serpico repeated his allegations to Sheridan, but nothing was said about the prior overtures to Kriegel, Walsh, and Fraiman.

Sheridan duly repeated the charges to his superiors, including Deputy Chief Inspector Jules Sachson, and then, on October 9, 1967, Sheridan, Sachson, and others met with Walsh to inform him, presumably for the first time, of Serpico's accusations. Walsh did not let on that he knew anything about Serpico or his charges. He authorized an investigation that led to a grand jury inquiry, run by Bronx District Attorney Burton Roberts. Indictments were returned and convictions obtained against several Seventh Division plainclothesmen. Frank Serpico had finally gotten someone to listen to him.

Serpico's testimony consumed a full day, and triggered the expected flurry of media attention.

The second day's testimony began with Inspector Neal Behan. Behan was a particularly credible witness, with an impeccable reputation for rectitude— he was, for example, given to organizing religious retreats for his comrades. Behan generally corroborated Serpico's testimony, but disagreed with him on one important point. Behan recalled that Serpico had given him only general information during their first meeting in January 1967 and had not come forth with specifics, for Behan to take to Walsh, until April. That meant that Walsh's inaction would have lasted five or six months, rather than nine. Moreover, Jay Kriegel, who Serpico said was also told in April, would have had little reason to suspect police inaction because, as far as he knew, Walsh had just been given, for the first time, information on which he could act.

In my view, it is probable that Serpico and Behan each honestly believed that his own recollection was accurate. In any event, under either version, the police department and City Hall did nothing to follow up on Serpico's charges for at least five months.

I had decided, with the Commission's approval, to reward the hard work put in by our two young volunteer lawyers, Warren Colodner and Paul Ford, by giving them the opportunity to question witnesses. Ford would question Behan, and Colodner would handle the next two witnesses, Inspector Sheridan and Deputy Chief Inspector Sachson. Colodner, as a young litigation associate at

Cahill Gordon, had handled a witness or two in depositions, but Ford, who was just beginning to be trained in corporate law at Cy Vance's law firm, had never questioned a witness in any proceeding. It would be his first time—ever. The night before the testimony, Ford was, at 11:00 P.M., still in our offices, going over his notes. Dropping in to ask him how it was going, I was told that he was fully prepared and ready to go. I asked him if he was nervous. Ford, who was sitting rigid in his chair, declared in a strained voice, "Of course not." I put on a regretful frown. "That's too bad," I said. "I guess I'm going to have to take the witness away from you." He looked up at me, startled. "This is your first witness," I continued. "You will be doing the questioning on live television before thousands of viewers. If you're not nervous right now, you're no good for the job." He dissolved in his chair with a huge sigh of relief. "God, I'm glad you said that," he exhaled. "I'm nervous as hell." I told him that he would be fine.

Ford's witness, Behan, was the first one up in the morning. Ford did a nice job, and his photograph appeared prominently on page three of the *New York Daily News* in the early bird edition of that paper, which came out the next morning. The picture was immediately replaced, in the next edition, by Colodner's. The fact that not too many people read the early bird edition did not bother Ford very much, because it was the only edition of the newspaper distributed in his hometown, New Haven, Connecticut.

The remainder of the second day's testimony was largely taken up by Bronx County District Attorney Burton Roberts. Roberts, while conceding Serpico's role in coming forth with information of corruption in the first place, was less than complimentary about Frank's cooperation thereafter: "This man [Serpico] didn't want to wear a wire," testified Roberts. "This man didn't want to testify. This man didn't want to go to the Grand Jury. [He] did not want to be marked lousy."

Sidney Cooper, who was not called to testify, had often confirmed to us Serpico's reluctance to become involved in any investigation of his accusations.

Frank never argued much with this characterization. He made no bones about the fact that he did not consider himself a "shoofly." He was willing to report what he had come upon. Investigating the information, he said, was the job of those who were paid to do that kind of work.

On the third day the commissioners heard from John Walsh. The forty-year veteran policeman, who had been first deputy under five police commissioners, had a fierce reputation of intolerance for police wrongdoing. He testified that he had "dropped the ball" by not following up on Serpico's allegations, or even seeing him. "I had planned to see Serpico," he said, "but I failed to do it." Purporting not to recall Neal Behan's informing him of Serpico's charges in January and again in February 1967, Walsh conceded that

Behan told him about them in April. He explained his subsequent inaction by claiming, "I was not going to interfere with Serpico . . . to disturb him, to prod him in any way, might upset him." Claiming that he somehow relied on Behan to bring the subject up again, Walsh testified that, when that didn't happen, "the incident left my mind."

Whit Knapp was not satisfied. "Why the hell did you wait six months before checking with Behan?" he asked.

Walsh did not answer.

Arnold Fraiman testified on the fourth day of the hearings. Like Walsh, he baldly admitted doing nothing about Serpico's charges, without offering any real explanation as to why. Denying the claim that he had called Serpico a "psycho," Fraiman said, "No, not a psycho. Certainly unusual. His manner and appearance were unusual, and what he had to say was unusual."

Fraiman stated that he had not viewed Serpico's charge—that an entire plainclothes unit, in which Serpico himself served, was corrupt—as "important" enough for his agency to investigate. When pressed, he conceded that on other occasions the DOI had considered ten-dollar payoffs to non-police City officials be "important" enough to warrant investigation.

Fraiman also tried to excuse his inaction by claiming inadequate manpower, but he was confronted with his prior testimony that his normal procedure, when he found himself too undermanned to pursue a matter, was to refer it to a district attorney. His only reason for not doing so in Serpico's case was, he said, Serpico's desire for "secrecy." Even if he really would have felt bound by any such restriction, it made no sense that Serpico, who was loudly trying to get people to act on his charges, would have imposed it.

David Durk also testified on the fourth day of the hearing, backing Serpico's version of events, adding that Kriegel had told him that nothing would be done about Serpico's charges until summer was over. The mayor needed to have police support during what was predicted to be a "long, hot summer" of racial tensions. He ended his testimony with an impassioned prepared statement, calling for reform of the Department and ending in a dramatic flourish, as he strode from the room, without waiting for any of the usual concluding formalities.

On the final day of the hearings, the Commission heard from Howard Leary and Jay Kriegel.

Leary claimed that he had never been told about Serpico's allegations. His testimony was, like the testimony he gave in executive session, confused and at times difficult to comprehend.

Jay Kriegel was the last witness to testify before the Commission. He denied that City Hall had deliberately delayed doing anything about Serpico's charges until summer was over. He claimed that he had given Mayor Lindsay "general" information about the corruption reported by Serpico but, at the specific request of Serpico and Durk, had deliberately withheld the fact that Serpico had made additional charges about the Department's doing nothing to follow up on the information. This testimony conformed with the mayor's statements, made to us in the meeting Whit and I had with him prior to the hearings. But it conflicted with Kriegel's own testimony, taken in executive session the previous June. At that time, Kriegel had testified that he had indeed told the mayor that Serpico was claiming that his allegations were being ignored by the Department.

Confronted with this inconsistency, Kriegel had little explanation, beyond insisting that his current testimony was accurate.[2]

With Kriegel's testimony, the Commission's public hearings were over. Later, the Commission's final report stated:

Although Walsh, Kriegel and Fraiman all acknowledged the extreme serious-ness of the [Serpico] charges and the unique opportunity provided by the fact that a police officer was making them, none of them took any action. No seri-ous investigation was undertaken until some months later when Serpico went to his division commander. . . . First Deputy Commissioner Walsh, whose reputation in the Department was that of an implacable corruption fighter, inexplicably took no action whatsoever for at least six months. . . . The May-or's Office did not see to it that the specific charges made by Serpico were investigated. No effective actions were taken to find out why the Department had delayed investigating the charges, or to explore the broader significance of a situation which indicated undiscovered corruption among the police.[3]

---

2. Later, after the hearings were over, Frank Hogan's Manhattan District Attorney's Of-fice began an investigation into whether Kriegel's testimony was perjurious, on an "in-consistent testimony" theory. The case was a tenuous one because Kriegel could defend himself simply by claiming that his recollection had changed. The investigation came to naught, partially because I alerted the prosecutor that, due to our never getting re-authorized by the City Council, an argument could be made that we did not have the power to administer an oath at our public hearings. If Kriegel was not technically un-der oath at our proceedings, there could be no perjury.

3. *Knapp Commission Report on Police Corruption* (New York: Braziller, 1973), pp. 203–204.

24

AFTERMATH

The hearings were finally over. Now we had to close shop, organize our files for presentation to various law enforcement authorities, and write a final report, which would detail what we had found, and what might be done about it. During the year that it took to accomplish all of this, I returned to Cahill Gordon and found my partners to be most tolerant of my spending virtually all of my time working on Commission matters, chiefly the final report.

Ironically, prominent among the many criminal investigations spawned, directly or indirectly, by our efforts, was the Manhattan grand jury investigation of our own pivotal informant/undercover operative/witness/equipment supplier/technical advisor Teddy Ratnoff. We had struggled to make sure that, in his efforts on our behalf, Teddy could not represent to anyone that he was our agent and spoke on our behalf. We were confident that he would use such a misrepresentation for nefarious purposes. We were right, but not careful enough. Teddy apparently absconded with the electronic equipment used in our hearings, having convinced those with whom he dealt that he worked directly for the Commission.

In investigating this transgression, the Manhattan District Attorney's Office explored broadly Ratnoff's various activities, including his relationship with Xaviera Hollander. This inquiry gave me my first and only opportunity to meet the renowned Madame who had unwittingly been so instrumental in our success. I was visiting Assistant District Attorney Ken Conboy, who was handling the Ratnoff investigation. He was in later years to become a deputy police commissioner and a federal judge. "There is someone here, today," said Conboy, "whom I think you have never met—Xaviera Hollander." He introduced us. "Oh my," she gushed. "You are much more attractive than you appear on television." I blushed (only inwardly, I hope) at the compliment, until I thought about it and realized that Xaviera's judgments about such things were not exactly discriminating.

Conboy's investigation resulted in Ratnoff's indictment on a number of charges. He jumped bail and fled to England, where he was indicted again for other misbehavior, which had nothing to do with the Commission. Ratnoff wound up doing prison time on both sides of the Atlantic.

For several months after the hearings, it was necessary to deal with the publicity we had created. The hearings had attracted enormous local, and even national, attention in the press and on radio and television. The gavel-to-gavel live television coverage on the local public channel was augmented by heavy coverage on commercial television and radio news shows, both local and national, which regularly carried hearing excerpts "at the top" of the news. The hearings had received repeated front-page treatment in all local newspapers and were the subject of news reports and analyses in major national magazines and on TV "background" shows.

I had found it interesting, during the hearings, to observe firsthand the influence of bias on some of the media coverage. There were, of course, pro-cop newspapers and publications that at first tried to soft-pedal the impact of our hearings. Most of them quickly succumbed to their basic urge to make money. Like us or not, the Commission was hot copy. Of course, when we stubbed our toe—as with our mistaken exposure of Captain Mazen's name on a hotel Christmas list—publications that didn't like us gleefully emphasized the story. Most media leanings, however, were in our favor. The *New York Times* had a particular interest in our success. David Burnham was, at the time of our hearings, being considered for a Pulitzer Prize for his *Times* article about Serpico.[1] Clearly, his chances of winning improved if the hearings that resulted from his story turned out well. The *Times* assigned Burnham to cover the hearings. He would have been less than human if he didn't—even subconsciously—present our efforts in just a little bit of a favorable light.

Both Whit Knapp and I were called upon for a number of speaking engagements. There were interviews, speeches, television talk shows, articles, public debates, book offers, and even movie proposals. I got one proposition to become the host of a television talk show. I was invited to appear on,

---

1. He was beaten out by the *Times*'s Pentagon Papers coverage.

among others, the *Today* show and the *Dick Cavett Show*, a national late-night talk-variety predecessor to today's Leno and Letterman shows, which devoted an entire evening to the Commission.

On another occasion, after our report had been issued, I was asked to appear on a national television show, *The Advocates*, hosted by a law school classmate of mine, Michael Dukakis, who would later run for president of the United States. The show's format was a debate of a public issue in which each side called witnesses, in a trial setting. The witnesses testified to conflicting points of view on the issue in question. Dukakis was the master of ceremonies. The show on which I appeared was an "up or down" debate about the legality of sports betting. Our report had noted, without taking sides regarding the underlying social issues, the unremarkable fact that if gambling were legalized, police corruption would diminish. Putting aside the subtleties of our position, I found myself arrayed, in the show, on the side of a notorious gambler, Jimmy the Greek. We both were presented as witnesses in favor of gambling at sporting events. Our opponents were the head of security for the National Football League and a renowned former Michigan football star, all-time great, Heisman Trophy–winner Tommy Harmon. I'm not sure who won the debate, but our show did not change the sports-betting landscape in the United States.

One category of appearance took first priority. I let it be known that I welcomed invitations to speak to cops. On such occasions, of which there were a number, usually at precinct houses, I did not presume to deliver an address, but simply made myself available for questions. I did the best I could to make it clear at the outset that everything was off the record, and that hostile inquiries were not forbidden, but expected. Supervisory officers were excused, to reduce inhibitions. "No shooting," I would admonish, "but anything else goes." Then I would do my best to field usually emotional, always heartfelt, and sometimes legitimate challenges to our procedures, findings, and very right to exist. When the grilling had run its course, I would make a challenge of my own that invariably brought my audience up short: "Can any of you tell me of any description of a pattern of corruption—given by Phillips or the other witnesses—that wasn't true?" The usual response: silence.

At one gathering of cops, a group of sergeants, I had withstood the usual barrage for about an hour, when a large, formidable African American, sitting toward the front, stood up, turned to face his comrades, and pretty well silenced the room: "Bullshit," he snapped. " I've been on the job for twelve years, and I know—and you all know—that the Knapp Commission didn't get half of what's going on."

Amidst the whirl of appearances and speeches was a debate, put on by one of the local colleges, pitting me against Nat Hentoff, director of the New York Civil Liberties Union, a consistent critic of the Commission. I had been a member of the American Civil Liberties Union since before I was a prosecutor, but the New York affiliate had always seemed to me to be a little far-out. Now I was to meet Hentoff to defend the propriety of the methods we had used in our investigation and public hearings.

I had always been amused to observe people with strong, sometimes impassioned, views on the subject of the rights of an accused person undergoing a 100 percent reversal of their supposedly fundamental views when a police officer was accused. "Law-and-order" conservatives, who normally had little use for a defendant's claims that his rights had been abused, suddenly discovered the Fifth Amendment and other Constitutional guarantees. Liberals, who showed unbounded enthusiasm and creativity in discovering sometimes hyper-technical ways in which the rights of an accused had been violated by governmental authorities, somehow became impatient when such rights were asserted by a cop. But the New York Civil Liberties Union, about as liberal an organization as could be found in those days, was true to its colors. For them, what was good for the ghetto dweller was good for the police officer as well. They took this position when we first went into business, and stuck to it throughout.

As we faced off against each other, Hentoff had one unexpected advantage. Seated in the front row of the auditorium, with his arms crossed over his chest, a stony glare directed at me, was a man I had admired most of my adult life, and whose judgment I had come to trust implicitly—Benjamin Spock, MD. He was the author of a best-selling paperback book giving parents advice on how to raise their children. Like all of our friends, my wife and I had always turned quickly to this well-indexed "Bible" whenever a child-rearing problem arose. It was uncanny how often Dr. Spock's book contained the correct answer. I had never met the man, but I had looked up to him for years. Now here he was, staring at me with obvious disapproval, if not malevolence. Oh well, my children were almost grown, and we wouldn't be talking about raising kids.

In his criticism of the Commission, Hentoff focused chiefly on two points: our failure to provide for cross-examination at our public hearings, and the fact that our agents used recording devices concealed on their bodies, without getting warrants. I answered that providing cross-examination was impractical—who and how many would cross-examine each witness? How and by whom would the cross-examiners be selected? And, most important, how could we have maintained our policy of protecting the privacy of individuals by not mentioning names, when delving into the specifics of names, places, and times would be the essence of any competent cross-examination? Not having the answers to these questions, we had not attempted to provide for cross-examination of our witnesses.

As for getting warrants before using recording devices, there was no procedure that would have allowed us to do so. New York and federal law allowed anyone, law enforcement agent or not, to transmit or record a conversation to which he was a party. We did not need a judge's approval, and no judge would have given it, had we asked. There was simply no procedure for getting a warrant.

I suspect, as is usual in such events, no one's mind was changed when it was over, but the dialogue was civil. I felt I had a moment of satisfaction at Hentoff's inability to answer me when I asked if he could think of a single law enforcement investigative technique that the NYCLU had not, at some time or other, opposed. Was he really against investigating crime altogether? Of course not. Hentoff's wife told me, after the debate, that she had asked him that question herself. He hadn't answered her, either.

When it was all over, Dr. Spock made me feel good by shaking my hand.

On another occasion, Whit, Warren Colodner, and I met in preparation for the debate and to draft a written response in the *New York Law Journal*, to an article on the same subject that had appeared in the *Village Voice*. At one point in the discussion, Colodner expressed a view with which Knapp did not agree. As he occasionally did, Whit expressed his disagreement emphatically, raising his voice and making pejorative remarks about Colodner's reasoning.

When the session was over, and I was alone with Knapp, I said to him that I thought he had been very unfair to Warren, who was, after all, a volunteer. I said that there had been no reason for Whit to raise his voice and, incidentally, I thought that Warren had been correct on the merits of what he had suggested.

Whit, characteristically, was quick to admit a mistake. "He should know me well enough by now," he grumbled, "to realize that when I raise my voice like that, I don't know what I'm talking about." Whit then telephoned Colodner to repeat what he had said to me and to apologize profusely.

My "fifteen minutes" of personal notoriety faded rapidly. For a time, my constant television and press exposure resulted in my having what reporters told me was a high "recognition factor"—strangers recognized me in public. The unaccustomed attention was not always for the best—on one occasion I heard someone bellow, from a block away on a crowded street, "Hey, Armstrong—BOOOOOOO!" But it wasn't too long before the rush of activity and public recognition had pretty well run its course. One Saturday morning, dressed informally, I was riding the elevator to my office at Cahill Gordon, in the company of a man in working clothes, who looked at me quizzically. "Hey, fella," he said, "don't I know you from someplace?" He paused thoughtfully. "Don't you work for ConEd?" On another occasion I was accosted by someone who apparently thought he recognized me. Obviously searching his memory, he asked, haltingly, "Aren't you—aren't you—aren't you—Michael Knapp?" Whit took particular delight in this anecdote, and repeated it often.

Presumably, one concrete benefit I might derive from all the publicity I received would be legal business that would come my way as a result. I'm sure my partners at Cahill Gordon thought so. In fact, I only had one offer of business that I could directly attribute to my service with the Knapp Commission. An inmate at the Tombs, the correctional facility servicing the State Court in Manhattan, requested that I represent him on a charge of murdering his last lawyer. I declined.

A principal job, once the hearings were over, was to pull together and organize all of the information we had gathered. It was a formidable task. As we put our files in order, we also shared them with police and federal authorities interested in making cases against individuals.[2] The attorneys who had served for varying periods during the investigation assisted by preparing summaries of areas on which they had worked, and two smart young law students, Patricia Farren and Susan Lissitzyn, volunteered to help.

For the job of actually writing our final report, it was clear that we needed the help of a professional writer. I could pull material together and write some first drafts, and the commissioners, particularly Whit Knapp, were available for editing, but the basic job of putting things down on paper required a full-time professional hand. For that purpose we retained a writer, Margo Barrett, the sister of the young law school graduate who had helped us at the outset of our investigation. Fiery and, like her sister, attractive as well as bright, she was no mere scribe, and was not shy about engaging in vigorous debates with various commissioners—especially Sprizzo—over wording or interpretations of the testimony. We had many lively editing sessions.

The Commission's report was issued in two stages. The first, in August 1972, was prepared for the purpose of meeting the intense public demand for conclusions to supplement the Commission's hearings. It set forth a brief summary of our investigation and presented our recommendations. The sec-

---

2. The Department's Internal Affairs Division examined 310 "cases" involving 627 police officers.

ond stage, issued in December 1972, comprised the main Commission report, incorporating the first report and presenting the details of what we
had done.[3] Focusing on the theme of the pervasive atmosphere of corruption
we had found, the report was 283 pages in length and contained a detailed
account of the Commission's investigative activities, summaries of the testi-
monies of the witnesses who appeared at the hearings, analyses of the various patterns of corruption we had found to exist, and comments on what
we considered to be the ineffective ways the Department dealt with the problems, as well as our detailed recommendations for reform.

At last Marty Danziger had his treatise, albeit not quite the academic
work he had thought he was paying for with Law Enforcement Assistance
Administration money.

Reactions were predictable, including that from PBA President Robert
McKiernan, who characterized the report as "a fairy tale told by thieves."
Elaborating, McKiernan asserted, "Your conclusions are contemptible. The
statement that a sizable majority of police officers are engaged, to some degree, in corruption ranks with some of the foulest statements in my memory."
The report got a wide circulation with police and in law enforcement libraries, and it apparently reached an even broader readership. For example, I was
traveling in Moscow in the early '80s at the height of the Cold War, and had
occasion to be in the American-Canadian Information Agency. There, in their
small library of radical American historical and literary works—such things
as the autobiography of revolutionary Angela Davis—I found a well-worn
copy of the *Knapp Commission Report*. I guess the Soviets liked the picture
of corruption we painted, thinking it to be the norm in American society.

---

3. Each of these reports was given, a day or so in advance, to "trusted" members of the
   press on a strict "embargo" basis. The newspeople could look the report over and have
   some time to prepare their stories, but they promised faithfully that they would not go
   public before the release date. In each case, one of the reporters violated the embargo,
   and in each case no justification was given, beyond a simple desire to "scoop" the competition. Obviously, not only cops were susceptible to giving in to temptation. One
   newsman who had not given in was the *New York Post* reporter, Carl Pelleck, who had
   regularly covered our activities. When I called to tell him that I felt obligated to let him
   know that one of his colleagues was probably in the process of violating the embargo,
   he responded, "I promised not to release the report. I have it in the trunk of my car. It's
   going to stay there. I don't care if anyone, even my editor, tells me otherwise."

25

PHILLIPS—EPILOGUE

There was yet another chapter to be written in the saga of Bill Phillips. One day in February 1972 I got a puzzling call from Chief Sidney Cooper. He wanted to know if I was aware of anything "unusual." Talking in circles, which Cooper never did, he hinted that something was in the works and that I would find out about it—soon.

A day or so later I found out what Cooper was talking about, when I got a furious phone call from Bill Phillips.

"They're pinning a fucking murder on me," Phillips ranted. He had just come from a confrontation at the District Attorney's Office. They had accused him of the 1968 murders of a pimp and a prostitute. He had not yet been arrested, but they clearly were about to pounce. Phillips was hysterical with rage. He screamed that it was a frame, engineered by the DA's office and the cops, and demanded that I arrange immediately for him to take a lie detector test, and that the detective in charge of the case against him also take one. I calmed Phillips down as best I could and told him I would look into the matter.

I didn't believe the prosecutor might himself be involved in a corrupt attempt to avenge Phillips's testimony against the police—but I was perfectly willing to accept the notion that cops themselves might engineer such a frame. Maybe my attitude sprang from the fact that I had been a prosecutor, not a cop.

I called former Knapp Assistant Counsel Nick Scoppetta, now working on the Leuci cases in the U.S. Attorney's Office. As an ex–assistant district attorney in Frank Hogan's office, Scoppetta would be able to help us figure out what was going on. I laid out to him the facts as Phillips had told them to me, and offered my speculation that an overenthusiastic assistant district attorney might have allowed himself to be pressured by some cops out to "get" Phillips. "Who is the assistant on the case?" Scoppetta inquired. "I dunno," I replied. "Some guy named John Keenan."

"Oh, shit," said Scoppetta.

Nick explained to me that Keenan was the most accomplished and respected assistant in Hogan's office, probably in the state. Keenan would never overreach, and it was extremely unlikely that he could be duped. Scoppetta acknowledged that anyone could make a mistake, but in Keenan's case, it was extremely unlikely.

The crime of which Phillips was now suspected was an unsolved double murder that occurred on Christmas Eve, 1968. On that evening, a man wearing a green sweater shot three people as they sat on a couch in an eleventh floor apartment on 57th Street off Third Avenue, where a pimp named Sam Goldberg did business. The victims were Goldberg and Sharon Stango, a seventeen-year-old prostitute, both shot dead; and Charles Gonzales, Stango's customer, who had been shot in the arm and the chest, but survived.

According to Gonzales's statements at the time, the killer was in the apartment, heatedly dunning Goldberg for an unpaid $1,000 debt, when Stango and Gonzales emerged from a bedroom. The killer ordered all three to sit on a couch. He then produced a pistol and coolly fired once at Goldberg and then twice at Stango, killing both of them instantly. Turning to Gonzales, he fired again. Gonzales flailed his arms in front of himself, and the bullet went through his forearm, into his chest. As Gonzales slumped to the floor, the killer turned and walked out of the apartment.

Badly wounded, Gonzales crawled to the door and out into the hallway, desperately looking for help. Thirty feet down the hall, waiting for the elevator, he saw someone, who turned to look at him. It was the killer. Gonzales froze in terror. Then, without shooting again, the killer got on the elevator, leaving Gonzales alone in the hall. Taking the elevator to the main floor, the killer calmly walked out past the doorman, mentioning to him that there was a disturbance on the eleventh floor.

The five-year-old case came to light because a detective who had worked on it, John Justy, revisited the file after seeing Phillips testify on television. He said that Phillips's testimony about Xaviera Hollander and other East Side prostitutes rang a bell with him. Justy dug out an old "wanted" flyer in the 1968 killings, containing an artist's sketch of the suspect. It wasn't a very good sketch, but it bore a resemblance to Phillips. The investigation was reopened. Witnesses were re-interviewed and Gonzales, the survivor, was brought in to identify Phillips.

On two occasions, Phillips was called to the District Attorney's Office, ostensibly to discuss a corruption case on which he was working. Instead, his conversations were held in a room with a see-through mirror. Gonzales picked him out. The doorman had died in the meantime, but another eyewitness said that he saw Phillips leaving the building.

Part of the case against Phillips came out of his own mouth. In describing his various activities, he had told us about shaking Goldberg down on a few occasions not significant enough to be included in his televised testimony. He also mentioned Goldberg to IAD investigators who debriefed him after the hearings. It seemed to me that if Phillips had killed Goldberg, he hardly would have told us, much less IAD, about any link to him, but his admission was considered by the prosecution to be an important piece of incriminating evidence.

I met with Phillips to discuss what to do. He was in a rage and claimed to be absolutely convinced that the police department and the District Attorney's Office were deliberately framing him. When the murders took place, he said, he had been at a family Christmas Eve party. Justy and the D.A. were making the whole thing up.

I told Phillips that I was sure that the District Attorney's Office was not involved in a frame and, from what I was hearing about Keenan, the odds were greatly against a setup engineered by detectives behind his back. But it wasn't necessary to think in terms of a frame in order to believe that Phillips was innocent. Mistakes happen in law enforcement, and prosecutors are occasionally wrong. I believed Keenan was wrong. It simply didn't make sense for Phillips to have committed this murder.

To begin with, Gonzales's identification was suspect. He had consumed an estimated twenty-three beers on the day of the shootings, and he had watched Phillips testify on television during the Knapp hearings without recognizing him as the man who had shot him.

Nor did the description of the killer on the original police flyer fit Phillips: "5 feet 9 inches, 165 pounds, appears to be of Italian heritage, pock-marked face." Phillips was 6 feet one inch tall, 195 pounds, with an Irish face and a clear complexion. Jurors deciding Phillips's guilt or innocence were not permitted to consider this discrepancy. The sketch on the wanted poster was admitted into evidence, but the printed description of the killer was not.

Moreover, I was convinced that if Bill Phillips committed a murder, he would do it right. I could not conceive of the man federal prosecutors had dubbed "Cool Hand Luke" putting himself in a position of terrible risk for very little reward. It was not his style to commit a highly visible murder, virtually in his own backyard, under circumstances where he was bound to be remembered by the doorman and likely to be seen by neighbors and passersby. These were his stamping grounds. He was known in the area and, as a police officer, would be particularly susceptible to being identified.

Anyway, even if Phillips might be considered capable of doing this kind of a killing, he would never do it merely because he had been stiffed for $1,000. Phillips's philosophy was to threaten and extort, using as much pressure as he could to get as much money as he could but, if he was unsuccessful, he merely shrugged, and moved on to another "mark." He had been double-crossed a thousand times in his career and for amounts a lot more than $1,000. It did not make sense to me that he would put himself in tremendous jeopardy merely because some pimp didn't pay a relatively minor debt.

I also found it significant that the killer had left a live witness. When Gonzales lurched, bleeding, into the hall just before the elevator arrived, the killer stared at him—and got on the elevator. Apparently he didn't think quickly enough to shoot one more time. Phillips would have. I once asked Phillips what he would have done if, having blown away two people and putting a bullet into a third, he saw his wounded surviving victim stumble out into the hall while he was waiting for an elevator. "You have used four bullets," I said to Phillips. "You have one or two left." "What do you do?" For Phillips, the answer was obvious. "Are you shitting me? I would have plugged that fucker right between the eyes." In my mind, a convincing reason for thinking that Phillips was innocent of this particular murder was not that he was incapable of a cold-blooded killing, but that he was.

Years later I was told a story that planted in my mind a small seed of doubt about Phillips's innocence. I ran into one of the cops who had investigated the Stango-Goldberg murders. He told me that Gonzales, the survivor, had mentioned to him a detail that had never found its way into the police reports. Gonzales said that when he had crawled, wounded, into the hall and found the killer waiting for the elevator, he and the killer looked at each other squarely for a split second. Then the elevator arrived at the floor and the killer stepped into the car. As he did so, he waived at Gonzales and said, "Merry Christmas." Few men would be capable of shooting three people, two of them to death, and then extending seasons' greetings to the third as he lay bleeding in front of him. Phillips was one of the few.

In any event, when Phillips was first accused, my thoughts focused on what could be done to help him. Consideration had to be given to selecting a defense lawyer. I recommended that he get either a young former assistant district attorney from Hogan's office, or F. Lee Bailey, the prominent Boston trial lawyer.

I knew Bailey slightly, from dealing with him on cases when I was a prosecutor. He had a reputation for flamboyance, due in no small part to publicity he generated himself in out-of-court statements. But in reality Bailey's courtroom manner was quite formal and subdued. He was extremely effective and a brilliant cross-examiner. Most of all, Bailey was known for his investigative approach to a criminal case. Unlike many lawyers who would try the case pretty much from the file available to them, Bailey believed in aggressively searching for evidence, and he employed some highly competent detectives to help him in such efforts. I told Phillips that if he really was innocent, Bailey would be a good bet because he would focus hard on finding out who really did the murders. Of course, I reminded Phillips, if he was guilty, it would not be in his best interest to hire a lawyer who would be likely to dig up the truth. Phillips called up Bailey and asked him to take his case.

Bailey was intrigued by the matter but, he said, he would take it only if he himself became convinced that Phillips had not committed the crime. He said this not out of any feeling of compunction about defending guilty people, but because his reason for taking this particular case would be the challenge presented if Phillips were indeed innocent. The chance that he might actually find the real killer in this highly publicized case was a genuine lure. It would partially make up for the fact that he could not hope to collect anything near his normal fee, if indeed he got anything.

Bailey questioned Phillips at length and had two lie detector tests administered to him. He concluded that Phillips was telling the truth, and agreed to take the case.

Motions and pretrial practice dragged on through most of the rest of 1972, while the Knapp Commission was writing its report. As the Interim Report, scheduled for release sometime in August 1972, neared completion, Phillips's trial began.

The trial was a showcase. The nationally famous F. Lee Bailey against prosecutor John Keenan, equally renowned among those who knew the criminal justice system. Bailey himself later characterized Keenan in one of his books as "the best local district attorney I ever came up against." In later years, Keenan was to hold a succession of important, high-level positions, culminating in his becoming a federal district court judge in the Southern District of New York. Students from law schools all over the city came to watch the trial, as did many others who remembered Phillips's televised testimony of a year earlier.

By all accounts, including the prosecutor's, Bailey's performance at trial lived up to his assessment of himself. For example, eyewitness-victim Gonzales was utterly destroyed in a forty-five-minute cross-examination. On the evening after Gonzales's testimony, I had occasion to talk to Keenan's number-two man, Ken Conboy, who morosely reported that Bailey had left Gonzales in rubble. However, Keenan did not take Gonzales's destruction as fatal to his case, which rested chiefly on other, largely circumstantial testimony.

I was asked to testify briefly for both sides on technical matters having to do with the Commission's work. To prepare my defense testimony, I went to Bailey's suite in the Gramercy Park Hotel. The trial had been going on for a couple of weeks, and when I arrived, Bailey was relaxing with a customary drink. With him were his latest girlfriend, two of his detectives, the local New York lawyer assisting on the case, three or four other hangers-on—and Phillips. Outside the door, and downstairs in the hotel lobby, were armed federal agents, assigned to protect Phillips as long as the presumption of his innocence lasted.

Phillips was resplendent in a single-piece leisure outfit—bright red in color.

"Bill," I jibed, "you've got half the mobsters in New York, and maybe a few cops, looking for you so they can put a bullet in you. Do you have to walk around looking like a bulls-eye?"

Before Phillips could answer, Bailey broke in. "Anyone afraid of an acquittal in this case would shoot me, not him."

Bailey's lady companion squealed, "Oh, no, Lee, don't say that."

As the trial progressed, so did the Commission's Interim Report. It became apparent that there was at least a possibility that the report might come out at about the time the trial was ending, and that publicity about it might affect the jury's deliberations. Whit Knapp had talked to Mayor Lindsay and ascertained that Lindsay was going to be traveling a good deal of the time over the summer. It was felt necessary that the mayor be in town, so that the report could be presented to him personally. A specific date was selected: Monday, August 7, 1972. The date was timed to coordinate with the mayor's scheduled return from a trip. Our information at that time was that the Phillips trial would be over at least a week before then. It did not work out that way.

The Phillips trial dragged on, longer than expected. In the final frenzy of putting our Interim Report together, we no longer paid much attention to the trial.

Advance copies of the Interim Report were given to select members of the media before the planned Monday release. It was necessary, particularly for serious newspapers, to have the lengthy report in advance, so that it could be read, digested, and excerpted in a meaningful way. Everyone agreed to an "embargo"—they would not publish the report or leak it prior to Monday morning.

It never dawned on anyone to keep the District Attorney's Office abreast of our publication schedule. Neglectfully, we had not made a point of informing them of the Monday release date. John Keenan first learned of it on the Friday before. At the same time, it became apparent that the Phillips case would likely go to the jury on the following Monday, just when the report was to be released. On the day they would begin deliberating, after which they would be sequestered, out of reach of the media, jurors would probably be greeted in the morning by tabloid headlines about the Knapp Commission. Keenan and Hogan were not unreasonable in thinking that this publicity might help a defendant who had presented himself throughout the trial as the persecuted hero of the Knapp Commission investigation. They were furious.

Knapp called me on Friday afternoon to tell me that he was leaving for Nantucket. It was up to me to handle Hogan. So, when Hogan called, fuming, I tried to point out to him that the report's release date had been picked weeks earlier, to meet Mayor Lindsay's schedule. I explained that, back then, we thought the Phillips trial would be well over by the time the report was made public. I don't think he believed me. He demanded that I call around to the press and change the release date. By now it was late on Friday afternoon, and I knew that the suggestion was a practical impossibility. Even if we could get to everyone to whom we had given "embargoed" copies, the chances of their agreeing to a delay were nil. Reporters might cooperate with a normal "hold" agreement, for a specified release date. They would never agree to a delay for the sole purpose of accommodating a prosecutor. The result would be more publicity—concerning what the press would call an attempted cover-up. Hogan wanted to explore the idea of getting a court order. My feeling was that such an attempt would fail, and would increase the publicity even more. But I said I would discuss it with Knapp, who would be getting into Nantucket in an hour or so, where he could be reached by phone.

While we waited, the issue became effectively moot. We learned that the local NBC-TV channel, contrary to the explicit promise made to me by the reporter to whom I had given the report, was, even then, breaking the embargo. The reporter's only excuse was that NBC-TV was down in the ratings. They had already leaked the story, and would go with the full treatment on the Saturday night news, at 6:00 P.M. That would necessarily release everyone from the "embargo," and it would be in all the papers the next day, Sunday. The timing was even worse from Hogan's point of view, but it was beyond our control.

Sunday's *Daily News* headline, covering the whole front page, was "KNAPP REPORT SAYS COPS CORRUPT." The Phillips jury began its deliberations the next day. Hogan was enraged. He considered himself betrayed by Knapp, and the incident so rankled him that he did not speak to Knapp until shortly before Hogan's death, a year and a half later.

The jury wound up deadlocked 10 to 2 (or 9–3, according to the prosecution team) in favor of acquittal. It may have been the *News* headline, or Bailey's superb cross-examination of Gonzales, or the lack of credible evidence of guilt; but Phillips was, for the time being, still free.

Both Keenan and Bailey were unavailable when it came time to try Phillips a second time. Keenan had left the office temporarily, to be chief assistant district attorney in Queens County. He was replaced by a seasoned prosecutor named Jack Litman, who in later years was to become a well-known defense attorney. Bailey's place was taken by a local lawyer named Henry Rothblatt. Litman was no John Keenan, but he was nevertheless an accomplished prosecutor. Rothblatt, on the other hand, was a courthouse joke. His incompetence was a thing of legend in the New York Bar. For example, Judge Thomas Murphy, in another case, had interrupted some particularly inept questioning to ask, incredulously, "Mr. Rothblatt, are you being paid?" Rothblatt lived up to his reputation in his defense of Bill Phillips. Instead of 10–2 for acquittal, the jury voted unanimously to convict.

The conviction was affirmed in state court, but later reversed in federal court when it was discovered that one of the jurors had applied for a job in the District Attorney's Office during the trial, and Litman had not seen fit to inform the judge of that fact. A federal district court judge ruled that Phillips had been denied his right to a fair jury, and the Federal Appeals Court agreed on different grounds—prosecutorial misconduct. However, the Supreme Court of the United States ruled that the error had been harmless. Phillips began serving a sentence of twenty-five years to life.

While in prison, he became a model prisoner, earning several academic degrees and becoming a highly effective jailhouse lawyer, representing fellow inmates. At one point, he called me on the telephone and said, "Hey Mike, you'd better tell Keenan and those guys to get me out of here, because I'm doing a lot of harm. You should see the humps that I am representing and getting released." As a result of these efforts on behalf of his fellow inmates, he was featured in a major article in the lawyers' trade magazine, *The American Lawyer*, and in an NBC television segment. Ellen Fleysher, the reporter who filmed the TV interview, came back shaking her head. "This guy is amazing," she said. "Ten minutes after I meet him, he's advising me on my love life."

The indomitable quality of Phillips's wit was demonstrated yet again when he sent a note to be read at the twentieth reunion of Knapp Commission friends and personnel held at the Merchants Club in 1992: "I regret I cannot personally be with you tonight, but the Department of Corrections had other plans for me. Thank you, and good evening from Auburn Prison."

Phillips served thirty-three years in prison, being rejected for parole the first four times he applied. The parole boards all agreed that his prison record had been stellar, and that he represented no threat to society, but refused parole on the ground of the "seriousness" of his crime. In his first two appearances before the parole boards, Phillips continued to deny his guilt. Then, faced with the fact that paroles are not given to those who do not express remorse, he finally "admitted" his crime. He was still twice denied parole because he could not discuss with enough particularity the circumstances of what had happened on the occasion of the murders. To the parole board, this failing, once again, demonstrated his lack of remorse.

One might suppose that the inability to describe the details of a crime scene on the part of a sharpster like Phillips, who knew that his freedom depended on his ability to do so, would indicate not so much a lack of remorse as a lack of guilty knowledge about the crime. Phillips was perfectly well aware that he could obtain a parole only by convincingly admitting his crime and expressing his sorrow for having committed it. Had he actually been in Goldberg's apartment on Christmas Eve, 1968, he could easily have described what happened in excruciating and even colorful detail, perhaps softening his culpability a bit by claiming to have been drunk. It may be that his inability to do so indicates that he wasn't there.

In any event, after thirty-three years in prison, Phillips finally obtained his parole in 2006, after a change in the governorship in New York State had apparently eliminated a virtual blanket order against granting paroles in capital cases.

26

SPECIAL PROSECUTOR

In its report, the Commission's main recommendation was the establishment of a Special Prosecutor's Office for the criminal justice system in New York City to monitor the district attorneys in their anti-corruption efforts and, when necessary, to conduct its own investigations. We suggested that the governor select, and the attorney general appoint, a special prosecutor with jurisdiction throughout the City of New York over matters involving the whole criminal justice system.

Our thought was that a police department covering all five boroughs needed a prosecutor's office to watch it that had jurisdiction over the same area. Each of the five district attorneys would still have primary jurisdiction over corruption cases, but the Special Prosecutor's Office would function in areas where efforts by an independent body seemed needed.

Members of the public who, rightly or wrongly, did not trust their local district attorney to investigate vigorously the police with whom his office worked so closely would have a place to take complaints. In other cases there might be an actual conflict of interest involving a district attorney's office and a particular target of an investigation. Also, there had been specific hints that some district attorney's offices deliberately "took it easy" investigating cops. Whitman Knapp remembered a specific admonition by then–District Attorney Thomas Dewey to that effect. In such cases, the special prosecutor could step in.

We suggested that the new office have jurisdiction over not just cops, but judges and lawyers in the criminal justice system as well, including the five

City district attorneys. It seemed fair not to single out just the police as needing monitoring. Not surprisingly, our recommendation did not sit well with the district attorneys. Frank Hogan, still particularly irked by the fact that the Interim Report was released just as the Phillips case was going to the jury, stated that he was "infuriated" and that his office has been "defamed." Bronx District Attorney Burt Roberts labeled the Commission's observation that the district attorneys were too close to the cops a "cheap shot." Queens District Attorney Thomas Mackell called the report a "damnable lie." We had anticipated these reactions.

Commissioner Murphy at first publicly endorsed the report's recommendation for a special prosecutor but, faced with the district attorneys' reactions, later modified his position, saying, "I don't have a firm position." Robert McKiernan, president of the PBA, predictably branded the whole report—without bothering to read it—"contemptible."

While the philosophy and broad outlines of our proposed Special Prosecutor's Office were laid out in our report, the undiscussed details of its implementation were of course formidable. It would be up to Governor Nelson Rockefeller to decide whether he agreed with our recommendation and, if so, how he wanted to go about structuring the machinery to bring it about.

In the rush of things, we had committed a real faux pas—we neglected to consult the governor. We just issued our report, without warning Rockefeller that we were going to call upon him, publicly, to take what he was later to characterize as "the most important administrative action during my Governorship." Having unceremoniously dumped the issue into the governor's lap, we waited to see what he would do.

Then one morning Whitman Knapp got a telephone call. It was Governor Rockefeller, asking if we could come up that afternoon to his New York office on 55th Street to discuss our recommendation. As we headed uptown, Whit and I agreed that the governor was simply covering his bases. He would great us with a characteristic "Hiya, fellas," chat with us politely for a half-hour or so, and then proceed to do whatever it was he had in mind. But when we got to Rockefeller's office, it became clear that he was not just putting on a show. Present were Attorney General Louis Lefkowitz, Lieutenant Governor Malcolm Wilson, State Investigations Commissioner Paul Curran, Special Aide to the Governor Maurice Nadjari, and two or three other high-level gubernatorial advisors. This was for real. The group, including Rockefeller, turned resolutely to the task of hammering out specific plans for the new Special Prosecutor's Office. It took three days of hard work.

Our commission had recommended an office with chiefly an oversight function, leaving primary jurisdiction in all cases to the local district attorney's offices. We thought that the special prosecutor should have the power to investigate, convene a grand jury, and issue subpoenas, but would only use those powers in circumstances where a conflict existed with one of the district attorney's offices, or some other special circumstance applied. An alternative plan, put forth by Maurice Nadjari, called for a full-fledged prosecutor's office, with a first-line mandate to search out corruption in the criminal justice system.

The three-day effort was one more new experience for me. I had never before had a governor—much less one named Rockefeller—get me coffee. The governor finally opted for Nadjari's model—a full-blown prosecutor's office, with a budget of $4 million, consisting of about two hundred attorneys and investigators (the number was later pared down to a still-sizable thirty-five attorneys and an equal number of detectives). The office was to have its own grand jury, a specially assigned judge, and carte blanche to go after corruption anywhere it could be found in New York City's criminal justice circles.

As the first Special Prosecutor, the governor selected Maurice Nadjari. He appeared to be a logical choice. Nadjari had had long experience in the Manhattan District Attorney's office, where he was known as an able, aggressive prosecutor. He had worked with the governor on a study of the organization of City government, and had held a number of posts related to criminal justice, including chief assistant district attorney in Suffolk County, New York.

I should have seen that something troubling was brewing simply by observing Nadjari's overeager advocacy of a large, powerful Special Prosecutor's Office. Another warning signal was the identity of the man he picked to be his chief assistant—Joe Phillips, the overbearing Manhattan prosecutor who had tried to strong-arm me into surrendering Bill Phillips during the middle of Phillips's undercover work. The final tip-off should have been the magnificent new offices that Nadjari set up to house his operation, which covered the entire fifty-seventh floor of Two World Trade Center. For himself, Nadjari constructed a huge, corner office overlooking New York Harbor, with a large adjoining private conference room. Looking around these accommodations, which matched those of senior partners in the largest law firms in the city, I recalled our commission's decision not to paint the walls in our run-down offices because it seemed inconsistent for corruption fighters to seek unnecessary comforts.

Nadjari turned out to be a disaster. Aided and abetted by Judge John Murtagh, an unabashedly pro-prosecution judge who was assigned to the Special Prosecutor on a permanent basis, Nadjari began a rampage. For the next three years, judges, prosecutors, and defense counsel were subjected to high-handed and invasive, but well-publicized, prosecutions, often based on the shakiest of evidence and the flimsiest of legal theories.

The "highlight" of Nadjari's crusade was the indictment, in 1973, of Queens County District Attorney Thomas Mackell. Mackell and his son-in-law, who worked in the Queens District Attorney's Office, were charged with conspiring to cover up a supposed scheme to obstruct justice by individuals working in Mackell's office, including his son-in-law. They had been the victims of a Ponzi scheme that was under investigation by the Bronx District Attorney Burton Roberts, and were charged with failing fully to cooperate with the investigation of the scheme.

Tommy Mackell was a large, gregarious man, in the true tradition of Irish politicians. Immensely popular in Queens County, he was given to attending social events where he entertained one and all with his near-professional-quality Irish tenor singing voice. He had three songs—"Danny Boy," "My Yiddishe Momma," and "O Solo Mio." Having neatly covered the major ethnic groups in Queens County, Mackell would be free to "work the room" and mollify those of any ethnic or religious persuasion that may have been left out. A kind and generous man, with a keen political eye, Mackell had even been spoken of as a possible gubernatorial candidate. Now he stood indicted by Maurice Nadjari for supposedly not being completely candid with his fellow district attorney from the Bronx. Mackell and his people may have been a little embarrassed at having been "taken" by the con man who duped them, and consequently may not have been as forthcoming to investigators as they might have been. Regardless, it was no criminal case by anyone's measure—except Maurice Nadjari's. But Mackell was forced to resign as district attorney in order to defend himself in court.

Mackell's resignation resulted in an interesting opportunity for me. Rockefeller and I had gotten to know each other during the marathon sessions in his office, when the Special Prosecutor's Office was created. Indeed, he had offered me the job before giving it to Nadjari, but I felt it might look odd for me to accept a position that was created at the suggestion of a commission of which I had been chief counsel. Anyway, I needed to get on with making a living in private practice. Now, Rockefeller asked me to replace Mackell. This time I accepted, on the condition that I would only serve for the less-than-one-year period until a new DA would be chosen, in a special election.

In an additional twist, I recruited, as my chief assistant, John Keenan, whom I had met under the inauspicious circumstance of his engineering the indictment of Bill Phillips. Keenan was clearly the best man to help me in a job I knew absolutely nothing about—running a local District Attorney's Office. I still thought he had been wrong about Phillips and he obviously had serious reservations about me, but we grew to work well with each other and eventually became fast friends.

Under the baleful judicial supervision of Nadjari's pet judge, Murtagh, Mackell was convicted in 1974. But the next year the conviction was emphatically reversed in the Appellate Division, Second Department. The court threw out the conviction on both the law and the facts, finding that Nadjari's legal theory was specious and that the facts did not add up to Tommy Mackell's having done anything wrong. Moreover, the Court took the unusual step of dismissing the indictment outright, rather than providing for a new trial.[1]

Mackell's vindication came too late of course to save his political career. But it did serve to put the brakes on Nadjari's headlong progress. Other cases of his began to come apart.

Nadjari's final downfall, three years after his appointment, was messy. Hugh Carey had become governor and, after hearing endless complaints of Nadjari's excesses, decided to remove him. Carey let it be known that he intended to replace Nadjari with Manhattan District Attorney Robert Morgenthau.

Nadjari attempted a pre-emptive strike. He announced that he had been undertaking an ongoing investigation of the governor himself. Carey was supposedly protecting himself from this investigation by getting rid of the man who was conducting it. Since Nadjari was technically an appointee of the attorney general, not the governor, he obviously hoped to put Attorney General Lefkowitz, a Republican who had held the office for sixteen years, in a position where it would be awkward for him to follow the apparently politically motivated instructions of a Democratic governor attempting to save himself.

But this time Nadjari had overplayed his hand. It quickly became clear that the so-called charges against the governor were totally specious and had been dreamed up only after Nadjari had been told that he was to be fired. Nadjari had falsely claimed that the charges were already under investigation at the time the governor announced that he would be dismissed. When these

---

1. The Court's opinion stated: "The prosecutor was guilty of constant and patent disregard of the basic rules of evidence . . . [and] repeatedly attempted to introduce irrelevant evidence . . . although representing that he would not refer to hearsay and conclusory statements. . . . Nevertheless [did so and] . . . continuously intimidated witnesses by shouting at them without so much as one word of reproval from the court."

Two concurring judges were even more outspoken, characterizing the case as "an absurd miscarriage of justice."

facts became publicly known, Nadjari was finished. He slipped back into private life and was not heard from again on the public scene.

Governor Carey's notion that Nadjari should be replaced by Morgenthau didn't make much sense. No one could question Morgenthau's competence—he was on his way to establishing himself as a legend, ultimately serving thirty-four years as district attorney—but part of the duties of the Special Prosecutor's Office was to oversee the City's district attorneys, and Morgenthau was one of them. There was no suggestion that he would resign as district attorney in order to assume the position of overseeing, among others, his own office. Carey did not think this conflict was important. After Nadjari, he just wanted the best man for the job.

However, in order to allow Morgenthau to hold both jobs, a special bill had to be crammed through the state legislature. Carey could handle this without too much difficulty, but it would take some time, maybe a few months. It was then that I found myself drawn into what turned out to be an extremely awkward situation.

I had completed my tour as Queens District Attorney and was busy getting back to work in my office at Cahill Gordon, when the phone rang. It was Bob Morgenthau. He said he was in his office, discussing the problem of the special prosecutor with some people, and asked me to join the group. I went right over and found Morgenthau surrounded by half-dozen or so of the top politicians and law enforcement people in the city, including John Keenan. They were engaged in a lively discussion of the pros and cons of the governor's plan to name Morgenthau as special prosecutor.

Asked for my opinion, I said that I thought it was a bad idea. With all due respect to my ex-boss, for whom I—like everyone—had the greatest regard, I didn't think he should wear two hats. He would be in the position of monitoring himself. My views were duly noted.

Of immediate practical concern was the fact that, assuming Morgenthau were to be appointed, it would take months to engineer the necessary ratification by the state legislature. What was needed, in the meantime, was an interim Special Prosecutor.

It didn't take long for me to realize that the supposed search for a sacrificial lamb, to serve for as long as three or four months as special prosecutor, was not as open a question as I had been led to believe. I had been summoned, not to join in the decision-making process, but to be pressured into taking the job.

This point was driven home when Morgenthau's secretary came into the room to say that the governor was on the phone. I saw the jaws of the trap closing.

Sure enough, after a few words on the telephone, Morgenthau turned to me, "The governor would like to talk to you." I had never met Governor Carey and had only limited exposure to movers and shakers like governors of New York. I was quite deferential when I picked up the phone. Carey greeted me warmly and proceeded to explain that he needed me to fill a vital position.

I explained that I had already turned down Governor Rockefeller's offer to fill the position when it was established, because among other things it didn't seem appropriate for me to have recommended the creation of a job that I then proceeded to occupy. Carey met that by pointing out that his offer was only temporary. While Rockefeller had presumably been requesting me to make a career change, Carey was merely asking me for a short-term sacrifice for the good of the state. I muttered something about having to check with my partners. Morgenthau got back on the phone and, after a few words, it was determined that he and several of the attending luminaries, together with Keenan and me, would immediately fly up to Albany to consider the matter further with the governor.

The discussion proceeded with Carey, in his pool house at the gubernatorial mansion. I stated my willingness to do what he asked, but advised him that I thought that the whole idea of selecting Morgenthau as special prosecutor was not a good one, and that instead he should pick someone else. My candidate was John Keenan, whose name had been prominently mentioned for the job.

Carey professed to be on the fence, and said that, in any event, that he had to travel to New York City that night to discuss the matter with Attorney General Louis Lefkowitz. He was the one who actually had to make the formal designation. Without Lefkowitz's acquiescence, it could not be accomplished. Keenan and I were put up in the Governor's Mansion, while Carey headed off to New York City.

I recall being amused at the changes in the mansion since the one other time I had visited there—when Rockefeller was governor. Then, Picassos and Mondrians had hung on the walls of the main living room. Now, in the same room, I noticed a child's pull-toy under the sofa.

At about three o'clock in the morning, Carey returned and woke us to say that he was pretty sure that Lefkowitz would go along with the idea. They were going to go ahead with a press conference that had been tentatively planned for that morning.

Carey still maintained, as we walked to the press conference after breakfast, that he had not finally made up his mind. Then he took the podium in front of an assemblage of reporters and television cameras to announce his selection of Morgenthau, his intention to seek legislation to facilitate that choice, and his temporary appointment of me as special prosecutor for the interim period.

The next day I had to explain to my partners how my picture wound up on the front page of the *New York Times*, accepting yet another public position, when I had assured them that I had returned to private practice permanently.

It quickly turned out that I need not spend any time or effort justifying my acceptance of the new position. Upon reflection, Lefkowitz had agreed with those of us who felt that appointing Morgenthau was not a good idea, and had exercised his prerogative of blocking the step by refusing to appoint me as interim special prosecutor. When Lefkowitz called me to explain that there was nothing personal about his action, I recalled a line from James Cagney's movie portrayal of George M. Cohan and said to him, "My wife thanks you, my children thank you, my partners thank you, and I thank you."

Foiled by Lefkowitz's refusal to go along with him, Carey did the right thing and appointed John Keenan as special prosecutor.

The smoke cleared from the conflagration that had been Maurice Nadjari's rise and fall, and John Keenan moved in to restore order. Among professionals, there was not a more respected law enforcement figure in the country. This reputation was important, because Keenan was faced with the tasks of not only restoring the Special Prosecutor's Office, but convincing everyone in the public and the criminal justice system that he had indeed done so. By the time Keenan stepped down, three years later, the office was a respected part of the law enforcement effort in New York, acting vigorously when required to do so and cooperating with other law enforcement agencies.

The Special Prosecutor's Office continued to play an important part in the battle against corruption in New York City under the leadership first of Roderick Lankler, a former assistant D.A. in Frank Hogan's office, then, Thomas Duffy, a former assistant in the Queen's District Attorney's Office, and, finally Charles ("Joe") Hynes, who was later to cap his career by being elected district attorney in Brooklyn, a post he still holds. In 1991, for budgetary reasons, Governor Mario Cuomo was forced to disband the office. Although it had been priced out of existence, it had done its job well. Cuomo would have been well advised to find the money somewhere to allow it to continue.

27

REFLECTIONS

Four decades after the creation of the Knapp Commission, it seems useful to reflect on what it accomplished and its impact, if any, on the New York City Police Department. Some—including Frank Serpico, in recent years—have complained that nothing really worthwhile was achieved because no high-level police brass or political figures went to jail. Others point to the relatively few criminal convictions that ultimately resulted from the Commission's work. Still others note that in 1992, just twenty years after the Knapp Commission ended, another commission, under the esteemed leadership of State Appellate Court Judge Milton Mollen, found extremely serious conditions of corruption to exist in the Department. Perhaps the Knapp Commission simply took its turn, without meaningful effect, in the recurring cycle of police corruption exposés that have occurred approximately every twenty years since 1894.

I think not.

I believe the Knapp Commission was responsible for a fundamental reform in the Department in one major respect, and the Mollen Commission followed, twenty years later, with another. To this day, the Department remains better for the efforts of both.

It is accurate to observe that the Knapp Commission did not definitely prove corruption on the part of any high-level police officer or politician. It had neither the resources nor the mandate to make cases against individuals, highly placed or otherwise. Rather, the Commission's task was to discover what "patterns" of corruption, if any, existed in the Department, and we actually did our best, in our hearings and in our report, to avoid reference to any individual by name. Those caught in our net were really incidental to our task.

Individuals did of course become involved.[1] Our chief witnesses were corrupt police officers whom we had uncovered. Their testimony was itself a breakthrough, shattering the myth of the "blue wall of silence." Approximately thirty indictments were quickly obtained on the strength of Bill Phillips's revelations alone, only to be compromised when Phillips was convicted for murder. Most of those cases were supported by tapes and surveillance testimony, but the prosecutors decided that they could not be pursued because Phillips himself would be unavailable, or unpersuasive, as a witness.

Indictments, and convictions, resulted from other Commission efforts: the meat robbery, the "Tank and Slim" operation, and the federal investigation involving Bob Leuci all led to specific charges against many individual wrongdoers. The Commission exposed the individual misdeeds and mistakes of many people, in and out of the Department, including ranking police bosses and political figures, who bore responsibility for letting conditions get the way they were. A number of top-level mayoral and police personnel, including former Police Commissioner Howard Leary, former First Deputy Commissioner John Walsh, and mayoral aide Jay Kriegel, were required to testify publically to explain their conduct, making the point that integrity in a police department requires vigilant dedication on the part of departmental and political leaders. But the Commission's charge was not to catch individuals, and its success, if any, lay elsewhere.[2]

The Knapp Commission's contribution was to use the weapon of public exposure to help bring about the elimination of the general, pervasive climate of corruption that existed in the Department at that time. "Grass eaters" then comprised the vast majority of New York City cops. Minor gratu-

---

1. Sometimes unfairly, as with Lieutenant Mazen, who was allowed to testify at the public hearings to permit him to react to an inadvertent and erroneous reference to him made in a document that had been displayed in the hearings.
2. No list of accomplishments of the Knapp Commission would be complete without mention of the disparate literary endeavors that the Commission's work spawned or heavily contributed to. Most prominent, of course, was Peter Maas's book, *Serpico*, followed by Robert Daley's *Prince of the City*, about Bob Leuci; Leonard Schecter's *On the Pad*, about Bill Phillips; L. H. Whittemore's *The Super Cops*, about "Batman" and "Robin"; Robin Moore's *The Happy Hooker*, about Xaviera Hollander; and *The Patrolman: A Cop's Story*, by Edward Droge.

ities and payoffs were a way of life, so prevalent that any officer who did not indulge was usually considered to be, like Frank Serpico, a "weirdo." We even heard of officers who lied about engaging in corrupt acts that they hadn't done, just to be thought of as being "one of the boys." The layer of corrupt fog that enveloped the Department had a significance beyond the sum of the individual criminal acts from which it arose. This atmosphere robbed Department members of the public respect to which their many worthwhile and heroic actions otherwise entitled them. Also, the general acceptance of "grass eater" corruption created fertile ground in which the more menacing "meat eaters" could breed. While we found no statistics convincingly linking the general crime rate to corruption, it seems logical that members of the public are less likely to respect the law if they have no respect for the police officers who are sworn to enforce it.

Particularly insidious was the fact that the pressures that naturally lead to corruption in a police force are to some degree seductively understandable. When confronted by overly righteous critics of cops and their foibles, Chief Sidney Cooper would trot out a hypothetical that he used for the purpose of suggesting that even clear wrongdoing can be rationalized.

"You are a sergeant, in charge of a half-dozen men," Cooper would say. "A confidential, undercover informant, whose identity you absolutely cannot disclose, tells you that an organized crime underboss by the name of, say, Joe Salerno is personally going to steal a particular truck, loaded with valuable merchandise, from a Brooklyn waterfront area warehouse parking lot. The crime is to occur at 3:30 A.M. the following Tuesday night.

"On that evening you conceal your men in the parking lot, and at exactly 3:30 A.M. a shadowy, unidentifiable figure makes his way through the darkness and jumps into the very truck that your informant had said would be stolen. As your men close in to make the arrest, the truck speeds away, escaping through an exit you had overlooked. You and your men leap in your own cars and, with lights and sirens at full blast, give chase through the deserted streets surrounding the warehouse.

"Within minutes, you find the truck, a few blocks from the warehouse parking lot. You fan out, looking for Salerno, and, after a while, find him walking down a lonely street a number of blocks from the abandoned truck. As you shove him against a wall to frisk him, he reaches in his pocket and produces a $1,000 bill. 'Let me go,' he says.

"You are being asked to accept $1,000 for not committing a crime. The only way you would be able to make a case against Salerno would be to 'put him back in the truck'—that is, to testify falsely that you caught him there. He is offering you $1,000 to do what the law requires—release him."

In advancing his hypothetical, Cooper was not saying that the police officer should take the money. He merely sought to point out that a major difficulty with dealing with the problem of police corruption is the fact that sometimes things aren't entirely black or white. To an underpaid cop, perhaps with debts, sick family members, or an overdue mortgage, accepting money from a well-heeled criminal in return for merely doing his duty—which he intended to do anyway—might not seem so reprehensible.

The dark, irrepressible humor that may be the single unifying characteristic among members of the New York City Police Department was illustrated by the reactions of two ex-cop friends of mine when I told them Cooper's hypothetical. "I know what I would have done," said one of them. "I'd have taken the $1,000 and *then* put the guy back in the truck." My other friend added, "And, you never know what might be in the truck."

The cynical humor that seems to come with policing need not overwhelm the pride that, if allowed to flourish, is also a natural part of the job. Pride in his job should lead a cop to feel that he is above taking tips and that he should recoil from a proffered gratuity, not let it become so ordinary that he accepts it without thinking. A routine bribe is beneath notice unless it is seen to be beneath contempt.

Fundamental to the attitude in the Department is the respect—or lack of it—that the cops feel for themselves. I believe all evidence indicates that the 80 percent of police officers who Frank Serpico said wished to be honest took the opportunity afforded by the Knapp Commission exposures, and the departmental reforms that followed, to become that way. The intense negative publicity that our commission brought to bear on conditions that had previously been deliberately ignored by police brass, politicians, and the public had the effect of facilitating a change in the climate in which the Department operated. This change was brought about not merely by the Commission's identifying patterns of corruption, but by the intense publicity attending these exposures. What had been a dirty secret, known to most but ignored by all, could no longer be brushed aside. The legendary Sidney Cooper was quoted in the *New York Times*: "We [police brass] used to sit around discussing corruption with all the enthusiasm of a bunch of little old ladies talking about venereal disease. Now, Knapp has made us deal with it."

The public wanted action, so the mayor and other politicians did too. Reform-minded Police Commissioner Patrick Murphy was free to crack down with new anti-corruption controls and investigative methods. Federal authorities and the new Special Prosecutor's Office, recommended by the Commission, also weighed in against corruption in the criminal justice system.

Now cops actually got arrested for being corrupt. Superior officers, from chiefs to sergeants, faced discipline for corruption occurring under them, even if they weren't aware of the wrongdoing until it was exposed. If they didn't know, they should have. So supervisors all up and down the line put the screws to subordinates, letting them know that their boss was not about to take blame for what they did. Occasions of corruption were nipped in the bud. A cop on the street could still be corrupt, if he was so inclined, but now it was a lot more difficult, and he had to lie about what he was doing, not brag about it.

On an anecdotal level, I heard from many people I encountered that the Department had indeed changed. Federal and local anti-corruption officers, bar-owners, storekeepers, small merchants, regular cops: all attested to the fact that the "good old days" were gone. I have been told that for quite some period, many in the Department actually measured time as "Pre-Knapp" and "Post-Knapp." Some time after the Commission I met and befriended an ex-cop—one of the very best—who asked me, with a twinkle in his eye, "Why did you have to mess up a good thing?"

This sea change in the Department was specifically noted by the Mollen Commission in its report in 1994:

> Unlike the situation a generation ago, this Commission can confidently re-port that the vast majority of New York City police officers are honest and hard working and serve this city with skill and dedication each day. (Mollen Commission Report, p. 1)

While the Mollen Commission found no remaining indications of systemic "grass eaters" in the Department of 1992, they also found that, during the twenty years since Knapp, the "meat eaters" had gotten substantially worse. The reason apparently lay in the increase in drug traffic. Cops growing up in a more permissive drug culture were not as offended by illegal drug sales as had been their elders, and became more prone to getting caught up in drug-related graft. At the time of Knapp, many police officers recoiled from getting involved with drugs in any way. Times changed, and as society got more accustomed to the use of drugs, so did the cops. In an often-described typical "slide" into narcotics-related corruption, a cop first skimmed excess narcotics from a dealer he arrested, having no purpose other than to use the drugs for paying informants. Since any cash given an informant would be used to buy drugs, why not shortcut the process? Then the informant began demanding more drugs than he could reasonably consume himself, so the cop found him-self in the position of supplying a supplier. From there it was a short step, for some, to require the informant to share some of his profits. The police officer had become a drug dealer!

This gradual "slide" of honest police officers into crime may have accounted for some of the corrupt cops exposed by the Mollen Commission, but most of them appear to have needed no persuasion. They were real "meat eaters," completely willing, even eager, to commit crime. The Mollen Commission's findings did not purport to gauge how widespread such criminal behavior was throughout the Department. Focusing on one major pocket of "meat eater" activity, the Commission found that cops were selling hard drugs and viciously brutalizing anyone—including other cops—who got in their way. A Knapp "meat eater" had been a crooked cop who took money to allow serious criminals to operate. By the time of the Mollen Commission, a "meat eater" had come to mean a cop who was himself a crook—in actual competition with those he was supposed to arrest.

As the Mollen Commission Report said:

> While the systemic and institutionalized bribery schemes that plagued the Department a generation ago no longer exist, a new and often more invidious form of corruption has infected parts of this city, especially in high-crime precincts with an active narcotics trade. Its most prevalent form is not police taking money to accommodate criminals by closing their eyes to illegal activities, as was the case twenty years ago, but police acting as criminals, especially in connection with the drug trade. . . . Thus, while more limited in extent, police corruption has become more serious and threatening than ever before.   (Mollen Commission Report, p. 2)

This was not a problem that could be cured by mere public exposure or disciplinary pressure. These miscreants were common criminals, sometimes very sophisticated ones. They had to be caught, and it was up to the Department to have in place the means to do so.

So Mollen focused on the Department's machinery for dealing with serious police crime. The Commission concluded that the Department's anti-corruption machinery had utterly broken down. "In the face of this problem, the Department allowed its systems for fighting corruption virtually to collapse" (p. 2).

As a result of the Mollen Commission's efforts, the Internal Affairs Division, responsible for combating corruption, was completely reorganized and strengthened. It was upgraded to bureau status, becoming the Internal Affairs Bureau (IAB), and was heavily staffed and supplied. Service in IAB was now a definite career track, rather than a disgraced backwater. Officers were drafted to serve in IAB for a set period, so that there was less cause for other cops to look upon them, derisively, as traitors. The Bureau was run with vigorous efficiency, having access to the latest technological investigative tools. It had the full support of both the Mayor's Office and the police commissioner.

The Mollen Commission made clear, as had Knapp, that an essential for maintaining a corruption-free police department is strong, knowledgeable leadership—chiefly on the part of the police commissioner. Put someone like World War II general George Patton or Green Bay Packers' football coach Vince Lombardi in charge of a police department and corruption should not be a problem. As star running back Paul Hornung said of Lombardi, "When the coach says 'sit down,' you don't even look to see if there's a chair." Cops respond to that kind of leadership.

The Mollen Commission also recommended a return to an independent monitor, such as the Special Prosecutor's Office, which had been abandoned a number of years earlier. Mayor Rudolph Giuliani responded by establishing the Mayor's Commission to Combat Police Corruption. Unlike the Special Prosecutor's Office, set up in the wake of the Knapp Commission, this commission would have no investigative or prosecutorial power. Its budget was dramatically smaller than had been the Special Prosecutor's, having a permanent staff of only about six people. Its job was not to make cases on its own, but merely to oversee the efforts to that end undertaken by the Department.

In a sort of return to first causes, the initial chair of this new commission, appointed in 1995, was one of our hardy Knapp Commission crew of twenty-five years before—Nick Scoppetta. After a few commissioners took their turns, the wheel came around to me. I have been chair of this commission since 2005. From this vantage point, my personal view is that the attitude throughout the Department seems fundamentally hostile to the kind of systemized graft that had been a way of life almost forty years ago. Leadership is firm. The pads are gone. There are some "grass eaters," but they are few, and not in favor with their comrades. As for the "meat eaters," there will always be some criminals operating in police uniforms, but well-oiled machinery—and the will to use it—now exists to root them out.

It appears that the twenty-year cycle may have been broken. Unless some startling revelations surface shortly, the twenty-year mark since the Mollen Commission will pass without the need for yet another inquiry. Knapp largely disposed of the "grass eaters." Mollen shaped the machinery to deal with the "meat eaters." As long as Department leadership remains strong and vigilant, there should be no need for any more commissions.

INDEX

The Advocates (television show), 221
after-hours clubs. *See* nightclubs
al-Hafeez, Humza, 79
Alessi, Al, 203
Armstrong, Joan, 7, 39, 190–191
Armstrong, Michael: appearances and speaking
    engagements by, 220–224; invitation
    to be chief counsel, 6; invitation to be
    Special Prosecutor, 238, 241, 242; Mayor's
    Commission to Combat Police Corruption,
    249; meeting Hollander, 219–220; meeting
    the mayor, 7–10; opinion of Mayor Lindsay,
    8; Pressman television interview of, 37–39; as
    Queens County District Attorney, 238–239,
    240; reflections on Knapp Commission,
    243–249
Ash, Carol ("Flash"), 18, 20, 135
Aurellio, Dick, 9, 207

Bailey, F. Lee, 229, 230, 231, 233
Barrett, Elizabeth ("Lisa"), 19, 32, 157
Barrett, Margo, 224
Barrett Smith Shapiro and Simon, 134
bars and restaurants, Commission investigation
    of, vii, 21, 36–37, 47, 57–58, 75, 119, 133,
    162, 172, 180, 183, 183n1
"bat cave," 160
"Batman and Robin," 78–82, 164, 166, 168,
    244n2

Bauman, Arnold, 6, 33, 135
Beame, Abe, 8
Beane, Anne, 19, 135
Behan, Cornelius "Neal," 214, 215, 216
Blitzblau, Paul, 20
"blue wall of silence," viii, 13, 113, 187, 195, 244
Board of Estimate hearing, 11
bodegas, police payoffs by, 35–36, 193
Broderick, Vincent, 10
Bruh, Brian: about, 42, 134, 137, 145; Burkert
    affair, 75; Droge operations, 164; Germaise
    operations, 108, 111, 112; Hollander
    operation, 44, 89; Leary subpoena, 136;
    Phillips operations, 89, 113, 146, 148, 158,
    171
Buckley, William F., Jr., 28–30
Bureau of Narcotics, 17
Burkert, George: operations involving, 51–56,
    72–74, 75; testimony of, 169, 200–201
Burnham, David, 1, 2, 79, 180, 181, 220

Caban, Desiderio, 131
cabarets. *See* nightclubs
Cahill, John, 124–125
Cahill Gordon Reindel & Ohl, 124, 126, 134,
    219, 224, 240, 242
Carey, Hugh, 239, 241
Carros, George, 62, 64, 67, 68, 71
Century Club, 24

"Cheech," 120

Cipriani, Ralph: about, 134, 137, 146; Droge operations, 116, 164, 166; gambling and, 194; Phillips operations, 148, 158, 171; testimony of, 194

Clark, Ramsey, 212, 214

Colodner, Warren, 134, 170, 178, 210, 215–216, 223

Community Attitude Survey, 32

Conboy, Ken, 219, 220, 231

concealed recorders or transmitters, 40–46

Condon, Richard, 161, 167, 170, 174

construction sites, 21, 35, 75, 79, 123, 133, 183, 184, 193, 201, 203

Cooper, Everett, 194

Cooper, Sidney, 27, 28, 119, 124, 166, 167, 207, 209n1, 216, 226, 245–246

Cuomo, Mario, 242

Curran, Henry, 4

Curran, Paul, 236

Daley, Robert, 168, 173, 173n1, 204

Danziger, Marty, 24, 25, 225

Davidson, Barbara, 197

DeSapio, Carmine, 14

Dewey, Tom, 3

DiPietro, "Colly," 146

Donovan, Jim, 46–48, 49, 50, 116, 203

Doyle, Jim, 130, 131, 174

Dreyfus, Larry, 89, 99, 181–182

Droge, Edward: book by, 244n2; operations involving, 115–122, 163–168; suspension of, 204–207; testimony of, 169, 195–197

Duffy, Thomas, 242

Dukakis, Michael, 221

Durk, David: about, 2, 61, 209; Leuci operations, 62, 63, 69–70; Serpico's testimony, 214, 215; testimony of, 210, 217

electronic surveillance equipment, 40–41, 43, 44, 67, 127, 159, 167, 219

ex-cops, as Knapp Commission agents, 18

Fanelli (policeman), 148, 149, 150

Farby (gambler), 129

Farren, Patricia, 224

Figueroa, Nicholas, 15, 35

Foley, Joe, 117, 205

Foran, Phillip, 214

Forcelon, Mary, 102

Ford, Paul, 134, 135, 215

Fraiman, Arnold, 214, 217, 218

free meal cases, 58–59, 84, 172, 173, 174, 183, 201–202

Fullilove, H. Earl, 203

funding, for Knapp Commission activities, 9, 10–11, 13, 23, 25, 132

fundraising, for Knapp Commission, 24–25, 132

Galante, Carmine, 146

Gallagher, Cornelius, 17

gambling, 1–2, 13, 21, 81, 129; Cipriani testimony, 194; Droge and, 120; legalization of, 221; "Little Artie," 148, 149, 150, 188; New York Police Seventh Division squad, 2; numbers racket, 2, 13, 61–71, 86, 151, 156, 184, 194; "on the pad," 2; payoffs, 2, 193; Phillips and, 129, 130, 150, 151, 158, 163, 184, 185, 187, 192, 193, See also police corruption; police payoffs

Gasner's Restaurant, 58

Germaise, Irwin, 100, 104–109, 112, 182

Giuliani, Rudolph, 249

Gold, Eugene, 81, 163, 164, 167

Goldberg, Arthur, 5–6

Goldberg, Sam, 227

Goldstein, Herman, 29

Gonzales, Charles, 227, 228–229

graft, vii, viii, 1, 46, 66, 75, 78, 82, 84–85, 112, 118, 119, 128, 129, 130, 139, 150, 161, 171, 183–184, 188, 189, 193, 195, 196, 201, 202, 203, 247, 249; bars and restaurants, vii, 21, 36–37, 47, 57–58, 75, 119, 133, 162, 172, 180, 183, 183n1; construction sites, 21, 35, 75, 79, 123, 133, 183, 184, 193, 201, 203; nightclubs, vii, 36–37, 47, 183, 193; numbers racket, 2, 61–71, 86, 151, 156, 184, 194; prostitution, 21, 41, 42, 43, 47, 89, 93, 100, 123, 150, 177; tow truck operators, 51–56, 169, 200–201. See also gambling; narcotics graft; police corruption; police payoffs

"grass eaters," vii, 28, 75, 119, 121, 122, 163, 243, 247

Great Plains Packing Company, Inc., 47–50

Greenberg, David, 78–82, 163–165, 166–167, 168

Gross, Harry, 4, 50

Group 6 (23rd Precinct), 140

gypsies, 59–60

Hanson, Mark, 58, 202

Hantz, Robert, 78–82, 163–165, 166–167, 168

Happy Hooker (Moore), 244n2

Hentoff, Nat, 222
hippies, 14, 20
Hiss, Alger, 29
Hogan, Frank, 3, 126, 232, 233, 236
Hollander, Xaviera, 43–45, 88, 109, 112, 179,
    181, 182, 185, 219–220, 244n2
homosexual prostitution hangouts, 47
"hooker" operation, 41–45. See also prostitution
Hornung, Paul, 249
Hynes, Charles "Joe," 165, 167, 168, 242

Impellizzeri, Julius, 134, 137, 140, 146, 147, 158
Internal Affairs Bureau (IAB), 249
Internal Revenue Service, 16, 17, 18, 42, 134
investigative team, 13–15

Jannotta, Alfonso, 75–77, 113, 130
"Jewish Max" incident, 214
"Joe Cuba," 185
"Joe Tough Guy," 128, 129, 151, 152–153
"Johnny Cigar," 185
Johnson, Sue, 21
Justy, John, 227

Keenan, John, 227, 228, 230, 231, 232, 233, 238,
    240, 241, 242
Kiernan, Ed, 198, 225, 236
Knapp, Whitman: about, viii, 3, 24, 46, 137, 178,
    204; appearances and speaking engagements
    by, 220, 223; on Durk, 69; formation of
    commission, 3–4; fundraising by, 24–25,
    133; Knapp Commission investigations, 7, 8,
    12, 13, 14, 15, 20, 22, 24, 62, 131, 202–203;
    Knapp Commission public hearings, 178,
    179, 185, 204; Leary testimony, 137–138;
    Leuci operations, 62, 67; Lindsay and, 10,
    231; physical appearance of, 3; Rockefeller
    and, 236; suspension of Phillips and Droge,
    204–207; threats on life of, 190
Knapp Commission: academia and, 29–30;
    accomplishments of, 244; administrative
    issues, 27; announced formal establishment
    of, 10; attorneys, 14–15; author's reflections
    on, 243–249; borrowed agents for, 16–18,
    133; cars for Commission use, 18–19; choice
    of commissioners, 4–6; compensation
    for team members, 6, 13; diversity on, 13;
    ex-cops on, 18; expense of farewell party,
    137–138; executive session of, 33; focus of,
    12; formation of, 3; funding of, 9, 10–11,
    13, 23, 25, 132; fundraising efforts, 24–25,

132; history of, viii, 3; investigative team
    of, 13–15, 133; loss of Scoppetta, Carros,
    and Neuman, 61–71; media coverage of,
    37–39, 60, 131, 174, 175, 177, 178, 180, 185,
    186, 198, 201, 202, 214, 216, 220, 227, 228,
    241; "neighborhood investigators," 13–14,
    20; office, 18; organizational plan of, 13;
    patterns of corruption, discovering, 12;
    as possible whitewash, 4–6; problems in,
    133–138; public charges against, 37; radio
    ad for, 32; staffing of, 12–26, 133; subpoena
    power, 25, 26, 32–33, 135, 136; support staff
    for, 14, 18, 19, See also Knapp Commission
    activities; Knapp Commission hearings
Knapp Commission activities: bars and
    restaurants investigations, 21, 36–37, 47,
    57–58, 75, 119, 133, 162, 172, 180, 183,
    183n1, 192, 202; "Batman and Robin,"
    78–82, 164, 166, 168, 244n2; bodegas
    investigations, 35–36, 193; construction
    sites, 21, 35, 75, 79, 123, 133, 183, 184,
    193, 201, 203; Droge operations, 115–122,
    163–168; early activities of, 27–34; electronic
    eavesdropping equipment, 40, 41, 43, 44, 67,
    127, 159, 167, 219; free meal cases, 58–59,
    172, 173, 174, 183, 201–202; Germaise
    operations, 105–109, 111, 112; "great meat
    robbery," 47–50, 203; gypsies and, 59–60;
    Hollander affair, 43–45, 88, 109, 112, 179,
    181, 182, 185, 219–220, 244n2; homosexual
    prostitution hangouts, 47; "hooker"
    operation, 41–45; Leuci operations, 61–71,
    71n1, 113, 123n1, 124, 126, 130; meat theft
    investigation, 47–50, 203; nightclubs, vii,
    36–37, 47, 183, 193; Phillips operations,
    88–104, 112–114, 123–132, 133, 148–162,
    244; Police Department files review, 30, 31,
    38; Tank and Slim, 139–146, 169, 199–200;
    tow truck operator payoffs, 51–56, 169,
    200–201; undercover work, 53–55; wearing a
    wire, 53–56, 114, 131, 140, 165
Knapp Commission hearings (first set), 169–210;
    advertising of, 173–174; Alessi testimony,
    203; bomb threats, 186; Burkert testimony,
    169, 200–201; Cipriani testimony, 199–200;
    criticism of, 198; Droge testimony, 169,
    195–197; Fullilove testimony, 203; Hanson
    testimony, 202; Logan testimony, 169,
    198–199; Mazen testimony, 202–203;
    McGowan testimony, 203–204, 208; media
    coverage of, 176–177, 185, 189, 201, 220;

Phillips testimony, 169–174, 175, 178–194, 244; preparation for, 169–177; purpose of, 208; reaction to, 198, 210; Tank and Slim, 199–200

Knapp Commission hearings (second set), 210–218; Behan testimony, 215–216; Durk testimony, 217; Fraiman testimony, 217, 218; Kriegel testimony, 217–218, 218n2, 244; Leary testimony, 136, 138, 217, 244; Roberts testimony, 216; Serpico testimony, 169, 210–215; Walsh testimony, 216–217, 218, 244

The Knapp Commission Report on Police Corruption, viii, 218, 218n3; issuance of, 224–225, 225n3, 231–232, 233; reactions to, 225, 236; recommendation of Special Prosecutor's office, 235; writing of, 224

Kriegel, Jay, 2, 9, 212, 213, 215, 217–218, 218n2, 244

Lankler, Roderick, 242

Laviano (policeman), 148, 149

Law Enforcement Assistance Administration (LEAA), 24

Leary, Howard: about, 10, 21; subpoena of, 136, 137–138; testimony of, 136, 138, 217, 244

Lefkowitz, Louis, 236, 239, 241, 242

Leuci, Robert, 61–71, 71n1, 113, 124, 126, 130, 244n2

Lexow Committee, 4, 4n1

Lindsay, John V., viii, 1, 2; funding for Commission activities, 23; Knapp Commission and, 4, 5; Knapp Commission hearings and, 212; meeting with author, 7–10; *New York Times* article and, 2–3

Lissitzyn, Susan, 224

Litman, Jack, 233

"Little Artie," 148, 149, 150, 188

loan sharks, 151

Logan, Waverly: operations involving, 83–87, 122, 139; testimony of, 169, 198–199

Lombardi, Vince, 249

"Louie Fats," 128, 129, 151, 153, 154, 155, 192

Luzzi (policeman), 150

Maas, Peter, 209, 209n1, 211, 244n2

Mackell, Thomas, 236, 238–239

Manton, Martin, 125

Mayor's Commission to Combat Police Corruption, 249

Mazen, Aaron, 202–203, 220, 244n1

McGovern, Joseph, 31

McGowan, Daniel, 30, 31, 32, 203–204, 208

McKenna, Jerry, 100–101, 160

McKiernan, Robert, 225, 236

"meat eaters," vii, 28, 121, 122, 124, 158, 243, 247, 248

meat theft investigation, 47–50, 203

media coverage: European, 197; of Knapp Commission, 37–39, 60, 131, 174, 175, 177, 178, 180, 185, 186, 198, 201, 202, 214, 216, 220, 227, 228, 241; of Knapp Commission public hearings, 176–177, 185, 189, 197–198, 201, 220

Mitchell, John, 126

Mollen Commission Report, 247–248, 249

Mollo, Silvio J., 14, 124, 125

Monserrat, Joseph, 5, 206, 207

Monsky, Mark, 72–73, 83

Moore, Robin, 244n2

Morgenthau, Robert, 14, 68, 240, 242

Murphy, Chief Patrick, 22, 23, 25, 46, 69, 70, 170–171, 173, 188, 189–190, 204–207, 246

Murphy, Judge Thomas, 29, 30, 233

Murtagh, Judge John, 237

"Muzzi," 156–157

Nadjari, Maurice, 236–241, 240n1

narcotics graft, 17, 66, 120–121, 128–130, 247–248; Leuci operations, 61–71, 71n1, 113, 123n1, 124, 126, 130; skimming off confiscated drug stash, 140; stolen merchandise exchanged for narcotics, 139–146, 169, 198–199; Tank and Slim, 139–146, 169, 198–199

National Association of Police Chiefs, 22

"neighborhood investigators," 13–14, 20

Nemic, Frank, 17–18, 46, 49

New York City: financial crisis, 23; transit strike, 8

New York City Police Department: First Division, 150, 171, 174; Third Division, 148, 150, 170, 188; Fourth Division, 148, 170, 188; Sixth Division, 184; Seventh Division, 2, 187, 214; Sixteenth Division, 158; 17th Precinct, 189; 19th Precinct, 183; 23rd Precinct, 140, 186; 25th Precinct, 192, 193–194; 80th Precinct, 119, 122; 84th Precinct, 166; 90th Precinct, 119; anti-corruption unit, 150; appointment of Chief Murphy, 22; "bat cave," 150; black community and, 78–82; "blue wall of silence," viii, 13, 113, 187, 195, 244; Bureau of Narcotics, 17;

detective squad, 192; "dunces," 86; files
of, 30, 31, 38; Group 6 (23rd Precinct),
140; headquarters of, 33–34; impact of
Knapp Commission post-Commission,
245–246; Intelligence Division, 30, 66;
Internal Affairs Bureau (IAB), 249; Internal
Affairs Division, 224, 248–249; Leary's
resignation, 21–22; Patrolman's Benevolent
Association (PBA), 11, 37, 39, 60, 131, 167,
168, 225; Prevention Enforcement Patrol
(PEP) Squad, 83, 85, 86, 198; Public Morals
and Administration Division (PMAD),
149; Sergeant's Benevolent Association,
33; Special Investigations Unit (SIU), 64;
Tactical Patrol Force (TPF Unit), 84; typical
plainclothesman's day, 2; Youth Squad, 188,
See also police corruption
New York Civil Liberties Union, 198
Newman, Sy, 62, 67, 68, 71
nightclubs (after-hour clubs; cabarets),
Commission investigation of, vii, 36–37, 47,
183, 193
numbers racket, 2, 61–71, 86, 151, 156, 184,
194

Obermaier, Otto: about, 14, 15, 62; Knapp
Commission activities, 16, 20, 27, 30, 31, 32,
34, 137; Knapp Commission hearings, 212;
Leary testimony, 138; Leuci operations, 66
obscene language, on television, 177
"on the pad," 2
On the Pad (Schecter), 209n1, 244n2
Ormento, "Big John," 146

Pacino, Al, 209
Parente, Ralph: Hollander operation, 42, 75;
Phillips operations, 89, 113
The Patrolman (Droge), 244n2
Patrolman's Benevolent Association (PBA), 11,
37, 39, 60, 131, 167, 168, 225
payoffs. See police payoffs
Pelleck, Carl, 225
PEP Squad. See Prevention Enforcement Patrol
(PEP) Squad
Percy, Charles, 103–104
Phillips, Joe, 160–161, 237
Phillips, William R.: about, 123; book about,
244n2; gambling and, 129, 130, 150, 151,
158, 163, 184, 185, 187, 192, 193; Knapp
Commission investigation, 88–104, 112–
114, 123–132, 133, 148–162, 179, 244;

murder indictment and trials, 220–233;
note on twentieth reunion of Commission,
233–234; parole, 234; prison time, 233,
234; suspension of, 204–207; testimony of,
169–172, 174, 178–194, 209n1, 244; transfer
to First Plainclothes Division, 171, 174–175
Pleasant Avenue (Harlem), 61, 151, 155, 175
PMAD. See Public Morals and Administration
Division
police corruption: black community and, 78–82;
free meals, 58–59, 172, 173, 174, 183, 201–
202; "grass eaters" and "meat eaters," vii,
28, 75, 119, 121, 122, 124, 158, 163, 243, 247,
248; history of, 4; numbers racket, 2, 61–71,
86, 151, 156, 184, 194; on-duty drinking, 39;
"on the pad," 2; payoffs, 2, 17, 35–37, 51–56,
66, 120–121, 169; policy operation, 86;
prostitution, 21, 41, 42, 43, 47, 89, 93, 100,
123, 150, 177; recordkeeping and, 30, 31, 38;
shakedowns, 51, 64, 82, 84, 132, 190, 194,
200; "shooflies," 13, 27; types of corruption,
vii–viii, See also gambling; graft; narcotics
graft; police payoffs
Police Department. See New York City Police
Department
police memo books, 38
police payoffs, 2; by bodegas, 35–36, 193; at
construction sites, 21, 35, 75, 79, 123, 133,
183, 184, 193, 201, 203; narcotics graft, 17,
66, 120–121; by restaurants and bars, 21,
36–37, 47, 57–58, 75, 119, 133, 162, 172, 180,
183, 183n1, 192, 202; by tow truck operators,
51–56, 169, 200–201, See also gambling;
graft; narcotics graft; police corruption
policy operation, 86
Pressman, Gabe, 37–39, 174
Prevention Enforcement Patrol (PEP) Squad, 83,
85, 86, 198
Prince of the City (Daley), 244n2
prostitution, 21, 41, 42, 43, 47, 89, 93, 100, 123,
150, 177
Public Morals and Administration Division
(PMAD), 149

Quill, Michael, 8

Ratnoff, Teddy: about, 175–176; electronic
equipment of, 40–41, 43, 44, 150, 156, 219;
Germaise operations, 105–109, 176; grand
jury investigation, 219; Hollander affair,
43–45, 88, 109, 112, 179, 181, 182; Leuci

operations, 67; Phillips operations, 88–104, 112, 126–127; prison time, 220

Reardon, James, 50

Redlich, Norman, 213

restaurants. *See* bars and restaurants

Ritchie, David, 69, 134

Roberts, Burton, 215, 216, 236, 238

Rockefeller, Nelson, 236, 238, 241

Roff, John, 131

Rogers, Jim, 81

Rooney, Paul: about, 14–15, 18; Knapp Commission activities, 16, 28, 30, 36; Knapp Commission hearings, 212; Leuci operations, 62, 63; Phillips operations, 113, 114

Rothblatt, Henry, 233

Ryder, John, 91, 92, 97, 100, 103, 181

Sachson, Jules, 215

Schecter, Leonard, 209n1, 244n2

Schweitzer, Justice Mitchell, 100, 103, 107, 182

Scoppetta, Nicholas: about, 15, 70, 249; Commission funding source, 24; Knapp Commission activities, 30, 32; Leuci operations, 62, 64, 66, 67, 68; Phillips prosecution, 226–227

Seabury Committee, 4, 4n3

Seedman, Albert, 172–173, 174

Sergeant's Benevolent Association, 33

Serpico, Frank: about, vii, viii, 1–2, 9; appearance of, 1; corruption reported by, 9, 21, 128, 208; Leuci operations, 61, 64; mentor of, 28; nonconformity of, 1; shooting of, 87; testimony of, 169, 210–215

Serpico (Maas), 244n2

Seymour, Whitney North "Mike", Jr., 68, 70, 123n1, 124, 125

shakedowns, 51, 64, 82, 84, 132, 190, 194, 200

Shaw, Edward "Mike", 68, 194

Sheridan, Phillip, 215

"shooflies," 13, 27

Silverman, Ira, 154, 155

Silverman, Theodore, 198

SIU. *See* Special Investigations Unit

Slim. *See* Tank and Slim

Smith, First Deputy Commissioner William, 22, 46, 49–50, 204, 207

Sontag, Marvin, 17

"Spanish Raymon," 185

Special Investigations Unit (SIU), 64

Special Prosecutor's Office, 235–242, 240n1

Spock, Benjamin, 222–223

Sprizzo, John, 135, 201, 206, 211, 212, 224

Squitieri, Arnold, 131

Stango, Sharon, 227

Starsky and Hutch (television show), 79

Stein, Stephen, 68–69

Stengel, Casey, 18

Stokes, Pat, 27

subpoena power, 25, 26, 32–33, 135, 136

The Super Cops (book; Whittemore), 80, 166n1, 244n2

Super Cops (movie), 79

surveillance equipment, electronic, 40–41, 43, 44, 67, 127, 159, 167, 219

Sweeney, John, 68, 134

Sweete, Veri, 19–20

Tactical Patrol Force (TPF Unit), 84

Tange, Daniel, 65, 67

Tank and Slim, 139–146, 169, 199–200

Target Blue (Daley), 168, 173, 173n1, 204

television coverage, 37–39, 60, 131, 175, 177, 178, 180, 185, 186, 198, 201, 202, 214, 216, 220, 227, 228, 241

Tendy, Bill, 146, 147

Thomas, Franklin, 5–6, 205

tow truck operators, police payoffs by, 51–56, 169, 200–201

TPF Unit. See Tactical Patrol Force

Troy, Matthew, 209, 210

undercover agents, 53–55, *See also* Phillips, William R.; Tank and Slim

U.S. Postal Service, 17

Vance, Cyrus, 5, 134, 205, 206

Walsh, John, 31, 87, 137, 214, 216–217, 218, 244

wearing a wire, 53–56, 114, 131, 140, 165

Weir, Lenny, 79, 82

Wells, Nettleton, 18

"West Indian Dave," 185

White, Gordon, 81, 108, 111, 112

Whittemore, L.H., 80, 166n1, 244n2

Williams, Milton, 15, 20, 36, 82

Wilson, Malcolm, 236

Wilson, Will, 68, 70

wiretapping racket, 157–158

wiretaps, illegal, 40, 66

Wyngate, Livingston, 20

Zimroth, Peter, 210